FBI

CAREERS

The Ultimate Guide to Landing a Job as One of America's Finest

Thomas H. Ackerman

JIST Works

FBI Careers: The Ultimate Guide to Landing a Job as One of America's Finest

© 2002 by Thomas H. Ackerman

Published by JIST Works, an imprint of JIST Publishing, Inc.
8902 Otis Avenue
Indianapolis, IN 46216-1033
Phone: 1-800-648-JIST   Fax: 1-800-JIST-FAX   E-mail: info@jist.com

Visit our Web site at **www.jist.com** for information on JIST, free job search information, book chapters, and ordering information on our many products!

Quantity discounts are available for JIST books. Please call our Sales Department at 1-800-648-5478 for a free catalog and more information.

Acquisitions and Development Editor: Lori Cates Hand
Interior Designer: Aleata Howard
Cover Designer: Nick Anderson
Page Layout Coordinator: Carolyn J. Newland
Proofreader: Jeanne Clark
Indexer: Tina Trettin

Printed in the United States of America
06 05 04   9 8 7 6 5 4

ISBN 1-56370-890-6

ABOUT THIS BOOK

The Federal Bureau of Investigation is one of the most sophisticated and well-respected organizations in the world. Since its formation in 1908, the FBI has protected the American people from enemies both domestic and foreign, while honoring and defending the Constitution and the rule of law. Over the years, "the Bureau" has placed a top priority on fighting threats to America's national security posed by terrorists and spies, while also combating organized crime, drug trafficking, white-collar crime, violent crime, and crimes against children. Although the FBI is known worldwide for being on the cutting edge of law enforcement technology and for using state-of-the-art equipment to fight crime, nothing is more important to the success of the Bureau than its most important resource—its employees. Simply stated, the 27,000 men and women of the FBI who serve as special agents and in professional support positions make the nation a better place for all of us—and for many there is no higher calling.

If the FBI sounds like the kind of organization you would like to make a career with, this book is for you. The Bureau's special agents and support personnel are given the best training possible and the opportunity to serve with a law enforcement agency that is unlike any other. To land a position with the FBI, you must be armed with accurate and up-to-date information. *FBI Careers* will guide you step by step through the rigorous selection process, including complete details on the positions, how to apply, and what to expect along the way. Whether you're interested in serving as a special agent, biologist, computer specialist, electronics technician, photographer, or in another area of expertise, this book will provide you with an overview of the positions, qualification requirements, and the training you can expect to receive. Most importantly, *FBI Careers* presents specific guidance on filling out application forms, improving your test scores, making a good impression during interviews, and many other strategies you can use to stand out from the crowd and get hired—even if your goal is to get a foot in the door by serving in an FBI internship.

It is widely known that competition for careers in the FBI is intense, regardless of the position. In order to succeed in your quest to join the ranks of the Bureau, you must carefully identify the steps you will need to take. The first step is to obtain an authoritative source of information that provides expert advice. The next step is to carefully chart a course to success. *FBI Careers* will provide you with the information and expert guidance you'll need to navigate your way to a career as one of America's finest!

—Thomas Ackerman

Dedication

In memory of Dixie, my mother,
who taught me the meaning of justice
—and to fight for it.

CONTENTS

PART 1

FBI Basics

CHAPTER 1

The History and Organization of the FBI

*Leadership is the art of accomplishing more than
the science of management says is possible.*

—*Colin Powell*

From its roots as the *Bureau of Investigation* in the early 1900s, the FBI has evolved from a force of 34 unarmed detectives to one of the most sophisticated and respected law enforcement organizations in the world. The Bureau now employs more than 27,000 personnel, including approximately 11,400 special agents, and serves as the principal investigative arm of the United States Department of Justice. In addition to conducting investigations, the Bureau offers cooperative services such as fingerprint identification, laboratory examination, police training, and the National Crime Information Center to duly authorized law enforcement agencies. Today's FBI is headed by a director who is appointed by the president and confirmed by the Senate for a term not to exceed 10 years. The Bureau has an annual budget of nearly $4 billion.

The mission of the FBI is "to uphold the law through the investigation of violations of federal criminal law; to protect the United States from foreign intelligence and terrorist activities; to provide leadership and law enforcement assistance to federal, state, local, and international agencies; and to perform these responsibilities in a manner that is responsive to the needs of the public and is faithful to the Constitution of the United States." Fulfillment of this mission requires a professional, skilled, and highly trained workforce to address a wide variety of challenges in an ever-changing environment.

The History of the FBI

The FBI originated from a force of special agents created in 1908 by Attorney General Charles Bonaparte during the presidency of Theodore Roosevelt. The two men first met years earlier, in 1892, when they spoke at a meeting of the Baltimore Civil Service Reform Association. Roosevelt, then United States Civil Service Commissioner, boasted of his reforms in federal law enforcement and his efforts to eliminate conflicts of interest in civil service hiring processes. Roosevelt spoke with pride of his insistence that Border Patrol applicants pass marksmanship tests, with the most accurate getting the jobs. Following Roosevelt on the program, Bonaparte responded, tongue in cheek, that target shooting was not the way to select the best-qualified people and announced an alternative plan: "Roosevelt should have had the men shoot at each other, and given the jobs to the survivors," he declared.

Roosevelt and Bonaparte did share the conviction that competence, not political connections, should determine who could best serve in government. Roosevelt became President of the United States in 1901 and appointed Bonaparte as attorney general in 1905. Three years later, on July 26, 1908, Stanley W. Finch was hired to manage an investigative unit of 34 special agents within the Justice Department. Finch's new investigative team consisted of former United States Secret Service agents and detectives. Both Bonaparte and Roosevelt, who completed their terms in March 1909, recommended that the agents become a permanent part of the Department of Justice. Attorney General George Wickersham, Bonaparte's successor, named the force the Bureau of Investigation on March 16, 1909.

Early Expansion of the Bureau

When the Bureau was established, there were few federal crimes on the books. The Bureau of Investigation primarily investigated violations of laws involving national banking, bankruptcy, naturalization, antitrust, peonage, and land fraud. Because the early Bureau provided no formal training, previous law enforcement experience or a background in the law was quite beneficial.

The first major expansion of the Bureau's jurisdiction occurred in June 1910, when the Mann Act was passed. Known also as the "White Slavery Act," this law made it a crime to transport women over state lines for immoral purposes. It also provided a tool by which the federal government could investigate criminals who evaded state laws but committed no other federal violations. Finch became Commissioner of White Slavery Act Violations in 1912, and former Special Examiner A. Bruce Bielaski became the new Bureau of Investigation Chief.

Over the next few years, the number of special agents grew to more than 300, complemented by another 300 support employees. Field offices existed from the Bureau's inception. Each field operation was controlled by a special agent in charge, who was responsible to Washington. Most field offices were located in major cities. However, several were located near the Mexican border, where they concentrated on smuggling, neutrality violations, and intelligence collection, often in connection with the Mexican Revolution.

During World War I, the Bureau's mission was broadened as the agency acquired responsibility for the Espionage, Selective Service, and Sabotage Acts, and assisted the Department of Labor by investigating enemy aliens. During these years, special agents with general investigative experience and proficiency in certain languages augmented the Bureau. In July 1919, William J. Flynn, former head of the Secret Service, became director of the Bureau and was the first to use that title. Three months later, the National Motor Vehicle Theft Act provided a means to prosecute criminals who previously evaded the law by crossing state lines.

Gangsters and the Prohibition Era

The period from 1920 to 1933 was characterized by gangsterism and the public disregard for Prohibition, the legislation that made it illegal to sell or import alcoholic beverages. This period, sometimes referred to as "the lawless years," created a new federal medium for fighting crime. However, the Department of the Treasury—not the Department of Justice—had jurisdiction over federal alcohol violations. The Bureau had limited success using its narrow jurisdiction to investigate gangsters during this period because its agents had neither arrest privileges nor the authority to carry firearms. Nonetheless, as a result of investigations involving the Ku Klux Klan, neutrality violations, and antitrust violations, the Bureau of Investigation gained stature.

William J. Burns was appointed director of the Bureau in August 1921. Later that year, Burns appointed 26-year-old J. Edgar Hoover as assistant director. Hoover had served the Department of Justice since 1917 and led the Department's General Intelligence Division, where he investigated suspected anarchists and communists. Hoover was appointed as head of the Bureau in May 1924. At that time, the agency had about 650 employees, including 441 special agents who worked in field offices in nine cities. Over the following six years, the number of field offices grew to 30, with divisional headquarters in New York, Baltimore, Atlanta, Cincinnati, Chicago, Kansas City, San Antonio, San Francisco, and Portland.

In an effort to professionalize the agency, Hoover immediately fired agents he considered unqualified, abolished the seniority rule of promotion, and introduced uniform performance appraisals. He also scheduled regular inspections of the operations in all field offices. In 1928, Hoover established the requirement that applicants for special agent positions had to be between the ages of 25 and 35. He also reaffirmed the Bureau's earlier preference for special agents with law or accounting experience, and established a formal training course for new agents. The following year, 27-year-old Edwin Shanahan became the first FBI agent to be killed in the line of duty when a car thief in Chicago murdered him.

During the early days of his directorship, Hoover also established the Identification Division in an effort to track criminals by matching their fingerprints. Although many large cities had already started their own fingerprint collections, law enforcement agencies across the country began contributing fingerprint cards to the Bureau in 1926. By the end of the decade, special agent training was institutionalized, the field office inspection system was solidly in place, and the National Division of Identification and Information was collecting and compiling crime statistics for the entire United States. In 1929, after the St. Valentine's Day Massacre occurred in Chicago, the Bureau conducted ballistics tests in the case, leading to the creation of the agency's Technical Laboratory, which would eventually become the FBI Laboratory. Originally, the small laboratory operated only as a research facility, although it eventually added specialized microscopes and extensive reference collections of guns, watermarks, typefaces, and automobile tire designs. These and other advancements gave the Bureau the tools it needed to end the "lawless years."

The Gangster Era Ends and the FBI Is Born

The stock market crash of 1929 and the Great Depression brought widespread unemployment, the collapse of many businesses and financial institutions, and an increase in crime. In response to the crime wave, President Franklin D. Roosevelt influenced Congress to expand federal law enforcement jurisdiction, and his attorney general fought an unrelenting campaign against rampant crime. At the same time, Hoover utilized the media to publicize the work of the Bureau to the American people. The Bureau of Investigation was renamed the United States Bureau of Investigation in July 1932.

The passage of several pieces of legislation during the early- and mid-1930s significantly enhanced the Bureau's jurisdiction. Responding to the kidnapping of Charles Lindbergh's son in 1932, Congress passed a federal kidnapping statute. Between September 1933 and July 1934, John Dillinger and his violent gang terrorized the Midwest—robbing eleven banks, killing ten men, and staging three jailbreaks—which earned him the title of "Public Enemy Number One." With gangsters such as Dillinger evading capture by crossing over state lines, Congress made robbery of a federally insured bank and interstate flight federal crimes, and also granted FBI agents statutory authority to carry firearms and make arrests. In July 1934, Bureau agents shot and killed Dillinger during a stakeout on Chicago's near-west side.

In March 1935, the agency changed its name to the Federal Bureau of Investigation. Four months later, the FBI National Academy was established to train police officers in modern investigative methods because at that time only a few states and localities provided formal training to their officers. The National Academy taught investigative techniques to police officials throughout the United States and, starting in the 1940s, to people from all over the world.

The legal tools Congress gave the FBI, as well as Bureau initiatives to upgrade its own professionalism, resulted in the arrest or demise of all major gangsters by 1936. By that time, however, Fascism in Hitler's Germany and Mussolini's Italy and Communism in Stalin's Soviet Union threatened American democratic principles. With war on the horizon, the FBI faced a new set of challenges.

The World War II Period

During the late 1930s, Germany, Italy, and Japan embarked on an unchecked series of invasions. In September 1939, Germany and Soviet Russia seized Poland, and Russia overran the Baltic States a short time later. Great Britain and France declared war on Germany, and World War II began. The United States, however, continued to adhere to the neutrality acts it had passed in the mid-1930s.

Meanwhile, the American depression continued, providing as fertile an environment for radicalism in the United States as it did in Europe. European Fascists had their counterparts and supporters in the United States in the German-American Bund, the Silver Shirts, and similar groups. At the same time, labor unrest, racial disturbances, and sympathy for the Spanish Loyalists presented an unparalleled opportunity for the American Communist Party to recruit supporters. The FBI was alert to these Fascist and Communist groups as threats to American security. Authority to investigate these organizations came in 1936 with President Roosevelt's authorization through Secretary of State Cordell Hull. A 1939 presidential directive further strengthened the FBI's authority to investigate subversives in the United States, and Congress reinforced it by passing the Smith Act in 1940, outlawing advocacy of violent overthrow of the government.

With the outbreak of World War II, the FBI's responsibilities escalated. Subversion, sabotage, and espionage became major concerns in the United States. The FBI responded by placing at least one agent in each of its 42 field offices who was trained in defense plant protection. In addition, the FBI also developed a network of informational sources, often using members of fraternal or veterans' organizations, to investigate potential threats to national security.

After France fell to the Germans in 1940, Great Britain stood virtually alone against the Axis powers. An Axis victory in Europe and Asia would threaten democracy in North America. Because of the Nazi-Soviet Pact, the American Communist Party and its sympathizers posed a double-edged threat to American interests. Under the direction of Russia, the American Communist Party vigorously advocated continued neutrality for the United States. In 1940 and 1941, the United States actively aided the Allies. In late 1940, Congress reestablished the draft, and the FBI was responsible for locating draft evaders and deserters.

After the Germans attacked Russia in June 1941, the FBI focused its internal security efforts on potentially dangerous German, Italian, and Japanese nationals as well as native-born Americans whose beliefs and activities aided the Axis powers. The FBI also participated in intelligence collection, with the Technical Laboratory playing a pioneering role. Lab staff cooperated with engineers, scientists, and cryptographers in other agencies to enable the United States to penetrate and sometimes control the flow of information from the belligerents in the Western Hemisphere.

Prior to the U.S. entry into the war, the FBI uncovered a major espionage ring. This group, the Frederick Duquesne spy ring, was the largest one discovered up to that time. The FBI was assisted by a loyal American with German relatives who acted as a double agent. For 16 months, the FBI ran a short-wave radio station on Long Island for him, learning what Germany was sending to its spies in the United States while controlling the information that was being transmitted to Germany. The investigation led to the arrest and conviction of 33 spies.

The FBI also engaged in sabotage investigations. In June 1942, two German submarines dropped off four saboteurs each in New York and Florida, all of whom had been trained in explosives, chemistry, secret writing, and how to blend into American surroundings. The FBI arrested the saboteurs, which helped to alleviate fear of Axis subversion and bolstered America's faith in the FBI.

On December 7, 1941, immediately after the Japanese attacked Pearl Harbor, Hawaii, the United States declared war on Japan. On that day, the FBI shifted into wartime mode and placed its Headquarters and all field offices on 24-hour schedules. The FBI immediately arrested previously identified aliens who threatened national security and turned them over to military or immigration authorities. On December 8, Germany and Italy declared war on the United States.

The FBI expanded substantially during the war, increasing its agent force from 896 in 1940 to about 4,000 by the end of 1943, and to 4,370 in 1945. During this period, the FBI's focus shifted from apprehending gangsters to investigating saboteurs and spies. In April 1945, Vice President Harry Truman took office as president after the death of President Roosevelt. Before the end of the month, Hitler committed suicide and the German commander in Italy surrendered. Although the May 1945 surrender of Germany ended the war in Europe, war continued in the Pacific until August 14, 1945. Although the war had ended and the world was once more at peace, hanging over the euphoria was a newly realized threat: atomic weaponry.

The Postwar Era

The threat of Communism continued after the war. In 1946, Joseph Stalin gave a public address in which he implied that future wars were inevitable until Communism replaced capitalism worldwide. Events in Europe and North America convinced Congress that Stalin was well on his way to achieving his goal, and Americans feared Communist expansion was not limited to Europe. In June 1945, the FBI raided the offices of *Amerasia,* a magazine concerned with Far Eastern affairs, where agents discovered copies of classified State Department and Navy documents, including some that were labeled "Top Secret." Several months later, Canadian officials arrested 22 people for trying to steal atomic secrets. By 1947, evidence existed that pro-Soviet individuals had infiltrated the American government. Previously, Americans felt secure behind their monopoly of the atomic bomb. Fear of a Russian bomb now came to dominate American thinking. The Soviets detonated their own bomb in 1949.

Counteracting the Communist threat became a paramount focus of government at all levels, as well as the private sector. Any public or private agency or individual with information about subversive activities was urged to report it to the FBI, and a poster to that effect was distributed to police departments nationwide. The FBI's authority to conduct background investigations on present and prospective government employees also expanded dramatically in the postwar years. The 1946 Atomic Energy Act gave the FBI "responsibility for determining the loyalty of individuals having access to restricted Atomic Energy data." Later, executive orders from Presidents Truman and Eisenhower gave the FBI responsibility for investigating allegations of disloyalty among federal employees. Considering that many suspected and convicted spies, such as Julius and Ethel Rosenberg, had been federal employees, background investigations were viewed to be just as vital as cracking major espionage cases. Despite the FBI's focus on subversion and espionage, and the time-consuming nature of background investigations, the Bureau's workforce did not expand until the Korean War in the early 1950s. After the end of the Korean War in 1953, the number of agents stabilized at about 6,200.

The FBI expanded its crime-fighting role in the postwar period through its assistance to state and local law enforcement agencies and increased jurisdictional responsibility. In March 1950, the FBI began its "Ten Most Wanted Fugitives" program to increase law enforcement's ability to capture dangerous fugitives. In addition, advances in forensic science and technical development enabled the FBI to devote a significant proportion of its resources to assisting state and local law enforcement agencies. For example, in the aftermath of the midair explosion of a plane over Colorado in 1955, the FBI laboratory examined hundreds of airplane parts, pieces of cargo, and the personal effects of passengers. It pieced together evidence of a bomb explosion from passenger luggage and then investigated the backgrounds of the 44 victims. Ultimately, agents identified the perpetrator and secured his confession. They then turned the case over to Colorado authorities, who successfully prosecuted it in a state court.

Civil Rights Investigations of the 1960s

In the 1960s, Congress enacted new federal laws that provided the FBI with new tools to fight civil rights violations, racketeering, gambling, and other offenses. These included the Civil Rights Acts of 1960 and 1964, the Crimes Aboard Aircraft Act of 1961, an expanded Federal Fugitive Act, and the Sports Bribery Act of 1964. Until the 1960s, the FBI had been reluctant to enforce civil rights violations.

The turning point in federal civil rights actions occurred in the summer of 1964, after the murders of three voting registration workers in Mississippi who were allegedly killed by members of the Ku Klux Klan. The Department of Justice ordered the FBI to investigate the incident, and the case against the perpetrators took years to proceed through the courts. The FBI arrested 19 suspects in December 1964, and all were indicted on federal civil rights violations one month later. After a trial was held in 1967, seven of the suspects were found guilty, including both a Klan leader and a Neshoba County sheriff's deputy. The investigation was dramatized in the 1988 movie, *Mississippi Burning*.

Other high-profile civil rights investigations in the 1960s focused on the 1963 murder of Medger Evers, who served as Mississippi Field Secretary of the NAACP, and the 1968 assassination of Martin Luther King, Jr. The FBI also investigated members of the Ku Klux Klan for the 1965 murder of Viola Liuzzo, a white civil rights worker from Detroit who was transporting African Americans from Montgomery to Selma, Alabama, after a four-day civil rights march. After four Klansmen were acquitted on state murder charges, federal prosecutors pursued civil rights charges against the suspects and three of them were convicted.

The FBI and Organized Crime

Involvement of the FBI in organized crime investigations also was hampered by the lack of federal laws covering crimes perpetrated by racketeers. After Prohibition, many mob activities were carried out locally or, if interstate, they did not constitute major violations within the Bureau's jurisdiction. An impetus for federal legislation occurred in 1957 with the New York State Police's discovery that many of the nation's best-known mobsters had met in upstate New York. The FBI collected information on the individuals who attended the meeting, confirming the existence of a national organized-crime network. Later the FBI persuaded mob insider Joseph Valachi to testify against the mob before a Senate subcommittee. Valachi's testimony provided the public with a firsthand account of *La Cosa Nostra,* the American "mafia."

On the heels of Valachi's disclosures, Congress passed two new laws to strengthen federal racketeering and gambling statutes to aid the Bureau's fight against mob influence. The Omnibus Crime Control and Safe Streets Act of

1968 provided for the use of court-ordered electronic surveillance in the investigation of certain violations. The Racketeer Influenced and Corrupt Organizations (RICO) statute of 1970 allowed organized groups to be prosecuted for all of their diverse criminal activities, without the crimes being linked by a perpetrator or all-encompassing conspiracy. Along with greater use of agents for undercover work in the 1970s and 1980s, these laws helped the FBI develop cases that put almost all of the leaders of major organized crime families in prison.

By the end of the 1960s, the Bureau employed 6,703 special agents and 9,320 support personnel in 58 field offices and 12 legal attaché offices. A national tragedy produced another expansion of FBI jurisdiction when President Kennedy was assassinated. This crime was considered a local homicide because no federal law addressed the murder of a president. Nevertheless, President Lyndon Johnson tasked the FBI with conducting the investigation, and Congress then passed a new law to ensure that any such act in the future would be a federal crime.

The Vietnam War Era

President Kennedy's assassination introduced a violent aspect of the era of the 1960s, known commonly as the Vietnam War Era. This period, which actually lasted into the mid-1970s, was characterized by idealism, but also by increased urban crime and a propensity for some groups to resort to violence in challenging the "establishment." Many Americans who objected to involvement in Vietnam or to other policies wrote to Congress or carried peace signs in orderly demonstrations. Nevertheless, others resorted to violent means and, in 1970 alone, an estimated 3,000 bombings and 50,000 bomb threats occurred in the United States. The emergence of antiestablishment groups who opposed the Vietnam War—coupled with the convergence of crime, violence, civil rights issues, and potential national security issues—ensured that the FBI played a significant role during this troubled period.

In May 1970, the FBI investigated the violent events at Kent State University, after the U.S. Army Reserve Officers Training Corps building was destroyed by fire and four students were killed by National Guardsmen during a Vietnam War protest. Four months later, a powerful bomb killed one student and injured others when it exploded at the Army Math Research Center at the University of Wisconsin. By 1971, with few exceptions, the most extreme members of the antiwar movement concentrated on more peaceable, yet still radical, tactics, such as the clandestine publication of *The Pentagon Papers*. However, the violent Weathermen and its successor groups continued to challenge the FBI into the 1980s.

The Watergate Scandal

FBI Director J. Edgar Hoover died in May 1972, just shy of 48 years as the FBI director. The next day his body lie in state in the rotunda of the capitol, an honor accorded only 21 other Americans. President Nixon appointed L. Patrick Gray as acting director the day after Hoover's death. Six weeks later, five men were arrested photographing documents at the Democratic National Headquarters in the Watergate office building in Washington, D.C., during a break-in that was authorized by Republican Party officials. Within hours, the

White House began its effort to cover up its role. The investigation disclosed that the burglars and two conspirators, G. Gordon Liddy and E. Howard Hunt, were linked to Nixon's reelection committee, and that five of the men had ties to the CIA. More than 300 FBI agents undertook an investigation.

In the midst of the Watergate investigation, the Senate Judiciary Committee held hearings for the confirmation of L. Patrick Gray as the permanent FBI director. During the hearings, Gray admitted to providing copies of files relating to the Watergate investigation to John Dean, who served as Nixon's legal counsel, and also to destroying documents related to the break-in that he received from White House staff. The controversy caused Gray to withdraw from consideration as FBI director, and he was replaced hours later by William Ruckleshaus, a former congressman and the first head of the Environmental Protection Agency. Ruckleshaus served as acting director for less than three months until Clarence Kelley was appointed director in July 1973. Kelley was serving as chief of the Kansas City Police Department when he received the appointment and had been an FBI agent from 1940 to 1961.

Three days after Kelley's appointment, top aides in the Nixon Administration resigned amid charges of White House efforts to obstruct justice in the Watergate case. Days later, two former members of Nixon's cabinet were indicted by a federal grand jury on charges related to the Watergate cover-up. Vice President Spiro Agnew resigned in October 1973, following charges of tax evasion. Then, following impeachment hearings that were televised to the American public, President Nixon resigned in August 1974. One month after Vice President Gerald Ford was sworn in as president, he granted an unconditional pardon to Nixon and vowed to heal the nation.

The Aftermath of Watergate

Director Kelley also sought to restore public trust in the FBI and instituted many policy changes that targeted the selection and training of FBI personnel, the procedures of investigative intelligence collection, and the prioritization of investigative programs. Kelley also responded to scrutiny by Congress and the media on whether FBI methods of collecting intelligence in domestic security and counterintelligence investigations abridged Constitutional rights. Kelley's most significant management innovation, however, was implementing the concept of "Quality over Quantity" investigations. He directed each field office to set priorities based on the types of cases most important in its territory, and to concentrate resources on those matters. Under J. Edgar Hoover, the Bureau had followed a quota system for the assignment of investigations in each office. Strengthening Kelley's concept, the FBI also established three national priorities, including foreign counterintelligence, organized crime, and white-collar crime. To address these priorities, the Bureau intensified its recruitment of accountants and expanded its use of undercover operations in major cases.

During Kelley's tenure as director, the FBI made a strong effort to develop an agent force with more women and one that was more reflective of the ethnic composition of the United States. By the late 1970s, nearly 8,000 special agents and 11,000 support employees worked in 59 field offices and 13 legal attaché offices. Kelley resigned in 1978 and was replaced by William Webster, who was serving as judge of the United States Court of Appeals for the Eighth Circuit.

Drugs, Corruption, and Terrorism in the 1980s

Webster's tenure as director was marked by efforts to modernize the FBI. Following a rash of terrorist incidents worldwide, he made counterterrorism a fourth national priority in 1982, and expanded FBI initiatives in the areas of foreign counterintelligence, organized crime, and white-collar crime. Part of this expansion was the creation of the National Center for the Analysis of Violent Crime at the FBI National Academy in 1984. The FBI solved so many espionage cases during the mid-1980s that the media dubbed 1985 "the year of the spy." The most serious espionage damage uncovered by the Bureau was committed by the John Walker spy ring and by former National Security Agency employee William Pelton.

The illegal drug trade severely challenged the resources of American law enforcement throughout the 1980s. To ease this challenge, in 1982 the attorney general gave the FBI concurrent jurisdiction with the Drug Enforcement Administration over narcotics violations in the United States. The expanded Department of Justice attention to drug crimes resulted in the seizure of millions of dollars in controlled substances, the arrests of major narcotics figures, and the dismantling of important drug rings. One of the most publicized, dubbed the "Pizza Connection" case, involved the heroin trade in the United States and Italy. It resulted in 18 convictions, including a former leader of the Sicilian Mafia. Then Assistant United States Attorney Louis Freeh, who was to be appointed FBI director in 1993, was key to successful prosecution of the case.

Webster also strengthened the FBI's response to white-collar crime, with particular emphasis on public corruption. From 1978 to early 1980, the Bureau conducted Operation ABSCAM to expose bribery and conspiracy by members of Congress. An FBI investigation undertaken throughout the 1980s focused on bribery within the Cook County Circuit Court in Chicago, resulting in the conviction of more than 90 corrupt judges, attorneys, police officers, and court employees. In 1986, following an FBI investigation that unveiled corruption in government procurement activities, dozens of Defense Department officials and contractors were indicted on charges of fraud, bribery, and other crimes. Between 1981 and 1987, the FBI also uncovered fraud surrounding the failure of almost 300 savings and loan institutions.

In 1984, the FBI acted as lead agency for security of the Los Angeles Olympics, and unveiled its Hostage Rescue Team as a force capable of responding to situations such as the tragedy that occurred in Munich at the 1972 games. In 1986, Congress expanded FBI jurisdiction to cover terrorist acts against United States citizens outside the United States. Three years later, the Department of Justice authorized the FBI to arrest terrorists, drug traffickers, and other fugitives abroad without the consent of the foreign country in which they resided.

In May 1987, Webster left the FBI to become director of the Central Intelligence Agency, and Executive Assistant Director John Otto became acting director. During his six-month tenure, Otto designated drug investigations as the FBI's fifth national priority. In November 1987, former Federal Judge William Sessions was sworn in as FBI director. Prior to his appointment as FBI director, Sessions had served as the chief judge of the United States District Court for the Western District of Texas, and also as a United States attorney for that district.

Under Director Sessions, crime-prevention efforts were expanded to include a drug demand–reduction program, and FBI offices nationwide began working closely with local school and civic groups to educate young people about the dangers of drugs. By 1988, the FBI employed 9,663 special agents and 13,651 support employees in 58 field offices and 15 legal attachés. In response to a 40 percent increase in violent crime over the previous 10 years, Director Sessions designated the investigation of violent crime as the FBI's sixth national priority program in 1989.

The Post Cold War Era

The dismantling of the Berlin Wall in November 1989 brought down the Iron Curtain—the final act in the Cold War—and the Soviet Union was dissolved in December 1991. The FBI reassessed its strategies in defending national security, now no longer defined as the containment of Communism and the prevention of nuclear war. It reassigned 300 special agents from foreign counterintelligence duties to violent crime investigations in January 1992. By creating the National Security Threat List, the Bureau changed its approach from defending against hostile intelligence agencies to protecting U.S. information and technologies. It also defined expanded threat issues, including the proliferation of chemical, biological, and nuclear weapons; the loss of critical technologies; and the improper collection of trade secrets and proprietary information. As President Clinton was to note in 1994, with the dramatic expansion of the global economy, "national security now means economic security."

Two events occurred in late 1992 and early 1993 that were to have a major impact on FBI policies and operations. In August 1992, the FBI responded to the shooting death of Deputy U.S. Marshal William Degan, who was killed at Ruby Ridge, Idaho, while participating in a surveillance of federal fugitive Randall Weaver. In the course of the standoff, Weaver's wife was accidentally shot and killed by an FBI sniper. Eight months later, at a remote compound outside Waco, Texas, FBI agents sought to end a 51-day standoff with members of a heavily armed religious sect who had killed four officers of the Bureau of Alcohol, Tobacco, and Firearms. Instead, the compound burned to the ground from fires lit by members of the sect. Eighty people, including children, died in the blaze. These two events set the stage for public and congressional inquiries into the FBI's ability to respond to crisis situations. In July 1993, following allegations of ethics violations committed by Director Sessions, President Clinton removed him from office and appointed Deputy Director Floyd Clarke as acting FBI director.

Reorganization and International Cooperation

Louis Freeh was sworn in as director of the FBI in September 1993. He had served as an FBI agent from 1975 to 1981 in the New York City field office and at FBI Headquarters before leaving to join the United States Attorney's Office for the Southern District of New York. Freeh prosecuted many major FBI cases, including the notorious "Pizza Connection" case and the "VANPAC" mail-bomb case. He had been appointed as a United States District Court judge for the Southern District of New York in 1991.

Freeh moved quickly to reorganize and streamline Headquarters operations. Selected divisions and offices were merged, reorganized, or abolished. He then ordered the transfer of 600 special agents serving in administrative positions to investigative positions in field offices. Freeh also emphasized law enforcement cooperation as a necessary way to combat domestic and international crime, and in 1999 the FBI placed Osama Bin Laden on its "Ten Most Wanted" list for his alleged involvement in the 1999 bombings of United States embassies in Africa. In 1994, Freeh led a delegation of high-level diplomatic and federal law enforcement officials to meet with senior officials of 11 European nations on international crime issues, and also announced the opening of an FBI legal attaché office in Moscow. By the end of 2000, the Bureau established legal attaché offices in Hungary, Ukraine, Poland, and Romania.

FBI investigations during the early- to mid-1990s included the Archer Daniels Midland international price-fixing conspiracies and the attempted theft of Schering-Plough and Merck pharmaceutical trade secrets. At the time, the United States Department of Justice characterized the Archer Daniels Midland investigation as the largest criminal antitrust case in U.S. history. In 1996, Congress passed the Economic Espionage Act, enabling the FBI to significantly strengthen its investigations involving the theft of trade secrets and intellectual property.

In December 1988, an explosion on board Pan Am flight 103 above Lockerbie, Scotland, caused the deaths of 259 passengers and 11 people on the ground. The FBI investigated the incident along with Scottish authorities. The investigation, which involved the U.S. intelligence community and numerous foreign law enforcement agencies, was one of the most extensive international investigations ever conducted by the Bureau. In January 2001, three Scottish judges convicted a Libyan national of murder for planting a bomb in a suitcase on the New York–bound flight.

Director Freeh initiated many changes to prepare for evolving criminal challenges, including formation of the Critical Incident Response Group in 1994 and the ground breaking for its new state-of-the-art FBI forensic laboratory in 1999. He also initiated a comprehensive and integrated FBI response to nuclear, biological, and chemical crisis incidents.

Fighting Domestic Terrorism: America's "New War"

As the 20th century came to a close, terrorism on U.S. soil shocked the nation and the world. In 1995, the bombing of the Alfred P. Murrah Federal Building in Oklahoma City was the worst terrorist attack ever to occur in the United States, killing 168 people and wounding nearly 700 more. The FBI initiated one of the most intensive investigations in its history, which led to the arrests and convictions of Timothy McVeigh and Terry Nichols. McVeigh was later sentenced to death and executed, and Nichols received a sentence of life in prison.

Between 1994 and 1997, six Muslim fundamentalists were convicted for the bombing of a parking garage at the World Trade Center complex in New York City. Six people were killed and more than 1,100 were injured. The FBI led a coordinated law enforcement effort to determine who was responsible for the terrorist incident.

Over the years following the Oklahoma City and World Trade Center bombings, funding in support of FBI counterterrorism programs tripled from $97 million in fiscal year 1996 to $301 million in 1999. To consolidate FBI counterterrorism initiatives, Director Freeh established the FBI Counterterrorism Division in 1999, and assigned the National Infrastructure Protection Center and the National Domestic Preparedness Office to the Division.

Louis Freeh retired from the FBI in June 2001. He was replaced by Thomas Pickard, who served as acting director for three months. Robert Mueller III, a former deputy attorney general for the United States Department of Justice, took over as FBI director on September 4, 2001.

Seven days after Mueller's appointment, on September 11, the FBI responded to the worst terrorist attacks the world had ever witnessed. On that morning, terrorists hijacked four commercial jets and crashed them into the World Trade Center in New York City, the Pentagon in Washington, D.C., and a field southeast of Pittsburgh. Around 3,000 people were killed in the attacks, including 343 firefighters and 71 law enforcement officers who gave their lives in the rescue attempts at the World Trade Center. The investigative response by the FBI included more than 7,000 agents and support personnel—about one in four of the Bureau's workforce—who worked around the clock. The FBI soon released photographs of 19 individuals believed to be hijackers of the four airliners—all of whom were killed in the attacks—and cautioned Americans to prepare for additional terrorist incidents within the United States and against U.S. interests overseas. Within three weeks, the Bureau also launched an investigation relating to anthrax exposures in Florida, New York, and Washington, D.C.

One month after the attacks, President George W. Bush signed an executive order establishing the Office of Homeland Security, to coordinate national strategy and strengthen protections against terrorist threats or attacks in the United States. Two days later, President Bush unveiled the Most Wanted Terrorists List, a new initiative similar to the FBI's Ten Most Wanted Fugitives Program, to spotlight the names and faces of terrorists who might be living, working, or hiding in the United States or overseas. The list combines the power of the media with the eyes and ears of millions of citizens around the world to fight against terrorism. Today, in the aftermath of terrorist incidents in the United States and around the world, the FBI has an enhanced capability to track the activities of foreign terrorist organizations maintaining a presence in the United States.

Preparing for the Future

Since its formation as a small group of investigators in 1908, the FBI has undergone myriad changes in technology, jurisdiction, and mission. To address the challenges it will face in the future, the Bureau must adapt to the ever-changing face of crime and strive to achieve even greater excellence. This can be accomplished through positive relationships with other law enforcement agencies, new scientific techniques to identify dangerous criminals who would otherwise evade law enforcement, and laws that enable the FBI to protect the civil rights of the nation's citizens. Perhaps the most critical resources the FBI will need to accomplish its mission in the future, however, will be its human resources: the special agents and support personnel it selects and trains to promote justice, act with fairness and compassion, protect the public, and uphold the Constitution.

The Organization of the FBI

The following sections present an overview of how the FBI is organized, including its jurisdiction and authority, its field offices, and its operational divisions.

Jurisdiction and Authority

The FBI serves as the principal criminal investigative arm of the United States Department of Justice. The Bureau is charged with investigating all violations of federal law except those that have been assigned to other federal agencies. Its jurisdiction includes a wide range of responsibilities in the criminal, civil, and security fields. Priority is given to investigations that affect society the most, including organized crime and drugs, domestic and international terrorism, white-collar crime, foreign counterintelligence, violent crime and major offenses, and civil-rights violations. The work that FBI special agents and support personnel perform has a daily impact on the nation's security and the quality of life for all United States citizens. Other law enforcement agencies of the Department of Justice include the Office of Inspector General (OIG), Drug Enforcement Administration (DEA), Bureau of Prisons (BOP), Immigration and Naturalization Service (INS), and United States Marshals Service (USMS).

Title 28 of the United States Code, Section 533, authorizes the attorney general to "...appoint officials to detect and prosecute crimes against the United States," and also to "...conduct investigations regarding official matters under the control of the Department of Justice...as may be directed by the Attorney General." Other federal statutes give the FBI the authority and responsibility to investigate specific crimes. The Bureau presently has investigative jurisdiction over violations of more than 200 categories of federal offenses. Throughout the 1980s, the illegal drug trade severely challenged the resources of American law enforcement. To ease this challenge, in 1982 the attorney general gave the FBI concurrent jurisdiction with the Drug Enforcement Administration over narcotics violations in the United States.

FBI special agents enforce more than 260 federal statutes, including those relating to organized crime, financial fraud, bank robbery, kidnapping, fugitive matters, and many other violations of federal laws. Information obtained through FBI investigations is presented to the appropriate United States attorney or Department of Justice official, who decides whether prosecution or other action is warranted.

The FBI routinely cooperates with other federal, state, and local law enforcement agencies on joint investigations and through formal task force operations. These investigations focus on organized crime, bank robbery, kidnapping, terrorism, motor vehicle theft, and other offenses. The Bureau also offers cooperative services such as fingerprint identification, laboratory examination, police training, and the National Crime Information Center to federal, state, and local law enforcement agencies. FBI Headquarters is located in Washington, D.C.

FBI Field Offices and Resident Agencies

The FBI's field offices are located in major cities throughout the United States and in San Juan, Puerto Rico. (See appendix J for a listing of FBI field offices.) There are 56 field offices located throughout the country. Coverage is divided according to population density, leaving some field offices with jurisdiction in surrounding states and others with jurisdiction over smaller geographic areas. For example, the Boston field office investigates criminal activity in Massachusetts, Maine, New Hampshire, and Rhode Island, whereas the Detroit field office has jurisdiction over Michigan only.

All but three field offices are headed by a special agent in charge (SAC), who manages the operations of the office. At the next level of supervision, SACs are supported by one or more assistants, each known as assistant special agent in charge (ASAC). Below the ASAC, supervisory special agents manage investigative squads, and relief supervisors take over in their absence. Due to their large size, the Los Angeles, New York, and Washington, D.C., field offices are managed by an assistant director in charge (ADIC). In these offices, the ADICs are assisted by SACs.

Field offices conduct their business from their facilities and through satellite offices known as resident agencies (RAs). The number of RAs under each field office varies, as does the territory they cover. For example, 11 RAs throughout Michigan report to the Detroit field office, and the number of counties served by these RAs ranges from 1 (for the Oakland County RA) to 21 (for the Bay City RA). Resident agencies, like field offices, are located where crime trends and available resources dictate.

Special agents assigned to field offices and RAs are organized into work groups known as squads. The responsibilities and focus of each squad depend on a number of variables, such as office size and the nature of investigations that are emphasized within the office. For example, various squads nationwide specialize in the investigation of violent crime, drug trafficking, organized crime, homicide, computer crime, financial institution fraud, white-collar crime, health-care fraud, interstate property crimes, and other offenses.

Headquarters Operational Divisions

The FBI is headed by a director, who is supported by a deputy director. Public Law 94-503, Section 203, provides for the appointment of the FBI director by the president with the advice and consent of the Senate. The FBI director's term is limited to 10 years. An assistant director heads each of the 11 Headquarters divisions (see below), as well as the Office of Professional Responsibility and the Office of Public and Congressional Affairs. The Office of the General Counsel is headed by the FBI's General Counsel, and the Office of Equal Employment Opportunity Affairs is administered by the Equal Employment Manager. Assistant directors of each division are supported by deputy assistant directors. FBI Headquarters divisions and offices usually are arranged along broad functional lines into sections, and then into smaller, more specialized work groups known as units.

The following sections provide an overview of the functions the FBI divisions carry out. An organizational chart showing these divisions and other operational sections, as of the January 2002 reorganization, is shown in figure 1.1.

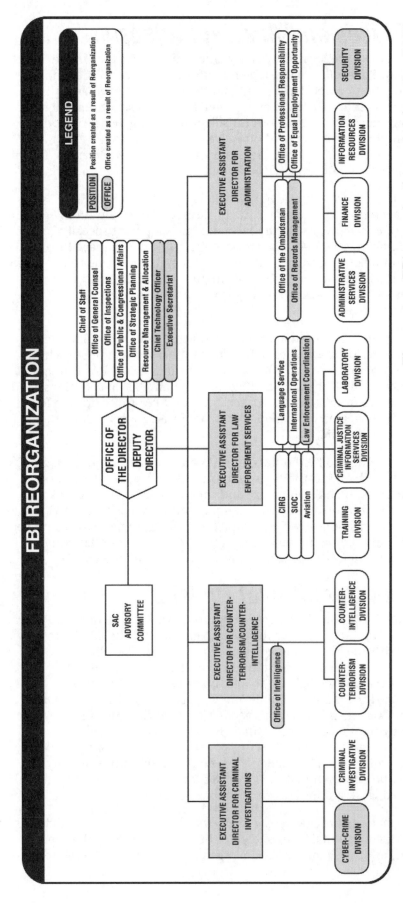

Figure 1.1: FBI organization as of January 2002.

Administrative Services Division

In addition to managing and providing executive direction in all aspects of FBI personnel management matters, such as personnel assistance, personnel benefits, and personnel selection, this division is responsible for the management and security of all FBI facilities. This division also manages all personnel-recruitment programs and selection systems, and oversees background investigations of applicants for FBI employment and employment with other agencies.

Counterterrorism Division

The Counterterrorism Division consolidates all FBI counterterrorism initiatives. The National Infrastructure Protection Center (NIPC) and the National Domestic Preparedness Office (NDPO) are assigned to this division. The NIPC serves as the U.S. government's focal point for threat assessment, warning, investigation, and response for threats or attacks against the United States' critical infrastructures. The NDPO coordinates all federal efforts to assist state and local first responders with planning, training, and equipment needs necessary to respond to an incident involving conventional or nonconventional weapons of mass destruction.

Criminal Investigative Division

The FBI's investigative mandate is the broadest of all federal law enforcement agencies. This division coordinates investigations into organized crime, including drug matters, racketeering, and money laundering; investigations of violent crimes, including fugitives, escaped federal prisoners (in some instances), unlawful flight to avoid prosecution, violent gangs, serial murders, kidnapping, bank robberies, crime of an interstate nature, crime on Indian reservations, theft of government property, and crimes against U.S. citizens overseas; investigations of white-collar crime, fraud against the government, corruption of public officials, health-care fraud, election law violations, business and economic frauds, and corruption crimes; and investigations of civil-rights violations.

Criminal Justice Information Services Division

Headquartered in Clarksburg, West Virginia, the Criminal Justice Information Services Division (CJIS) serves as the focal point and central repository for criminal justice information services within the FBI. This division provides state-of-the-art identification and information services to local, state, federal, and international criminal justice communities. The CJIS Division includes the Fingerprint Identification Program; the National Crime Information Center Program; the Uniform Crime Reporting Program; and the development of the Integrated Automated Fingerprint Identification System (IAFIS), a computer-based system that can store, process, analyze, and retrieve millions of fingerprints in a short period of time.

Finance Division

The Finance Division manages FBI budget and accounting matters, voucher and payroll functions, the procurement process, forfeiture and seized property processes, property management, automotive management, competition advocacy, relocation and transportation services, and Chief Financial Officers Act requirements.

Information Resources Division

The principal responsibility of the Information Resources Division is to provide centralized management and planning for information resources within the FBI. Architectures are developed and maintained that specify how information is to be collected, managed, and used. The architectures delineate the information that is essential to the Bureau's mission, as well as the systems needed to manage this data and the technical infrastructure needed to maintain them. Two engineering sections of this division provide technical expertise and equipment to collect data, conduct research into improved methods for conducting electronic and physical surveillance, and perform forensic examinations of certain evidence.

The IRD also developed the National Crime Information Center (NCIC) 2000 computer system, which is used by federal, state, and local law enforcement agencies to locate wanted and missing persons, vehicles, boats, guns, and other property. The enhanced system supports the transmission, storage, and search of photograph and fingerprint images from patrol cars and workstations to the NCIC central processor.

Inspection Division

The Inspection Division is responsible for examining the FBI's investigative and administrative operations to ensure their compliance with established rules, regulations, laws, and objectives. These examinations ensure that FBI personnel conduct themselves in a proper and professional manner. The Inspection Division also conducts organizational streamlining studies, process re-engineering and improvement projects, and program evaluations, and makes recommendations for improved organizational efficiency and effectiveness.

Investigative Services Division

The Investigative Services Division (ISD) coordinates the FBI's analytical capabilities and oversees the Bureau's crisis-management functions. The ISD includes an Information, Analysis, and Assessments section, which extracts information from case files and other sources to identify future trends and the means of preventing crime and threats to national security.

Laboratory Division

The FBI laboratory is one of the largest and most comprehensive crime laboratories in the world. It provides leadership and service in scientific solution and prosecution of crimes nationwide and is the only full-service federal forensic laboratory in the United States. Laboratory Division activities include crime-scene searches, special surveillance photography, latent-fingerprint examinations, forensic examinations of evidence, DNA testing, court testimony, and other scientific and technical services. The FBI offers these services free of charge to all law enforcement agencies in the United States and also provides training to other state and local crime laboratory and law enforcement personnel.

National Security Division

Coordination of investigative matters concerning foreign counterintelligence is the responsibility of the National Security Division. Activities of this division include investigations relating to espionage and overseas homicide, domestic security, and nuclear extortion. The division is also responsible for the FBI's Security Countermeasures Program, which includes background investigations and physical security issues, as well as the protection of foreign officials and guests.

Office of Equal Employment Opportunity Affairs

The Office of Equal Employment Opportunity (EEO) Affairs ensures equality of opportunity for all FBI employees and applicants and prohibits discrimination in employment based on race, color, religion, age, sex, national origin, disabled status, or reprisal for previous involvement in a protected activity. This office handles EEO-complaint processing, training, and monitoring of employment practices and policies. Additional responsibilities include the operation of special-emphasis programs relating to American Indians, Alaskan Natives, Asian Americans, Pacific Islanders, Black Affairs, Federal Women, Hispanic Employment, Selective Placement of individuals with disabilities (including disabled veterans), and Upward Mobility.

Office of the General Counsel

Legal counsel to the FBI director and other Bureau officials is provided by the Office of the General Counsel (OGC). In addition, OGC personnel research legal questions regarding law enforcement and national security matters and coordinate the defense of civil litigation and administrative claims involving the FBI, its personnel, and its records. OGC is comprised of the Legal Advice and Training Branch and the Litigation Branch.

Office of Professional Responsibility

The Office of Professional Responsibility (OPR) is responsible for the investigation of allegations of criminal conduct and serious misconduct by FBI employees. Additionally, OPR is responsible for the adjudication of cases of administrative discipline based on its investigation, determining whether the allegations have been substantiated, and making written findings and recommendations regarding what (if any) disciplinary action is appropriate. OPR is also responsible for setting policy and establishing procedures regarding the disciplinary process, and for monitoring its effectiveness to ensure that the ability of the FBI to perform its law enforcement and national security functions is not impaired.

Office of Public and Congressional Affairs

The Office of Public and Congressional Affairs communicates information on FBI investigations, services, programs, policy, and accomplishments to the public, Congress, and the news media. This office also manages relations with the electronic and print media; prepares FBI publications; answers verbal and written inquiries from the general public, scholars, and authors regarding the FBI; and operates the Headquarters tour.

Training Division

Located in Quantico, Virginia, the Training Division manages the FBI Academy, trains FBI special agents and support staff, and also offers courses to local, state, federal, and international law enforcement personnel. In addition to teaching responsibilities, FBI Academy faculty members conduct research and provide assistance to federal, state, and local law enforcement agencies on many topics and investigative techniques.

Legal Attaché Offices

The growth of international criminal activity and the authority granted by Congress has expanded the FBI's role in international investigations. Given the increasing international occurrences of illegal drug trafficking, organized crimes, espionage, terrorism, and white-collar crimes that affect U.S. citizens, the FBI establishes and maintains liaisons with principal law enforcement and intelligence organizations in many foreign countries.

The primary element of the FBI's international law enforcement initiative is the Legal Attaché (Legats) program. The Bureau has been assigning personnel abroad since World War II and presently has legal attaché staff stationed at more than 40 American embassies and consulates around the world. Special agents stationed overseas are among the Bureau's most experienced investigators and carry the titles of legal attaché, deputy legal attaché, or assistant legal attaché. With very few exceptions, they are fluent in the language of the country to which they are posted.

Legal attachés are overseen by the International Operations Branch of the Criminal Investigative Division at FBI Headquarters. That branch also is responsible for contacts with other executive-branch agencies, as well as the International Criminal Police Organization (INTERPOL) and foreign law enforcement officers based in Washington, D.C.

Chapter 2

Salary and Benefits

A wise man will make more opportunities than he finds. —Francis Bacon

FBI employees enjoy competitive salaries and a wide range of fringe benefits that are superior to those provided by many state and municipal government agencies and firms in the private sector. All full-time Bureau personnel receive health and life insurance coverage, paid holidays, vacation and sick leave, travel allowances, and injury-compensation benefits. In addition, FBI special agents are also covered under special salary and benefit programs. This chapter provides an overview of salary structures and the primary benefits available to FBI special agents and professional support staff.

Salary Structure and Rates

This section presents an overview of the pay system and salary progression procedures the FBI follows for its special agents and support personnel, including locality adjustments for those who serve in certain geographic areas.

The General Schedule Pay System

Although FBI personnel serve in Excepted Service appointments—meaning that they are part of an independent personnel system that is excluded from competitive civil-service procedures—the Bureau follows the General Schedule (GS) pay system for most of its employees, as do the vast majority of federal agencies. Most FBI jobs allow employees to advance from an entry-level pay grade to higher grades over a period of time.

Advancement to Higher Grades

The General Schedule consists of 15 grades, ranging from GS-1 to GS-15. Advancement to higher grades varies from one position to another. For example, the document analyst position covers a pay range from GS-7 through GS-12 and also provides for advancement to the next-higher grade level in one-year increments. Therefore, document analysts who are hired at the GS-7 level can advance to GS-9 after one year, then to GS-11 one year later, and to GS-12 after another year. Regardless of the position, employees must demonstrate work at an acceptable level of competence to qualify for advancement to the next higher grade. Of course, some positions allow for advancement to higher grades than others.

Within-Grade Increases

As shown in the following schedules, a salary range of 10 steps is provided within each grade, with employees normally starting at step 1 within a particular grade at entry level. Within-grade increases to the next step normally occur after 52 weeks of service in the first three steps in a grade, after 104 weeks in steps 4 through 6, and after 156 weeks in steps 7 and above. Employees who reach the highest possible grade in their position continue to receive within-grade increases until they "top-out" at step 10.

Special Agent Salaries

FBI special agents are hired at the GS-10 level and can advance to the GS-11, GS-12, and GS-13 grade levels in nonsupervisory assignments. Advancement from GS-10 to GS-13 is based on satisfactory performance and is noncompetitive. In order to obtain promotions to supervisory, management, and executive positions, special agents must compete with other candidates in formal application processes. Promotions are available to grades GS-14 and GS-15, and also to Senior Executive Service positions. Like most other federal criminal investigators, FBI special agents receive Law Enforcement Availability Pay (LEAP), which is an additional salary premium for unscheduled duty fixed at 25 percent of base pay.

Table 2.1 provides an overview of salaries for FBI special agents, including LEAP, based on 2002 General Schedule salary rates:

Table 2.1: Annual Salary for FBI Special Agents, Including Locality Pay for "Rest of United States" Geographic Areas (Based on 2002 General Schedule Salary Rates)

	Step 1	Step 2	Step 3	Step 4	Step 5	Step 6	Step 7	Step 8	Step 9	Step 10
GS-10	53,239	54,958	56,675	58,393	60,110	61,829	63,546	65,264	66,983	68,700
GS-11	56,606	58,494	60,380	62,266	64,153	66,039	67,925	69,811	71,698	73,584
GS-12	67,844	70,105	72,366	74,628	76,889	79,150	81,411	83,671	85,933	88,194
GS-13	80,678	83,366	86,055	88,744	91,433	94,121	96,810	99,499	102,189	104,878
GS-14	95,339	98,516	101,694	104,871	108,049	111,228	114,405	117,583	120,760	123,938
GS-15	112,144	115,883	119,621	123,359	127,098	130,836	134,575	138,314	142,053	145,829

Professional Support Personnel Salaries

Most FBI professional support employees are paid under the General Schedule pay system, at levels ranging from GS-1 to GS-15. Advancement to nonsupervisory, supervisory, and management positions varies from one position to another, depending on salary structures for each position. Professional support personnel are not eligible for LEAP because only federal criminal investigators are authorized to receive this premium pay. FBI blue-collar personnel, such as automotive workers and aircraft mechanics, are paid under the Federal Wage System, which includes the Wage Grade Schedule.

The following table provides an overview of salaries for FBI professional support personnel:

	Step 1	Step 2	Step 3	Step 4	Step 5	Step 6	Step 7	Step 8	Step 9	Step 10
Table 2.2: Annual Salary for FBI Professional Support Personnel, Including Locality Pay for "Rest of United States" Geographic Areas (Based on 2002 General Schedule Salary Rates)										
GS-1	16,032	16,567	17,100	17,630	18,165	18,479	19,003	19,535	19,556	20,051
GS-2	18,026	18,453	19,050	19,556	19,774	20,355	20,936	21,517	22,098	22,680
GS-3	19,667	20,322	20,977	21,632	22,287	22,943	23,598	24,253	24,908	25,563
GS-4	22,078	22,813	23,549	24,284	25,020	25,755	26,491	27,226	27,962	28,697
GS-5	24,701	25,525	26,348	27,172	27,995	28,819	29,642	30,466	31,289	32,113
GS-6	27,534	28,452	29,370	30,288	31,206	32,124	33,042	33,960	34,878	35,796
GS-7	30,597	31,617	32,638	33,658	34,678	35,698	36,718	37,738	38,758	39,779
GS-8	33,886	35,016	36,146	37,275	38,405	39,535	40,665	41,795	42,925	44,055
GS-9	37,428	38,675	39,922	41,169	42,416	43,664	44,911	46,158	47,405	48,652
GS-10	41,217	42,591	43,966	45,340	46,714	48,088	49,463	50,837	52,211	53,586
GS-11	45,285	46,795	48,304	49,813	51,322	52,831	54,340	55,849	57,358	58,867
GS-12	54,275	56,084	57,893	59,702	61,511	63,320	65,129	66,937	68,746	70,555
GS-13	64,542	66,693	68,844	70,995	73,146	75,297	77,448	79,599	81,751	83,902
GS-14	76,271	78,813	81,355	83,897	86,439	88,982	91,524	94,066	96,608	99,150
GS-15	89,715	92,706	95,697	98,687	101,678	104,669	107,660	110,651	113,642	116,633

Locality Payments

FBI personnel receive locality-based comparability payments, known as locality pay, for the difference between prevailing federal and private-sector salaries in the geographic location where they are employed. More than 30 metropolitan areas in the United States are designated as qualifying for locality pay. Personnel employed in all other areas receive locality pay according to the rate established for the "Rest of United States" category. Locality pay rates are adjusted annually.

Salary schedules shown in tables 2.1 and 2.2 include locality pay of 8.64% for calendar year 2002. Table 2.3 provides an overview of locality pay for personnel who are not employed in "Rest of United States" areas. Employees in these areas receive the difference between the Rest of United States rate and the rates shown in table 2.3. For example, personnel in Portland receive 11.64% locality pay—which is 3% higher than the Rest of United States rate—meaning that employees in Portland would be paid 3% more than those who work in "Rest of United States" areas.

Table 2.3: Locality Pay Adjustments for 2002.
Rates in Metropolitan Areas in Addition to the 8.64% "Rest of United States" Rate

City	Percent Adjustment
Atlanta	1.10%
Boston	4.93%
Chicago	5.94%
Cincinnati	3.45%
Cleveland	1.69%
Columbus	2.06%
Dallas	2.26%
Dayton	0.98%
Denver	4.70%
Detroit	6.07%
Hartford	5.47%
Houston	9.97%
Huntsville	0.44%
Indianapolis	0.21%
Kansas City	0.64%
Los Angeles	7.41%
Miami	3.81%
Milwaukee	1.41%
Minneapolis	2.92%
New York City	6.59%
Orlando	0.03%
Philadelphia	3.47%
Pittsburgh	0.88%
Portland	3.00%
Richmond	1.03%
Sacramento	3.35%
St. Louis	0.34%
San Diego	4.06%
San Francisco	10.40%
Seattle	3.13%
Washington, D.C.	2.84%

Paid Leave

All FBI personnel receive time off for vacations, sickness and medical care, maternity and paternity leave, holidays, and other purposes. The following sections give details on the FBI's paid leave policies.

Annual Leave

The Bureau's full-time employees accumulate paid annual leave for vacations or other purposes based on their years of federal service. Annual leave accrues at the rate of 13 days per year (four hours per pay period) for employees with fewer than three years of service, at 20 days per year (six hours per pay period) for those with 3 to 15 years of service, and at 26 days per year (eight hours per pay period) for personnel with more than 15 years of service. Employees are normally prohibited from carrying forward more than 240 hours of annual leave from year to year.

Paid Holidays

Full-time FBI employees receive paid leave for 10 holidays annually, including the following: New Year's Day, Martin Luther King's Birthday, Washington's Birthday, Memorial Day, Independence Day, Labor Day, Columbus Day, Veterans Day, Thanksgiving Day, and Christmas Day. If a holiday falls on Saturday, the preceding Friday is observed as the legal holiday for employees whose basic workweek is Monday through Friday. Similarly, holidays that fall on Sunday are observed on the following Monday. In the case of employees whose basic workweek is other than Monday through Friday, when a holiday falls on a non-workday, these personnel receive paid leave on the first workday before the holiday.

Sick Leave

All full-time FBI personnel earn 13 days of paid sick leave per year, in four-hour increments each biweekly pay period. Sick leave can be used for the following:

- Medical, dental, or optical examination or treatment
- Incapacitation
- To prevent the exposure of communicable diseases
- To conduct adoption-related activities
- To provide care for ill family members
- To make arrangements necessitated by the death of a family member or attend the funeral of a family member

Family and Medical Leave

Under provisions of the Family and Medical Leave Act of 1993, FBI employees can take up to 12 weeks of unpaid leave per year for the following occurrences:

- The birth of or care for a child
- The placement of a child with the employee for adoption or foster care
- The care of a spouse, son, daughter, or parent of the employee who suffers from a serious health condition

- A serious health condition of the employee that makes him or her unable to perform the essential functions of the position

Family and medical leave is available only to those who have served as federal employees for at least one year.

Maternity Leave

Women who want to take time off for maternity purposes—and then return to their positions—can be granted up to six months leave of absence. During the time the employee is physically incapacitated from duty, she is charged with sick leave. Annual leave and leave without pay can be used after a doctor has determined that the employee is able to return to duty.

Paternity Leave

Male employees can take up to five days of paternity leave to assist or care for their newborn or minor children while the mother is incapacitated for maternity reasons. This leave of absence is charged to the employee's sick leave balance. Up to an additional eight days of paternity leave may be allowed in certain circumstances.

Family Friendly Leave

Under Family Friendly Leave provisions, FBI employees can use up to 40 hours of sick leave per year to care for a family member or to arrange or attend an immediate family member's funeral. In certain circumstances, employees can use an additional 64 hours for these purposes.

Additional Leave Benefits

FBI employees are also eligible for leave to attend court either as a witness or member of a jury, for bone marrow or organ donations, to serve military obligations, or to vote in elections.

Health Care and Wellness Benefits

The FBI provides a comprehensive package of health benefits to ensure the physical and emotional well-being of its personnel. This section provides an overview of health insurance programs, on-site clinic services, counseling programs, and child-care services that are available to FBI personnel.

Federal Employees Health Benefits Program

Group health-care insurance is available to all permanent FBI employees through the Federal Employees Health Benefits Program (FEHBP), which is the largest employer-sponsored health insurance program in the world. The FEHBP offers the widest selection of health plans in the nation, including managed fee-for-service plans, point of service (POS) plans, and health maintenance organization (HMO) programs. Enrollees are granted coverage without medical examinations or restrictions relating to age or medical condition, and they can elect self-only or self-and-family protection. The government contributes between 60 and 75 percent toward the total cost of premiums, depending on the plan they have selected. Employees pay their share of premiums through a payroll deduction.

Health Care Programs Unit

The FBI offers a variety of occupational health services to its employees at the J. Edgar Hoover Headquarters Building, the FBI Academy, and the Bureau's 56 field offices. At FBI Headquarters, the Bureau's Health Care Programs Unit (HCPU) provides assessment and treatment of work-related injuries and illnesses, health counseling, referral service to physicians or hospitals, and emergency response in the clinic and throughout the building. The HCPU provides travel immunizations to employees, immunization injections to at-risk personnel, and health screenings for cholesterol, hypertension, and diabetes. The unit also offers educational classes on health and safety issues, such as basic cardiac support and first aid, weight reduction, smoking cessation, back care, safety in the workplace, health issues concerning men and women, proper nutrition, and other areas. Employees assigned to the FBI Academy and the Bureau's field offices are offered similar facilities that are staffed with experienced health-care professionals and specialty support staff.

Employee Assistance Program

The FBI Employee Assistance Program (EAP) is a service that is available to employees and their immediate families. The EAP is designed to address problems such as alcohol and drug abuse, marital difficulties, legal and financial concerns, and job stress that can adversely affect job performance, reliability, and personal health. The program is staffed by professional counselors who discuss and assess problems and provide short-term counseling. If needed, EAP counselors also provide referrals to other professional services and resources.

The EAP is a confidential program that is protected by strict confidentiality laws and regulations and by professional ethical standards for counselors. Details of discussions with counselors cannot be released without the written consent of the employee, and EAP records do not become part of any employee security or personnel record. There are no fees for EAP services.

Child Care Services

The availability of child care for FBI employees varies from one duty station to another. Personnel who serve at FBI Headquarters—which amounts to almost one-third of the Bureau's workforce—have access to "Just Us Kids," a child-development center operated by the United States Department of Justice. This center is located approximately two blocks from the J. Edgar Hoover FBI Building. It accommodates up to 68 children, ages three months to five years, and offers a tuition-assistance program for low-income families. Employees assigned to the Criminal Justice Information Services Division in Clarksburg, West Virginia, have access to a child-development center known as "Lasting Impressions" that operates at the FBI complex. In addition, many FBI field offices are located in federal office buildings that provide child-care services to federal employees. The Bureau also addresses the need for child care by maintaining listings of resources throughout the country.

Life Insurance

FBI employees can protect themselves and their families with life insurance, disability insurance, and professional liability insurance through a variety of programs. Insurance coverage is available to all FBI personnel, and participation is optional.

Federal Employees' Group Life Insurance

FBI special agents and professional support personnel are eligible to participate in the Federal Employees' Group Life Insurance (FEGLI) Program, a plan that offers both life insurance and accidental death and dismemberment coverage. Premiums are based on the employee's age and are paid through regular payroll deductions. FEGLI policies build no cash or loan value, and participants are not permitted to borrow against life insurance benefits. Participants can purchase additional life insurance to cover eligible family members, although accidental death and dismemberment coverage is not included. The amount of basic life insurance coverage is equal to an employee's annual basic pay, plus $2,000. The government pays approximately one-third of the premium for basic life insurance, and the remaining two-thirds is withheld from the employee by payroll deduction.

Other Sources of Insurance Coverage

FBI personnel can also purchase life insurance, accidental death and dismemberment insurance, disability insurance, and professional liability insurance through the Special Agents Mutual Benefit Association and the Special Agents Trust for Insurance. In addition, FBI employees can join the Employee Benevolent Fund, which pays their survivors $15,000 if they die while employed by the FBI, or the Special Agents Insurance Fund, which pays a $30,000 benefit.

Travel Allowances

FBI special agents and many professional support employees must travel on official business from time to time. The Bureau provides full reimbursement for airfare, lodging, rental cars, parking, taxis, and other expenses for travel throughout the United States and worldwide.

Reimbursement of Travel Expenses

FBI employees who travel on official business normally receive reimbursement for their transportation and lodging expenses, plus a daily allowance for meals and incidental expenses (M&IE). This allowance applies to travel undertaken during the course of investigative assignments, attendance in training programs, and other activities in furtherance of the Bureau's mission. Most hotel chains and many independent establishments offer discounted lodging rates for FBI employees and other government travelers. M&IE allowances are paid at a government-wide flat daily rate, which varies from one locality to another depending on prevailing costs in the area visited.

Death and Disability Benefits for Special Agents

The United States Congress enacted the Public Safety Officers' Benefits Act and the Federal Law Enforcement Dependents Assistance Act to provide benefits to the families of law enforcement officers whose deaths or disabilities are the result of injuries sustained in the line of duty. Congress has also enacted provisions to allow federal officers to attend funerals, during duty hours, for fellow law enforcement personnel.

Public Safety Officers' Benefits Program

The families of federal law enforcement officers, including FBI special agents, are eligible to receive death and disability benefits under the Public Safety Officers' Benefits (PSOB) Act, which was enacted to assist in the recruitment and retention of law enforcement officers and firefighters. The act was designed to offer peace of mind to men and women seeking careers in public safety and to make a strong statement about the value American society places on the contributions of those who serve their communities in potentially dangerous circumstances.

The PSOB program provides a one-time financial payment to the eligible survivors of public safety officers whose deaths are the direct and proximate result of a traumatic injury sustained in the line of duty. The program provides the same benefit to those who have been permanently and totally disabled by a catastrophic personal injury sustained in the line of duty if that injury permanently prevents them from performing any gainful work. Since 1988, the benefit has been adjusted annually to reflect the percentage of change in the Consumer Price Index. For example, the benefit amount increased from $146,949 in the 2000 fiscal year to $151,635 in 2001. The base amount was increased in 2002 to $250,000. After Consumer Price Index calculations, the FY 2002 figure was adjusted to $259,038.

Law enforcement officers eligible for PSOB program benefits include, but are not limited to, police, corrections, probation, parole, judicial, and other law enforcement officers of federal, state, county, and local public agencies, as well as the District of Columbia, the Commonwealth of Puerto Rico, and any U.S. territory or possession.

Federal Law Enforcement Dependents Assistance Program

Congress enacted the Federal Law Enforcement Dependents Assistance (FLEDA) Act of 1996 to provide financial assistance for higher education to the spouses and children of federal law enforcement officers killed or disabled in the line of duty. FLEDA benefits are intended for the sole purpose of paying for educational expenses, including tuition, room and board, books, supplies, and fees for dependents who attend a qualifying program of education at an eligible institution. Assistance under the program is available for a period of 45 months of full-time education or training, or for a proportional period for a part-time program.

Funeral Leave for Law Enforcement Officers

FBI special agents and other federal law enforcement officers may be excused from duty, without loss of pay or leave, to attend the funeral of a fellow federal law enforcement officer who was killed in the line of duty. Attendance at such a service is considered to be an official duty, and employing agencies are authorized under the United States Code to pay the costs of travel and subsistence for those who attend.

Retirement Benefits

Most federal civilian employees, including FBI professional support staff, are eligible to receive an unreduced retirement annuity at age 60 with 20 years of service, and at age 62 with five years of service. With 30 years of service, those who are covered under the Federal Employees' Retirement System (FERS), which includes most who were hired after December 31, 1983, can retire at age 55 to 57 depending on their year of birth. Employees who are covered under the Civil Service Retirement System (CSRS), the predecessor to FERS, can retire at age 55 with 30 years of service. There is no mandatory retirement age for FBI professional support employees. Special agents, however, must retire by age 57 because they are covered under special retirement provisions for law enforcement officers.

FERS is a three-tiered plan consisting of a Basic Annuity Benefit, the Federal Thrift Savings Plan, and Social Security. Upon completion of five years of civilian service, prior military service can be counted toward the service requirements under certain circumstances.

Basic Annuity Benefit

Retired FBI employees receive a basic annuity benefit based on the length of their federal service and their earnings history. If an employee reaches the minimum retirement age and has at least 20 years of creditable service, he can retire and begin receiving the basic annuity benefit immediately. This benefit is reduced if the employee retires under the age of 62, unless he retires under one of the following conditions:

- With 20 years of service at age 60

- With 30 years of service at the minimum retirement age

- Following an involuntary separation through no fault of the employee after completing 25 years of service (or 20 years if at least age 50)

An employee is also entitled to a basic annuity benefit at any age if approved for disability retirement, although some restrictions apply.

Federal Thrift Savings Plan

The Federal Thrift Savings Plan (TSP) is a retirement savings and investment plan for federal personnel that offers the same type of savings and tax benefits that many private firms provide under 401(k) plans. The TSP offers tax-deferred investment earnings, a choice of investment funds, a loan program, portable benefits on leaving government service, and a choice of withdrawal options.

As of 2002, employees could contribute up to 12 percent of their basic pay each pay period to a TSP account. This contribution limit will increase by one percentage point each year through 2005, to 15 percent, after which participants' contributions will be restricted only by annual limits prescribed by the Internal Revenue Code. The FBI matches each employee contribution dollar for dollar on the first 3 percent contributed, and 50 cents on the dollar for the next 2 percent. All contributions to an employee's TSP account earn interest and can be divided among five funds, including government securities investments (the "G Fund"), bond market investments (the "F Fund"), common stock investments (the "C Fund"), small capitalization stock investments (the "S Fund"), and international stock investments (the "I Fund"). Employees also have the opportunity to borrow against their TSP contributions.

An employee who leaves the government prior to retirement can either obtain a refund of their contributions or leave the contributions in his or her account and allow the account to earn interest. Employee contributions, agency matching funds, and earnings on all TSP accounts are deferred from income taxes until funds are withdrawn.

Social Security

All new FBI personnel are automatically covered under the Social Security system. An employee can apply for regular Social Security benefits as early as age 62. Disability Social Security benefits are conditionally available at any age.

Special Retirement Provisions for Special Agents

The majority of fully commissioned federal law enforcement officers are covered under special provisions that provide for voluntary and mandatory retirement at an earlier age than other government employees. These provisions apply not only to FBI special agents, but also to other law enforcement officers who serve in certain "covered" positions, including most criminal investigators, police officers, correctional officers, field personnel assigned to federal correctional institutions and military detention or rehabilitation facilities, and certain other law enforcement officers and security specialists. FBI special agents can receive an unreduced retirement annuity at age 50 with 20 years of federal law enforcement service, or at any age with 25 years of such service. Retirement is mandatory for FBI special agents at the end of the month in which they turn 57, provided that they have at least 20 years of law enforcement service.

PART 2

GETTING INTO THE FBI

CHAPTER 3

FBI Special Agent Career Opportunities

Courage is its own reward.   *—Plautus*

FBI special agents are recruited from a broad range of educational disciplines and professions and receive outstanding basic and in-service training to prepare them for unique challenges. In addition to conducting investigations and protecting the United States from foreign intelligence and terrorist activities, FBI special agents also provide leadership and assistance to law enforcement agencies in the U.S. and throughout the world. The Bureau has the largest force of criminal investigators of all federal law enforcement agencies, with almost one-half of its 27,000 personnel serving as special agents.

Investigative responsibilities of FBI special agents include more than 260 federal statutes that are divided among seven programs:

- Applicant matters
- Civil rights
- Counterterrorism
- Foreign counterintelligence
- Organized crime and drugs
- Violent crime and major offenders
- White-collar crime

Among the greatest challenges special agents face is involvement with high-profile cases, such as investigations relating to public corruption, bribery, kidnapping, air piracy, terrorism, and civil rights violations. These investigations demand skill, tact, and undaunted perseverance, and frequently require sensitive investigative methods, undercover operations, court-ordered electronic surveillance, and interaction with informants. The investigative techniques and strategies special agents use are subject to rigorous review and approval procedures.

Many investigations are conducted through task force or joint operations with other law enforcement agencies, through cooperation with law enforcement agencies in foreign countries, and with the assistance of assistant United States attorneys. Cases are prosecuted by United States Attorney's Offices located within the jurisdiction of the investigation.

This chapter provides insight into what it takes to become one of America's finest, as well as the types of investigative and special assignments that FBI special agents can expect throughout their careers.

Investigative Priorities

The FBI focuses its investigative efforts primarily on complex cases that have a major impact on the security and quality of life for U.S. citizens. In 1998, the FBI established a five-year strategic plan to set investigative priorities in line with a three-tiered structure. Tier 1 focuses on crimes that threaten national or economic security, while Tier 2 concerns criminal enterprises and public integrity offenses. Tier 3 includes violations against individuals or property. Within these tiers, the FBI presently categorizes its investigative priorities into the areas of applicant matters, civil rights, counterterrorism, foreign counter-intelligence, organized crime and drugs, violent crime and major offenders, and white-collar crime, each of which is detailed in the following sections.

Applicant Matters

The FBI conducts background investigations for all candidates for employment with the FBI, Department of Justice, Department of Energy, and Nuclear Regulatory Commission. The Bureau also conducts background investigations for presidential appointees who require Senate confirmation, and U.S. Court candidates.

Civil Rights

Violations of the Civil Rights Act of 1964, Voting Rights Act of 1965, Fair Housing Act, Equal Credit Opportunity Act, Freedom of Access to Clinic Entrances Act, and other statutes are the responsibility of the FBI's Civil Rights Program. Investigations pertaining to excessive use of force by federal, state, and local law enforcement officers also fall under the civil rights umbrella.

Counterterrorism

Congress has designated the FBI as the lead federal law enforcement agency for the investigation of incidents involving terrorism in the United States, as well as terrorist acts against U.S. citizens overseas. The FBI's Counterterrorism Program is responsible for the investigation of incidents involving weapons of mass destruction, threats against atomic energy, sabotage, hostage-taking, and civil unrest. The program's mission to combat terrorism is carried out through the Bureau's Counterterrorism Division, which includes the National Infrastructure Protection Center and the National Domestic Preparedness Office. The FBI conducts intelligence-gathering activities with the White House Office of Homeland Security, which was created by President George W. Bush days after the September 11, 2001, attacks on the World Trade Center and the Pentagon. The Bureau also coordinates counterterrorism activities with the Central Intelligence Agency and dozens of other federal agencies.

Foreign Counterintelligence

The FBI's foreign counterintelligence responsibilities revolve around preventing and investigating foreign espionage; economic espionage; international terrorism threats; weapons of mass destruction threats; and attacks on the nation's critical infrastructures, including communications, transportation, and banking systems. The FBI is the lead agency within the U.S. intelligence community for the investigation and prevention of foreign counterintelligence.

Organized Crime and Drugs

The Organized Crime and Drug Program targets complex organizations and criminal enterprises that engage in drug trafficking, money laundering, and both traditional and nontraditional organized-crime activities. Much of the Bureau's efforts in the program are carried out through nationwide joint task forces, including the Organized Crime and Drug Enforcement Task Force. The program also relies largely upon sophisticated investigative techniques, informants, and extensive criminal intelligence. Investigations involving labor racketeering often target violations under the Racketeer Influenced and Corrupt Organizations (RICO) statute.

Violent Crime and Major Offenders

Under the Violent Crime and Major Offenders Program, the FBI investigates kidnapping, assaults, crimes against children, extortion, bank robbery, consumer product tampering, crimes on Indian reservations, and unlawful flight to avoid prosecution. Investigations relating to assaults on the president, vice president, members of Congress, and federal officers are also targeted, as are crimes aboard aircraft, murder for hire, and criminal activity of street gangs.

White-Collar Crime

Economic crime investigations are among the Bureau's highest priorities. Offenses investigated under the White-Collar Crime Program focus on fraud against the government, health-care fraud, bank fraud and embezzlement, money laundering, corruption of public officials, environmental crimes, election law violations, and telemarketing fraud. The White-Collar Crime Program is the largest of the FBI's criminal investigation programs.

Qualifications for the Special Agent Position

Special agent applicants must meet a number of qualifications to be eligible for employment, including standards relating to citizenship, entry age, education, eyesight, hearing, and physical fitness, among others. These qualifications represent the first hurdle applicants must clear on the road to becoming an FBI special agent.

Basic Qualifications

The work of FBI special agents is rigorous and demanding—and sometimes dangerous. Special agents must be mentally and physically fit in order to perform surveillance and undercover work, conduct interviews and interrogations, execute search warrants, make arrests, and respond to critical incidents.

The position demands alertness, intelligence, and good judgement, whether special agents are involved in fact-finding tasks, working with informants, using sophisticated electronic investigative equipment, advising assistant United States attorneys, or testifying in court. To ensure that the FBI recruits qualified personnel who can face these challenges successfully, special agent applicants must meet the following qualifications to be considered for the position.

Citizenship

All applicants for special agent positions must be citizens of the United States or of the Northern Mariana Islands. Resident aliens of the U.S. and other noncitizens do not qualify for FBI employment.

Minimum and Maximum Age

Special agent candidates must be at least 23 years of age and must not have reached their 37th birthday at the time of appointment. The maximum entry age of 37 ensures that special agents will be able to complete 20 years of service by age 57, which is the mandatory retirement age. (Special agents must serve for at least 20 years to qualify for retirement.) The FBI advises anyone over the age of 36½ not to apply for a special agent position, considering the length of time it takes to test, process, and hire new agents.

Educational Requirements

Applicants must possess a bachelor's degree from a four-year resident program at a college or university accredited by one of the regional or national institutional associations recognized by the United States Secretary of Education. No particular major is required, unless an applicant wishes to qualify under the Accounting Program (see "Entrance Programs," later in this chapter).

Eyesight Requirements

Eyesight requirements include uncorrected vision not worse than 20/200 (on the Snellen scale) and corrected vision not worse than 20/20 in one eye and 20/40 in the other eye. All candidates must also pass a color-vision test. Applicants who have undergone surgical vision correction are evaluated on a case-by-case basis by the FBI's Health Care Programs Unit. The Bureau has accepted applicants who have had LASIK laser vision correction in the past, although these candidates must wait one year from the time of surgery to be considered as a special agent.

Hearing Requirements

An audiometer test is used to determine whether special agent candidates meet minimum hearing requirements. Hearing loss must not exceed: (a) average hearing loss of 25 decibels (ANSI) at 1000, 2000, and 3000 Hertz; (b) a single reading of 35 decibels at 1000, 2000, and 3000 Hertz; (c) a single reading of 35 decibels at 500 Hertz; and (d) a single reading of 45 decibels at 4000 Hertz.

Physical Fitness

FBI special agents must have the strength and endurance necessary to successfully deal with strenuous and dangerous situations. Therefore, applicants must be in excellent physical condition and deemed by the FBI's chief medical officer to be physically able to use firearms, participate in raids, execute defensive tactics, and perform other essential functions of the job. An extensive physical examination is required. Prior to appointment, each candidate's medical history is reviewed, and a determination is made about whether any medical issue or condition could possibly affect the applicant's ability to perform the basic functions of the position. Applicants must successfully complete a 1.5-mile timed run toward the end of the hiring process.

Driver's License

Special agent candidates must possess a valid driver's license.

Entrance Programs

The FBI fulfills its mission by employing a diverse workforce with a variety of talents. To this end, the Bureau requires special agent candidates to qualify under at least one of four entry programs, including Law, Accounting, Language, Computer Science, and Diversified. The following provides an overview of the entry requirements under each program:

- **Law.** To qualify under the Law Program, an applicant must have a law degree. (Juris Doctorate) from an accredited resident law school.

- **Accounting.** A bachelor's degree with a major in accounting or a related discipline is required under the Accounting Program. Applicants must be academically eligible to take the CPA examination. Those who have not passed the CPA exam will also be required to pass the FBI's accounting test.

- **Language.** To qualify under the Language Program, applicants must have a bachelor's degree in any discipline and be proficient in a language that meets the needs of the FBI. Candidates must also pass a language proficiency test that focuses on listening comprehension, reading comprehension, and translation. Applicants who wish to qualify under the Language Program are required to complete a Foreign Language Assessment Questionnaire (see appendix H for a copy of this questionnaire).

- **Computer Science.** To qualify under the Computer Science Program, you must have a B.S. in Computer Science or a related discipline; or any B.S. or B.A. degree plus certification as a Cisco Certified Network Professional (CCNP) or a Cisco Certified Internetwork Expert (CCIE).

- **Diversified.** Applicants who qualify under the Diversified Program must have a bachelor's degree in any discipline, plus three years of full-time work experience, or an advanced degree and two years of full-time work experience. The FBI does not consider internships, co-op positions, summer employment, or temporary employment as full-time work experience.

Automatic Disqualifiers

The FBI will automatically disqualify applicants from consideration for the special agent position under certain circumstances. Automatic disqualifiers include the following:

- Conviction of a felony.

- Use or sale of illegal drugs in violation of the FBI Employment Drug Policy (see chapter 4), or an applicant's misrepresentation of his or her drug history during the hiring process.

- Refusal to submit to FBI urinalysis drug testing.

- Failure of a urinalysis drug test.

- Default of a student loan that was insured by the U.S. government.

- Refusal to submit to an FBI polygraph examination.

- Failure to register with the Selective Service System, if required.

- Omitting, misstating, or falsifying any information—in writing or orally —to the FBI during the hiring process. (If the omission, misstatement, or falsification is discovered after hiring, the person may be subject to administrative or disciplinary action, or dismissal.)

- Unwillingness to be available for employment within 90 days of phase II testing or to report for New Agent Training within two weeks of completion of the application process.

- Unwillingness to accept a permanent or temporary assignment anywhere worldwide according to the needs of the Bureau.

Additional Requirements

Additional requirements for the special agent position include a willingness to carry firearms, a willingness to relocate, the ability to report for duty within 90 days of phase II testing, availability for duty at all times, and completion of basic training. The following sections give details on these additional requirements.

Willingness to Carry Firearms

Applicants must be willing to carry firearms and use them in training and life-threatening situations if they are hired as a special agent. All newly hired special agents are trained in the use and maintenance of firearms during the New Agent Training Program at the FBI Academy in Quantico, Virginia. Prior experience or proficiency with firearms is not required. Special agents must also agree to be armed or have immediate access to a firearm at all times when on official duty unless good judgment dictates otherwise, and to utilize deadly force should circumstances dictate.

Willingness to Relocate

Anyone appointed to the special agent position must be willing to relocate anywhere in the FBI's geographic jurisdiction. Although newly hired special agents normally are not assigned to permanent posts of duty outside the United States, they must be available for duty anywhere in the world.

Therefore, as a condition of employment, new special agents must sign a Worldwide Mobility Agreement (FD-918) indicating their willingness to accept a permanent or temporary duty (TDY) assignment anywhere worldwide according to the needs of the Bureau (see appendix F for a copy of this agreement). Applicants must also attest to their willingness to accept assignments anywhere in the FBI's geographic jurisdiction on the Application Checklist for the Special Agent Position (FD-869) early in the hiring process (see appendix A for a copy of this checklist). Normally, the FBI seeks qualified volunteers for assignments overseas.

Reporting for Duty

Applicants must be available for employment within 90 days of phase II testing and to accept no more than two weeks' notice to report for New Agent Training upon successful completion of the application process. Applicants must attest to their willingness to report for duty, as specified above, on the Application Checklist for the Special Agent Position.

Availability for Duty at All Times

Applicants must indicate their willingness to be available for duty around the clock, 365 days per year, according to the needs of the Bureau. Availability for duty may include weekends, holidays, overtime, or an irregular schedule. Special agents must work an average of 10 hours per day.

Completion of Basic Training

Newly hired special agents must successfully complete the 16-week New Agent Training Program at the FBI Academy in Quantico, Virginia, before being assigned to a post of duty. (See chapter 8 for additional details about initial and in-service training.)

Assignment of New Special Agents

Although new hires who land jobs with private companies—as well as with most federal law enforcement agencies—have the luxury of knowing in advance where they will be assigned, FBI special agents could end up almost anyplace in the United States after completing basic training. After reporting for duty, new agents are assigned to offices and investigative squads where they apply what they learned at the FBI Academy under the guidance of experienced agents. This section provides some insight into the assignment and work life of new FBI special agents.

Location of Initial Assignment

At the beginning of the New Agent Training Program, all special agent trainees are provided with a list of the FBI's 56 nationwide field offices. New agent trainees are asked to review the list and indicate where they would like to be assigned, in order of their preference from 1 through 56. Office assignments are based on the current staffing and critical specialty needs of the Bureau at the time. The Bureau notifies trainees of their office assignments during the sixth week of training, and about 70 percent receive one of their top 10 choices. Initial assignment to the trainee's hometown, however, is unusual.

Although trainees are allowed to rank-order the 56 field offices on their "wish list," assignments can also include any of the FBI's resident agencies. For example, if the Bureau were to honor a trainee's preference for the Detroit field office, the trainee could be assigned to a resident agency in Lansing, Grand Rapids, Bay City, or any other resident agency under the jurisdiction of the Detroit field office. New special agents normally remain at their first office of assignment for a minimum of four years.

Probationary Period

Newly hired special agents are required to serve a two-year probationary period. Preference-eligible veterans, however, are required to serve only a one-year probationary period. In either case, much of a special agent's first two years on the job are spent under the watchful eye of veteran special agents and supervisory personnel, who provide advice and guidance.

A Special Agent's Work Life

One of the most interesting aspects of FBI special agents' work lives is that their job is anything but routine. Whether they are reviewing business records at an FBI field office, conducting interviews at a local bank, executing a search warrant, or conducting surveillance throughout the night, the daily activities, work environments, dress code, and work hours of special agents can vary widely from one day to another.

Office Environment

Office and workspace in FBI field offices and resident agencies vary widely from one location to another. Many FBI offices are located in federal office buildings along with an assortment of other agencies. Being co-located with other federal offices in the same building has its advantages, as taking the elevator to another floor makes quick work of conducting interviews, reviewing files, or obtaining information from other federal agencies. Many Bureau offices occupy space in federal courthouses or post office facilities. Others rent office space within private buildings, and some have their own buildings. Special agents assigned to task-force operations often share offsite office space with personnel from other law enforcement agencies.

Personal workspace arrangements also vary from office to office. Some field offices provide desks in open "bullpen" areas, whereas others offer semi-private cubicles or private offices.

Dress Code

The dress code in FBI offices also varies, although this is more dependent on agents' activities than office location. When J. Edgar Hoover was FBI director, special agents were required to wear suits, along with white shirts and neckties that matched the color of their suit lining. It wasn't until 1972, when L. Patrick Gray was appointed director, that special agents were permitted to wear colored shirts. Today, agents are allowed to dress according to their day-to-day activities and assignments. For example, an agent who is conducting mobile surveillance is permitted to "dress down," and casual attire would be appropriate. Similarly, the execution of search or arrest warrants could call for either casual or tactical attire and equipment—such as raid pants, jackets with FBI markings, leather gear, and body armor—depending on the situation and environment. Agents are expected to wear business attire—such as a suit, dress, or pantsuit for females, and a suit or coat and tie for males—while in the office or working in a business atmosphere outside the office.

Work Hours

In consideration of rules relating to Law Enforcement Availability Pay, Congress requires FBI special agents and most other federal law enforcement officers to average a 10-hour workday. Most FBI special agents work 50 to 55 hours per week, although this can vary considerably during weeks in which surveillance or special operations are undertaken. Special agents often begin or end their workday away from the office. For example, if an agent is scheduled to meet with an assistant United States attorney or other law enforcement officers at 8:00 a.m., the agent probably could drive to the meeting site directly from home. In this case, time associated with the agent's commute to the meeting would count toward his or her 10-hour workday. The same holds true when returning home from activities in the field.

Equipment

Most special agents are issued a pager, a cellular telephone, a car that is equipped with law enforcement communications equipment, and a credit card to cover travel expenses. Many are also issued laptop computers. Presently, new agents are issued a .40 caliber semiautomatic pistol and soft body armor. FBI field offices are equipped with shotguns and submachine guns, so that there is one shoulder weapon per field agent nationwide. Members of special response teams are issued additional equipment according to their responsibilities.

Squad Assignments

FBI field office personnel are organized into various investigative squads that specialize in certain crimes, ranging from bank robbery to health-care fraud, public corruption, counterterrorism, and white-collar crime, among others. The variety of squads and number of assigned members varies from one office to another, depending largely on the size of the office, the nature of crime in the area, the existence of task force operations, or investigative priorities established by the FBI or United States Attorney's Offices. In addition, many offices combine the investigative responsibilities of various squads. For example, some offices combine organized crime and drug squads because these offenses often are committed by the same groups. Other offices have squads that combine the investigation of economic and environmental crimes, property crime with violent crime, or public corruption with government fraud. To provide its personnel with a broad range of investigative responsibilities and experiences, the Bureau tends to rotate special agents periodically from one squad to another throughout their careers.

Although not all-inclusive, the following sections provide examples of the functions carried out by many of the primary FBI squads presently operating at the Bureau's field offices.

Applicant Squads

FBI applicant squads are responsible for the recruitment and processing of candidates for employment with the Bureau, including special agents and professional support personnel. Among their primary responsibilities, applicant squads conduct background investigations for all FBI candidates who have been issued a conditional letter of appointment—from mail clerks to the FBI director. These squads also conduct background investigations for appointees to presidential cabinet posts, other presidential appointees, White House staff, and applicants for positions with the Department of Energy, Nuclear Regulatory Commission, Department of Justice, and United States Courts. Some applicant squads are also responsible for training, media relations, security programs, and other tasks.

Civil Rights Squads

The FBI is the primary federal agency responsible for investigating violations of federal civil rights laws. Investigations carried out by civil rights squads focus on hate crimes and discrimination cases which, based on their severity, cannot be addressed appropriately on local or state levels. Special agents assigned to civil rights squads maintain liaison with local, state, and federal law enforcement agencies and community and civic organizations to identify, detect, and deter all forms of discrimination, as well as acts of hatred and violence. Guidelines relating to federal civil rights investigations have been established by the FBI and the United States attorney general.

Civil rights squads investigate crimes involving racial and religious discrimination, and other violations under the Civil Rights Act of 1964; Color of Law violations, which focus most often on excessive force by law enforcement officers; and violations of the Church Arson Prevention Act. Investigations also focus on violations of the Freedom of Access to Clinic Entrances Act violations, which involves use of force, threats, or physical obstruction of persons seeking to obtain or provide reproductive health services; involuntary servitude and slavery cases; and discrimination in housing under the Fair Housing Act. Violations of the Voting Rights Act of 1965, Equal Credit Opportunity Act, and the Civil Rights of Institutionalized Persons Act are also investigated by the civil rights squads.

Computer Crime Squads

Illegal electronic intrusion into computer networks is a rapidly escalating crime and security risk. Businesses and government agencies are vulnerable to attacks that are designed to alter, steal, or destroy information in their computer systems. Such attacks could be devastating if launched on critical systems constituting the national critical infrastructures, including telecommunications, transportation, government operations, and emergency services. Computer crimes also include attempts to illegally transfer funds from financial institutions; financial crimes perpetrated on the Internet, such as investment and pyramid schemes; sales of illegally reproduced computer software; and fraudulent sales of other goods.

To address the problem, FBI computer crime squads investigate computer intrusions, attacks on computer systems and networks, data loss or data manipulations, and software copyright violations. These investigations may focus on white-collar criminals, terrorists, economic espionage agents, organized crime groups, and foreign intelligence agents—all of whom have been identified as "electronic intruders" responsible for penetrations of American computer systems and networks. Computer crime squads also are responsible for the forensic examination and analysis of computers and systems.

Counterterrorism Squads

The FBI is the lead federal law enforcement agency in the United States government's fight against international and domestic terrorism. FBI counterterrorism squads conduct sensitive intelligence and investigations to prevent terrorism before it occurs and to effectively and swiftly respond to terrorist acts. Crimes of terrorism can include bombings or other acts of violence, weapons of mass destruction, hostage taking, overseas homicide of U.S. citizens, sabotage, nuclear extortion, sedition, and crimes directed at federally designated special events such as the Olympic Games and presidential inaugurations.

FBI counterterrorism squads frequently participate in task-force operations with federal law enforcement agencies such as the Secret Service; Immigration and Naturalization Service; Customs Service; State Department Bureau of Diplomatic Security; Federal Protective Service; Naval Criminal Investigative Service; Internal Revenue Service; and the Bureau of Alcohol, Tobacco, and Firearms. Investigations and task-force operations are also conducted with other federal, state, and local law enforcement agencies, as well as firms in the private sector.

Drug Squads

In 1982, the attorney general assigned concurrent jurisdiction for enforcement of the Controlled Substances Act to the FBI and the Drug Enforcement Administration. FBI drug squads are responsible for the investigation of domestic and international trafficking, the laundering of illegal proceeds from drug trafficking, and acts of violence associated with drug trafficking. As tools of the trade, these squads utilize sophisticated investigative techniques and equipment, extensive criminal intelligence, and cooperation from other law enforcement agencies to disrupt and dismantle drug organizations and enterprises. In addition to seeking criminal prosecution of drug traffickers, FBI drug squads also concentrate on the seizure and forfeiture of assets used in or derived from criminal activity. These squads also coordinate investigative activities with agencies such as the Drug Enforcement Administration, Customs Service, Immigration and Naturalization Service, Coast Guard Investigative Service, USDA Forest Service, and other federal, state, and local law enforcement agencies.

Economic Crime Squads

Economic crime squads investigate a variety of financial crimes that significantly affect the community. These offenses range from telemarketing fraud to securities and commodities fraud, wire-transfer fraud, bankruptcy fraud, insurance fraud, investment fraud, lottery schemes, copyright and trademark violations, industrial and economic espionage, and pyramid schemes. Particular emphasis is given to the investigation of "con artists" who prey on unsuspecting victims using elaborate schemes. These schemes include get-rich-quick and prize scams; high-yield investment opportunities; and the issuance of bogus guaranties, performance bonds, and other financial obligations. Many FBI economic crime squads also investigate intellectual-property offenses, including copyright and trademark infringement. These include crimes such as the manufacture and sale of counterfeit designer apparel or computer chips, and piracy of computer software, videos, compact discs, tapes, or DVD recordings. Economic crimes may be investigated not only with the assistance of other law enforcement agencies, but also with cooperation from representatives of the securities industry, financial institutions, insurance companies, and other private firms, and government regulatory agencies.

Environmental Crime Squads

The Bureau has authority to investigate a full range of environmental crimes, including offenses that involve discharge of toxic substances into the air, water, or soil that pose a significant threat of harm to people, property, or the environment. Investigative priorities of FBI environmental crime squads include air and water pollution violations, discharges from industrial users, wetlands violations, spills of hazardous substances, illegal dumping, and the illegal importation and use of Freon. These investigations focus on violations of the Clean Air Act, Clean Water Act, Resource Conservation and Recovery Act, Toxic Substances Control Act, and other environmental statutes. FBI environmental crime squads also conduct investigations jointly with special agents of the Criminal Investigation Division of the Environmental Protection Agency.

Financial Institution Fraud Squads

Federal crimes involving federally insured banks, savings and loan firms, and credit unions are investigated by the Bureau's financial institution fraud squads. These investigations often focus on bank embezzlement, bribery of bank officials, check-kiting schemes, fraud involving checks and other negotiable instruments, counterfeit and stolen-check schemes, organized check rings, wire-transfer frauds, and loan and mortgage frauds. Organized groups involved in check-fraud and loan-fraud schemes are often involved in illegal money-laundering activities in an effort to conceal the proceeds of their crimes. The successful prosecution of bank failure cases is largely the result of task forces that have combined the efforts of FBI financial institution fraud squads and the resources of other federal law enforcement and regulatory agencies. Inasmuch as financial institution fraud cases periodically are tied to fraud in government programs, these investigations may be conducted jointly with special agents representing Office of Inspector General agencies.

Government Fraud Squads

Fraud against the federal government is costly not only for the government but for all taxpayers, and certain forms of fraud can pose grave risks to public safety. The government fraud squads investigate a wide range of fraud against the federal government, including offenses involving bribery of public officials involving contracts or procurement processes, collusion among government contractors, bid rigging, false or double billing, false certification of the quality of parts or of test results, substitution of bogus or otherwise inferior parts, antitrust matters, false claims, conflict of interest, and fraud in various public benefits programs. Government fraud cases are often investigated jointly with special agents representing various Office of Inspector General agencies.

Health-Care Fraud Squad

The Bureau has statutory authority to investigate all forms of fraud affecting government-sponsored health-care programs, including Medicare and Medicaid, as well as private insured health benefit programs. FBI health-care fraud squad investigations focus primarily on bribery, kickbacks, billing for services not rendered, false claims, managed-care abuses, and diversion of controlled substances, among other crimes. These offenses may be committed by physicians, hospitals, nursing homes, home health-care providers, medical equipment companies, laboratories, clinics, and others who provide goods and services to the health-care industry. FBI health-care squads often cooperate with other law enforcement agencies and private organizations to combat health-care fraud, including the Department of Defense—Defense Criminal Investigative Service, the Department of Health and Human Services—Office of Inspector General, the Drug Enforcement Administration, the Food and Drug Administration, the Internal Revenue Service, the Department of Veterans Affairs—Office of Inspector General, various state agencies, private insurance companies, and health-care industry associations.

Homicide Squads

In joining forces and combining investigative expertise with state and local police departments, FBI homicide squads focus on heinous and unsolved murders. These squads include agents with a solid background in violent crime investigations and a thorough knowledge of the Bureau's resources and capabilities, and police detectives who have extensive experience in investigating homicide cases. Homicides investigated by these squads frequently target drug-trafficking organizations and urban gangs. These investigations rely on a combination of scientific techniques, confidential informants, cooperative witnesses, and expert legal guidance from prosecutors and assistant United States attorneys to solve crimes.

Organized Crime Squads

The FBI's organized crime squads investigate sophisticated groups who conspire to violate federal laws for personal gain, including La Cosa Nostra (more commonly known as "the Mafia" or "the mob"), Russian and Eastern European criminal enterprises, Asian criminal enterprises and gangs, and other organizations. Special agents who investigate organized crime utilize a broad range of investigative techniques, but emphasize the use of informants, intelligence gathering, undercover operations, and obtaining evidence through court-authorized electronic surveillance. Investigations focus on criminal enterprises that engage in drug trafficking, money laundering, labor racketeering, and both traditional and nontraditional organized-crime activities. FBI organized crime squads participate with agencies such as the Drug Enforcement Administration, Internal Revenue Service, USDA Office of Inspector General, and other law enforcement agencies in conjunction with Organized Crime Drug Enforcement Task Force operations.

Property Crime Squads

Major thefts that affect interstate commerce are investigated by FBI property crime squads. These investigations often revolve around the interstate or worldwide transportation of stolen property by organized groups. Many of these groups steal high-value merchandise, such as art, jewelry, and motor vehicles, and market the goods nationally and internationally. During the course of these investigations, FBI special agents frequently come in contact with representatives of various manufacturers, distribution centers, warehouse facilities, trucking companies and terminals, airlines and air cargo firms, and railroad yards. The Bureau's property crime squads often conduct investigations jointly with the U.S. Customs Service; other federal, state, and local law enforcement agencies; and the National Insurance Crime Bureau, a private-sector organization that works with law enforcement agencies on behalf of insurance companies. Many of the Bureau's property crime squads also investigate theft or destruction of U.S. Government property, and crimes that occur on property owned by the government.

Public Corruption Squads

Public corruption investigations are among the most sensitive investigations the FBI handles. Investigations carried out by public corruption squads focus on the corruption of elected or appointed public officials on the federal, state, and local levels, including law enforcement officers, judiciary and executive department employees, and others in positions of trust. Generally speaking, public corruption occurs when a government official asks, demands, solicits, seeks, accepts, receives, or agrees to receive anything of value in return for being influenced in the performance of his or her official duties. Corruption schemes are secretive and characterized by unwritten agreements sealed with whispered conversations, handshakes, and under-the-table payments. These crimes often lack physical evidence, such as fingerprints or a "smoking gun," and rarely involve violent acts. Public corruption destroys public confidence in government and casts a cloud over the majority of public officials who are honest and hard working.

Violent Crime Squads

The Bureau's violent crime squads investigate a wide variety of criminal offenses, including bank robbery, armed robbery of commercial establishments, armored car robbery, burglary, extortion, kidnapping, homicide, assault on federal officers, sexual exploitation of children, interstate transportation of child pornography, and child abduction. In addition, many of the Bureau's violent crime squads locate and arrest fugitives and investigate crimes committed by violent street gangs. These squads frequently participate in task force operations with special agents and detectives of other federal, state, and local law enforcement agencies. The FBI also provides assistance to other law enforcement agencies with the behavioral profiling of violent felons and the investigation of serial murders.

Beyond the Initial Assignment

After gaining experience, FBI special agents can be assigned to a variety of special response teams, promoted to supervisory positions, or transferred to other field offices or Headquarters. In some cases, agents can work part-time to meet family obligations and other personal needs. This section provides an overview of opportunities that are available to veteran agents, as well discussion of the Special Agent Transfer Policy and part-time employment status.

The Special Agent Transfer Policy

As a condition of their employment, FBI special agents must be willing to be transferred to other offices according to the needs of the Bureau. By signing both the Worldwide Mobility Agreement and the Application Checklist for the Special Agent Position during the hiring process, applicants indicate their acceptance of the FBI's transfer policy. In 1996, the Bureau made significant modifications to the Special Agent Transfer Policy which, over the following two years, allowed more than 3,200 agents to transfer to offices where they preferred to work. As a result of the policy modifications, since 1996 the transfer of special agents who did not want to move has been extremely limited.

Presently, special agents who have worked in their first office of assignment for at least four years can be considered for a nonvoluntary rotational transfer to another office, depending on the Bureau's staffing needs at the time. However, those who remain in their first office of assignment for more than 10 years generally will not be considered for a nonvoluntary transfer. The FBI pays for personal moving expenses associated with nonvoluntary transfers.

Special Response Teams

Experienced and highly motivated special agents may have the opportunity to join special operational and enforcement response teams. Unlike squads, whose roles are to investigate particular types of crimes, the FBI's response teams are geared to deploy to crime scenes and critical incidents to locate and collect evidence or to intervene in dangerous situations. Special agents normally participate on response teams as collateral duty, meaning that their involvement is undertaken in addition to investigative responsibilities. Response team assignments require particular skills and abilities and offer ongoing advanced training opportunities. The following sections provide examples of special teams that special agents may join.

Scuba Team

The FBI scuba team consists of highly trained and experienced special agents who fulfill a variety of functions, although their primary responsibilities revolve around evidence recovery. Its members must be skilled enough to accomplish recovery missions in hazardous conditions and hostile underwater environments, under ice, in varying degrees of current, and along silty bottoms. The team was formed in 1981, under the FBI's chief of special operations, with an elite group of divers that included former Navy Seals. Using inflatable boats, metal detectors, sonar units, dive computers, underwater scooters, and other high-tech equipment, the team has participated in a number of high-profile operations. For example, its dive operations played a key role in search-and-recovery operations following the explosions of Pan Am 103 over Lockerbie, Scotland, in 1988 and of TWA Flight 800 over Long Island Sound in 1996. They also worked around the clock in support of the 1996 Summer Olympics in Atlanta. The team supports missions throughout the United States and anywhere in the world where the FBI has an interest.

Evidence Response Teams

Each of the FBI's 56 field offices has an evidence response team (ERT) that specializes in organizing and conducting major evidence-recovery operations.

These teams identify, collect, and preserve evidence during the execution of search warrants and at crime scenes involving bank robberies, kidnappings, bombing incidents, and other offenses. ERTs are staffed not only with special agents, but also with support personnel such as forensic anthropologists, evidence collection specialists, paralegals, language specialists, fingerprint specialists, and photographers. These specialists have responded to countless high-profile crime scenes, including the World Trade Center bombings in 1993 and 2001, the Alfred P. Murrah Federal Building bombing in Oklahoma City, Atlanta's 1996 Olympic Park bombing, and the Montana cabin used by Theodore Kaczynski—the "Unabomber." These teams undergo continuous training to develop and maintain their organizational and forensic skills.

Hazardous Materials Response Unit

A key component of the Bureau's efforts to prevent terrorists from using nuclear, biological, or chemical weapons in the United States is the Hazardous Materials (HAZMAT) Response Unit, which is based at the FBI Laboratory. Special agents and support personnel assigned to this unit respond to criminal acts and incidents involving the use of weapons of mass destruction and other hazardous materials. For example, in the wake of the terrorist attacks on the World Trade Center and the Pentagon on September 11, 2001, the HAZMAT unit participated in the investigation and recovery of a letter containing anthrax spores that was mailed to U.S. Senator Patrick Leahy in Washington, D.C. Since the unit's formation in 1996, its personnel have also responded to a variety of special events, such as Pope John Paul II's visit to the United States, the World Alpine Games, and the Super Bowl. Although the HAZMAT unit is based at the FBI Academy in Quantico, Virginia, it also trains, equips, and certifies FBI field office personnel for hazardous materials operations.

Hostage Rescue Team

The FBI's hostage rescue team (HRT) is a full-time tactical force that conducts high-threat rescue operations involving persons who are being held illegally by terrorists or other criminals. With headquarters at the FBI Academy in Quantico, Virginia, the HRT's special agents are prepared to deploy to any location within four hours of notification. Since being activated in 1983, its members have deployed on more than 200 occasions in support of incidents involving terrorism, violent crimes, foreign counterintelligence, and other matters. The team has performed missions involving hostage rescue, barricaded subjects, high-risk arrest and search-warrant operations, and dive-search operations. The HRT has also performed traditional law enforcement roles during hurricane-relief operations, dignitary-protection missions, tactical surveys, and in support of special events such as the Olympic Games, presidential inaugurations, and political conventions. Assignment to the HRT is open to all FBI special agents, and selection is based on their background and experience, as well as their performance during a rigorous two-week selection course. Once selected, team members undergo a four-month initial training program. Ongoing in-service training includes instruction in maritime operations from the U.S. Navy Seals, sniper tactics, explosives, nonlethal weapons, communications, and other subjects.

Crisis Negotiation Unit

The crisis negotiation unit (CNU) responds to significant crisis events world-wide. The FBI has approximately 340 crisis negotiators in the Bureau's 56 field offices who are trained to deploy to kidnapping and hostage situations, barricaded suspect incidents, suicide threat incidents, and other crisis situations. The CNU is responsible for the initial training of all FBI negotiators, which includes a two-week national negotiation course conducted at the FBI Academy. Its members also conduct research projects and case studies to expand the Bureau's capabilities to assess, manage, and successfully resolve critical events. The unit is based with all other critical incident response group units at the FBI Academy in Quantico, Virginia.

Special Weapons and Tactics Teams

Each FBI field office has a special weapons and tactics (SWAT) team, although the size of each team varies from one office to another depending on the geographical area covered, population density, and the potential for violent crime in the area. SWAT teams are well trained and specially equipped to conduct dangerous raids, rescues, and other missions. These operations could include drug raids, the execution of other high-risk search or arrest warrants, barricaded suspect situations, dignitary protection, and other specialized operations or critical incidents. The FBI also has eight technically advanced district SWAT teams that are configured to provide technical and operational support to field offices during major or protracted crisis situations. About 1,100 special agents are members of the Bureau's SWAT teams.

Canine Teams

The FBI has canine (K-9) teams that specialize in locating fleeing criminals, missing persons, explosives, and narcotics. Although the Bureau's K-9 teams are based at the New York field office and FBI Headquarters, they are prepared to respond to any FBI field office nationwide. Each K-9 team consists of a dog handler and a specially trained dog. The Bureau's dog handlers serve as special agents, special agent bomb technicians, or police officers. Chemical explosives detection dogs are trained to detect odors from a wide range of explosives, explosives residues, and firearms. Narcotics detection dogs search for drugs such as marijuana, hashish, cocaine, methamphetamine, and heroin. Search and rescue dogs are trained to track fleeing criminals and locate missing persons, cadavers, and others over many forms of terrain, under rubble or snow, and in a variety of climatic conditions. The teams train year-round and must be certified annually in their areas of expertise by organizations such as the North American Police Work Dog Association and the United States Police Canine Association. Certification is valuable not only for its affirmation that K-9 teams are performing up to standards, but also in the event that a dog handler is required to testify in court. Canine teams have provided support to many investigations, including the crash of TWA Flight 800 over Long Island Sound, as well as special events such as the Super Bowl and the Goodwill Games.

Promotion

Newly hired special agents advance from grade GS-10 to GS-11 after two years of service, from GS-11 to GS-12 after one additional year, and from GS-12 to GS-13 after two additional years. Promotion from GS-10 to GS-13 is contingent on agents successfully meeting performance standards and other criteria. Those who want to remain in nonsupervisory field investigative positions for the remainder of their careers will then climb the GS-13 step structure, "topping out" at GS-13 step 10.

On the other hand, agents who aspire to advance to supervisory and management positions typically serve as a relief supervisor before taking on full-time responsibilities as a squad supervisor. This allows special agents on the management track to obtain supervisory experience on an occasional basis while the squad supervisor is out of the office. Relief supervisor responsibilities are a collateral duty, meaning that an agent serving in this position must also maintain investigative assignments. Promotions to supervisory and management ranks are available at the GS-14 and GS-15 levels, and in the Senior Executive Service. Promotions often require a stint in FBI Headquarters.

Part-Time Special Agents

Since 1990, special agents who meet certain criteria have been able to convert to part-time employment status in order to address personal needs and family obligations. For example, a female agent could request a part-time schedule after returning from maternity leave and work three eight-hour days per week for a period of months or years. Presently, the FBI special agent part-time program permits agents to remain in part-time status for up to 10 years, while still maintaining active caseloads, squad assignments, and participation in training programs. The program allows the FBI to retain skilled agents who might otherwise have resigned.

Organizations for FBI Personnel

FBI employees can join a number of associations that provide a collective voice in employment issues, scholarships, financial assistance, insurance, legal counsel, recreation, and camaraderie. These organizations allow FBI personnel to address common concerns and needs that are unique to past and present members of the "FBI family."

FBI Agents Association

The FBI Agents Association (FBIAA) was founded in 1981 to protect and advance the interests of FBI special agents both within and outside the FBI. The association has promoted issues benefitting agents on matters such as Law Enforcement Availability Pay, due process during administrative inquiries, passage of the Federal Employees Pay Comparability Act, pay grade raises, and relocation benefits. FBIAA also maintains a college scholarship fund for the children and spouses of deceased agents. Member benefits include legal representation for administrative actions. The association's quarterly newsletter, *FBI Agent,* includes articles on current matters affecting FBI personnel, including legislative issues, legal representation, employee rights, and other topics. Membership is open to current and former FBI agents, including supervisors and managers. Approximately 70 percent of active FBI special agents are members of the FBIAA.

Special Agents Mutual Benefits Association

The Special Agents Mutual Benefits Association (SAMBA) provides group insurance coverage to active and retired employees of the FBI and other federal law enforcement agencies. SAMBA insurance products include a health plan, dental and vision coverage, personal accident insurance, life insurance, disability income protection, and long-term care insurance. The association also offers a legal services plan. The SAMBA Health Benefit Plan is part of the Federal Employees Health Benefits Program.

FBI Recreation Association

The FBI Recreation Association (FBIRA) is a nonprofit organization that encourages athletics, recreation, and overall fitness activities among FBI employees and the communities they serve. FBI special agents and support personnel are eligible to participate in FBIRA recreation and athletic programs—including softball, volleyball, and basketball leagues—and other activities. The association provides sponsorship funds to community athletic leagues, as well as other school and community activities. FBIRA also hosts an annual 5K run in memory of FBI Special Agent Jerry Dove, who was killed in the line of duty in 1986 during a shootout with bank robbery suspects in Miami.

Society of Former Special Agents of the FBI

The Society of Former Special Agents of the FBI was formed in 1937 to offer assistance to fellow agents and to support activities of the FBI. The society provides social opportunities for its members, hosts regional and national conventions around the United States, offers scholarships, and performs charitable activities. Since 1946, the organization's job-placement program has served as a clearinghouse for members seeking employment. Through a permanent trust fund and continued contributions, the society funds a variety of charitable programs, including college scholarships for the children and grandchildren of former agents, financial assistance to former FBI special agents and their families, and a program that provides gifts and pays travel expenses for terminally ill children. Other charitable activities include grants to other organizations that have performed services for the benefit of the society, a disaster relief program, and humanitarian service awards. The society publishes *The Grapevine,* a monthly journal that includes information on chapter meetings and activities, conventions, member achievements, awards, and other matters of interest to its members.

Society of FBI Alumni

In 1973, the Society of FBI Alumni was originally organized as the *Society of Former FBI Women,* to promote fellowship and support law enforcement causes on the local, state, and national levels. In 1992, the society modified its bylaws to allow men to join and changed its name two years later. Through its 1,500 members in 28 chapters nationwide, the society provides temporary financial assistance to members in need, and scholarships for the children and grandchildren of members. This organization maintains liaison with FBI Headquarters and field offices and the Society of Former Special Agents of the FBI. Its quarterly newsletter, *The Informant,* provides information on its annual convention, meetings, chapter news, society business, and other items of interest. Membership is open to special agents and support personnel who have served with the FBI for at least one year.

Federal Law Enforcement Officers Association (FLEOA)

The Federal Law Enforcement Officers Association (FLEOA) is a nonpartisan organization that represents nearly 20,000 federal law enforcement officers from about 60 agencies of the federal government. FLEOA provides its members with immediate expert legal advice and representation following critical incidents or other legal matters, and also works on legislative action and issues affecting federal law enforcement officers. FLEOA publishes *The Eighteen-Eleven,* a monthly newsletter that includes up-to-date information on legislative matters, member awards and accomplishments, articles of interest to the federal law enforcement community, and news relating to events and meetings held by various FLEOA chapters. The organization also funds grants to the survivors of federal law enforcement officers killed in the line of duty, financial assistance to disabled officers, educational scholarships, and charitable contributions. Membership is open to current full-time federal law enforcement officers, as well as certain former officers, retirees, and others who have an interest in promoting the objectives of FLEOA.

CHAPTER 4

The Special Agent Hiring Process

A journey of a thousand miles must begin with a single step.

—*Chinese Proverb*

The application process for FBI special agent positions is rigorous and time-consuming. It's very different from hiring processes followed in private industry, by police departments, or even by other federal law enforcement agencies. This chapter provides a step-by-step overview of the components in the hiring process, including the forms applicants encounter along the way. Additional information and specific strategies for carrying out a successful campaign for FBI employment are provided in chapter 7, "Standing Out from the Crowd." In addition, copies of FBI application forms are exhibited in the appendixes. Minimum qualifications for the special agent position—as well as automatic disqualifiers—are discussed in chapter 3, "FBI Special Agent Career Opportunities."

FBI Hiring Policies

The FBI application process is guided by a number of written policies to ensure not only that the Bureau hires the best and brightest to carry out its mission, but also to comply with employment laws and ensure that hiring decisions are based on merit principles. These policies address drug use, false statements, veterans' preference, equal employment opportunity, and applicants with disabilities, among other issues. The following sections discuss each of these topics in more detail.

FBI Employment Drug Policy

All applicants for FBI positions must meet the Bureau's Drug Policy Criteria in order to be considered for employment:

- An applicant who has used any illegal drug while employed in any law enforcement or prosecutorial position, or while employed in a position that carries with it a high level of responsibility or public trust, will be found unsuitable for employment.

- An applicant who is discovered to have misrepresented their drug history in completing the application will be found unsuitable for employment.

- An applicant who has sold any illegal drug for profit at any time will be found unsuitable for employment.

- An applicant who has used any illegal drug (including anabolic steroids after February 27, 1991), other than marijuana, within the last 10 years or more than five times in their life will be found unsuitable for employment.

- An applicant who has used marijuana within the past three years or more than a total of 15 times in their life will be found unsuitable for employment.

Failure to meet the preceding criteria will result in disqualification. In an effort to allow prospective candidates to provide a self-assessment of their eligibility under the FBI's drug policy, applicants are asked to answer the following questions:

1. Have you used marijuana at all within the last three years?

2. Have you used marijuana more than 15 times in your life?

3. Have you used any other illegal drug (including anabolic steroids after February 27, 1991) at all in the past 10 years?

4. Have you used any other illegal drug (including anabolic steroids after February 27, 1991) more than five times in your life?

5. Have you ever sold any illegal drug for profit?

6. Have you ever used an illegal drug (no matter how many times or how long ago) while in a law enforcement or prosecutorial position, or in a position that carries with it a high level of responsibility or public trust?

Anyone who answers "Yes" to any of these questions would be disqualified and should not apply for employment with the FBI. All Bureau personnel are subject to random drug screening throughout their careers.

False Statements

It is critical for applicants to be truthful throughout the application process. Any intentional false statement or willful misrepresentation will result in disqualification for the special agent position. In addition, if the misrepresentation is discovered after hiring, the agent may be subject to inquiry and administrative or disciplinary action up to and including dismissal.

Veterans' Preference

Certain applicants may be entitled to preference in the hiring process based on their service in the armed forces. To receive veterans' preference, applicants must have done all of the following:

a. Served on active duty.

b. Been honorably discharged from active duty in the U.S. Army, Navy, Air Force, Marine Corps, or Coast Guard.

c. Performed service that meets certain criteria.

To be considered for veterans' preference, applicants must present a DD-214 (Report of Separation from Active Duty) issued by the armed forces, the Department of Veterans Affairs (DVA), or the National Personnel Records Center of the National Archives and Records Administration. For additional information about the rights of veterans in the hiring process, including how and when veterans' preference is applied, contact either the DVA or the Applicant Coordinator at any FBI field office.

Applicants who want to receive veterans' preference must clearly identify their claim on application forms and other materials, including dates of service and campaign badges. Veterans entitled to preference who meet minimum qualifications will be contacted and asked to submit a copy of their DD-214 or a statement specifying the type of discharge, dates of service, campaign badges received and, if applicable, an SF-15 (Application for 10-point Veteran's Preference), together with the proof required by the form.

Applicants with Disabilities

The FBI is committed to satisfying its affirmative obligations under the Rehabilitation Act of 1973, to ensure that persons with disabilities have every opportunity to be hired and advanced on the basis of merit within the Department of Justice. The Bureau welcomes and encourages applications from persons with physical and mental disabilities and will reasonably accommodate their needs. Any applicant with a disability who requires an accommodation to complete the application process should notify the applicant coordinator of the nearest FBI field office. Notification should be in writing, including the need for the accommodation and medical documentation concerning the disability. Although the Bureau will make reasonable accommodations, applicants must be physically and mentally able to perform the essential functions of a special agent position in order to be hired.

Equal Employment Opportunity

Except where otherwise provided by law, the FBI cannot discriminate because of an applicant's color, race, religion, national origin, political affiliation, marital status, disability, age, sex, sexual orientation, membership or nonmembership in an employee organization, or on the basis of personal favoritism.

An Overview of Applicant Processing

It is important for special agent applicants to be aware of the hiring process sequence, application and testing procedures, factors that could exclude them from employment consideration, how final screening is carried out, and the application time frame. This section provides a snapshot of applicant processing. The remainder of the chapter covers each step of the process in greater detail.

Application, Testing, and Final Screening

The FBI special agent application process requires candidates to submit various application materials in a specific sequence. Those who meet minimum qualifications are administered a battery of written examinations in the first phase of the selection process. Candidates who pass the tests may be eligible for an interview based on their overall qualifications, competitiveness with other candidates, and the needs of the FBI. The interview and written exercise are conducted in phase II of the process, after which the applicant submits a detailed application for employment. To complete the process, final screening includes a security interview, background investigation, physical examination, drug screening, and polygraph examination.

Automatic Disqualifiers

Certain factors disqualify a candidate from selection as a special agent. Competitive candidates must be physically fit to participate in the demanding physical training conducted at the FBI Academy, and able to execute the duties of a law enforcement officer. All candidates must also meet a standardized weight-to-height ratio and/or body fat requirement to be qualified for appointment. (Appendix G is a chart of the desirable weight ranges and body fat requirements.) Candidates must also pass a physical examination to ensure that they are physically suited for the special agent position. Additional details relating to automatic disqualifiers are provided in chapter 3, "FBI Special Agent Career Opportunities."

Application Time Frame

The road from the preliminary application stage to completion of final screening takes at least nine months—although it often lasts more than a year—depending on a variety of factors, such as the number of applicants being processed and issues that arise during background investigations. Figure 4.1 is a flow chart showing the step-by-step progression of the process.

From Application to Appointment, Step by Step

The following sections provide a detailed explanation of each step in the journey from initial application to appointment as an FBI special agent.

Step One: The Preliminary Application Process

To begin the preliminary application process, applicants must submit to the FBI biographical details and information relating to their qualifications and background. Traditionally, applicants have completed various forms and submitted them by mail for processing. Since February 2002, however, candidates for special agent positions have had the option of applying for employment over the Internet. Those who apply online are asked to submit essentially the same information that is requested on the following paper forms:

- Application Checklist for the Special Agent Position (FD-869)
- Preliminary Application for Special Agent Position (FD-646)
- Special Agent Qualifications Questionnaire (FD-843)
- Applicant Background Survey (FD-804)

Candidates who want to apply by mail must send completed forms to the FBI field office nearest their residence. (A complete listing of FBI field offices, including addresses and phone numbers, is provided in appendix J.) The following sections provide summaries of the requested information.

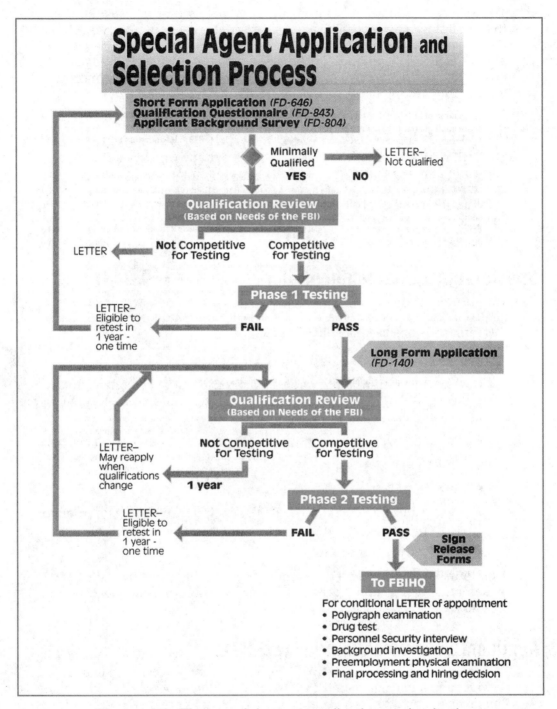

Figure 4.1: The special agent application and selection process.

Application Checklist for the Special Agent Position (FD-869)

The Application Checklist is a five-page form that lists specific qualifications that applicants must be willing and able to meet, as well as automatic disqualifiers. The checklist also lists specific job requirements for the special agent position and asks applicants to acknowledge that they have received and understand information about the position and hiring process. A copy of this form is provided in appendix A.

Preliminary Application for Special Agent Position (FD-646)

The Preliminary Application is also used to determine whether the applicant meets minimum qualification standards. This form requests minimal biographical information relating to military service, arrest record, employment history over the preceding three years, educational background, language proficiency, and prior drug use. A copy of the Preliminary Application is provided in appendix B.

Special Agent Qualifications Questionnaire (FD-843)

The Special Agent Qualifications Questionnaire is used to determine the competitiveness of each applicant. To make this determination, the Bureau reviews this form and considers the following factors:

- The investigative needs of the FBI at the time
- Academic qualifications, professional certifications or licenses (for example, CPA, law degree, engineering certificate, pilot's license), language proficiency, and direct supervisory experience
- Previous law enforcement, federal government, or military experience
- Professional work experience
- Awards, professional recognition, medals, and so on
- Successful completion of the FBI Honors Internship Program, community service, or volunteer work
- Veterans' preference

All information provided on this form is verified through future testing and background-investigation procedures. A copy of this form is provided in appendix C.

Applicant Background Survey (FD-804)

This form is used to obtain demographic information so that the FBI can provide summary demographic information in compliance with the Equal Employment Opportunity Commission's annual reporting requirements. Information supplied on the Applicant Background Survey is not used in selecting applicants for further processing and appointment. A copy of the Applicant Background Survey is provided in appendix D.

Further Processing

After the FBI receives these forms and online applications, candidates who are considered competitive for further processing are notified by the applicant coordinator from the FBI field office and may be scheduled for phase I testing. The applicant coordinator serves as the point of contact through the remainder of the hiring process. Applicants who are not considered competitive are sent a letter indicating that their applications will not be considered further.

Step Two: Phase I Testing

The first phase of the testing process consists of a battery of written tests, including a Biographical Data Inventory, a three-part Cognitive Ability Test, and a Situational Judgment Test. These are paper-and-pencil exams that are scored on a "pass or fail" basis. Applicants are not told their numeric scores. Applicants are notified in writing within 30 days whether they passed or failed the phase I test. Applicants who fail the exam may be eligible for a one-time retest. (See "Phase I Retest Policy," later in this chapter.) For additional details relating to these tests—as well as specific test-taking strategies—see chapter 7, "Standing Out from the Crowd."

Phase I Procedures and Rules

Rules and procedures for phase I testing include details on test location and scheduling, test materials and prohibited items, basic ground rules, and nondisclosure of testing information.

Test Location and Scheduling

Phase I testing is administered at various locations throughout the United States. Applicant coordinators or staffing assistants at each FBI field office coordinate the testing and inform applicants of the date, time, and location of their testing sessions. Test processing normally takes place in the office that covers the applicant's residence, place of education, or place of employment. Exceptions to this policy must be approved by FBI Headquarters officials. Candidates usually have a 30-day notice of scheduled testing dates, times, and locations. Applicants who are tardy will not be permitted to participate in the testing process because testing is conducted on a strict time schedule. The phase I test takes approximately four hours to complete.

Test Materials and Prohibited Items

Applicants must bring a driver's license to phase I and phase II testing for identification purposes. If an applicant does not have a photo on his driver's license, he must provide an additional form of photo identification. The FBI will not allow anyone to participate in the testing process without proper identification.

Candidates are not permitted to bring certain items to phase I or phase II testing sessions, including reference materials, dictionaries, pens or pencils, books, magazines, newspapers, briefcases, resumes, blank paper, pagers, cellular phones, tape recorders, cassettes, compact disc players, radios, calculators, cameras, and firearms, among other items.

Basic Ground Rules

Eating and drinking are not permitted during testing, but will be allowed during breaks. Smoking and chewing tobacco are not allowed. Candidates are permitted to use restroom facilities and telephones during breaks, but not during administration of the tests. Cheating is strictly prohibited.

Nondisclosure of Testing Information

To reduce the likelihood of giving other applicants an unfair advantage or disadvantage in the selection process, the FBI prohibits candidates from discussing any part of the tests and interview questions with anyone during or after tests. Applicants are required to sign a nondisclosure form at phase I and phase II testing. The FBI will disqualify anyone who violates the nondisclosure agreement. If this misrepresentation is discovered after hiring, the employee may be subject to inquiry and suitable disciplinary action, including dismissal.

Components of the Test

Phase I testing consists of three components:

- The Biographical Data Inventory
- The Cognitive Ability Test
- The Situational Judgment Test

The following sections give more details on each of these components.

The Biographical Data Inventory

The Biographical Data Inventory measures the following critical skills and abilities:

- Ability to organize, plan, and prioritize
- Ability to maintain a positive image
- Ability to evaluate information and make judgment decisions
- Initiative and motivation
- Ability to adapt to changing situations
- Physical requirements

This component includes 47 questions that the applicant must complete within 45 minutes, which allows most candidates to finish without being rushed. Answers are recorded on machine-readable answer sheets.

The Cognitive Ability Test

The Cognitive Ability Test measures mathematical reasoning, data analysis and interpretation skills, mathematical knowledge, attention to detail, and ability to evaluate information and make decisions. This test consists of three parts, which are timed separately under stringent time limits. Many individuals are unable to finish this segment in the time allocated.

Part One of the exam includes 25 questions that measure mathematical reasoning and problem-solving abilities. Candidates are given 29 minutes to answer the questions. Part Two measures ability to interpret data from tables and graphs. This 24-minute segment consists of 25 questions. Part Three measures ability to use learned mathematical relationships. Candidates have 22 minutes to answer 25 questions in this segment.

The Situational Judgment Test

The Situational Judgment Test measures critical skills and abilities, such as the ability to organize, plan, and prioritize; the ability to relate effectively with others; the ability to maintain a positive image; the ability to evaluate information and make judgment decisions; the ability to adapt to changing situations; and integrity. Many of these traits are also measured in the Biographical Data Inventory. Although the focus is similar in both tests, the Situational Judgment Test explores what applicants would do in hypothetical situations, whereas the Biographical Data Inventory examines applicants' behavior in actual situations in the past. In this test, candidates are faced with descriptions of problem situations and are asked to choose their *most likely* and *least likely* courses of action from among a number of alternatives. There are 33 descriptions of problem-solving situations in this 90-minute segment. Time limits for this portion of the test are not particularly demanding for most candidates.

Scoring of Phase I Testing

The phase I test is scored on a "pass or fail" basis. The FBI has established a passing score that will be applied uniformly to all applicants taking the test. The Biographical Data Inventory and Situational Judgment Test are each weighted as 40 percent of the total score, whereas the Cognitive Ability Test is weighted as 20 percent. For security purposes, the FBI does not release the passing score.

Candidates are notified within 30 days of the test as to whether they passed or failed, although the FBI does not disseminate actual test scores. Those who pass the phase I tests are advised to complete a detailed Application for Employment within 10 days, which is the next step in the selection process.

Phase I Retest Policy

Those who fail phase I testing may be eligible for one retest at least one year after their initial test date. The FBI does not allow applicants who have passed their 37th birthday (or who cannot be processed prior to their 37th birthday) to be retested. Due to the overwhelming volume of special agent applications, the FBI is able to offer retest opportunities only to those who are found to meet minimum qualifications and are the most competitive. An updated Preliminary Application and Special Agent Qualifications Questionnaire must be submitted before the applicant retakes the test. Applicants who want to retake the phase I test must contact their applicant coordinator.

Step Three: Application for FBI Employment (FD-140)

Applicants who pass phase I testing are invited to complete the next step in the process, which involves completing and submitting the detailed Application for Employment (FD-140) within 10 days. The FD-140 application is a 15-page form that requests information relating to birth and citizenship, places of residence, educational background, employment history, military service, references and social acquaintances, foreign travel, association membership, civil and criminal court record, financial status, relatives, roommates, drug use, and availability for employment. A recent full-face photograph of the applicant must be attached to the FD-140. A copy of this form is provided in appendix E.

The FBI reviews each FD-140 and determines the competitiveness of the applicants. Only the most competitive applicants are scheduled for phase II testing. Competitiveness is based not only on applicants' backgrounds, but also on the FBI's hiring needs at the time. In other words, not all applicants who pass the phase I test will be selected to continue in the hiring process. Candidates who are permitted to continue are notified by their applicant coordinator of the date, time, and location of phase II testing.

Step Four: Phase II Testing

The phase II testing process consists of a structured interview and a written exercise. Candidates who successfully complete this segment of the hiring process receive a conditional offer of employment and must be available for employment within 90 days of the testing.

Phase II Procedures and Rules

Testing procedures are similar to those followed in phase I testing. Arrangements for phase II testing are coordinated by either applicant coordinators or other staff. These personnel notify applicants of the date, time, and location of phase II testing sessions. Candidates usually are given 30 days' notice prior to testing. The phase II test takes approximately three hours to complete. As with phase I testing, applicants must bring a driver's license to the phase II test. If an applicant does not have a photo on his driver's license, he must provide an additional form of photo identification. Applicants are prohibited from discussing any part of the Structured Interview or Written Exercise with anyone and must sign a Nondisclosure Form prior to taking the test.

The Structured Interview

The Structured Interview measures skills and abilities that are critical to the performance of FBI special agents. These include many of the skills and abilities that are also measured during phase I testing, although in a different format and setting. The Structured Interview focuses on the following abilities and characteristics:

- Ability to communicate orally
- Ability to organize, plan, and prioritize
- Ability to relate effectively with others
- Ability to maintain a positive image
- Ability to evaluate information and make judgment decisions
- Initiative and motivation
- Ability to adapt to changing situations
- Integrity
- Physical requirements

The interview is administered by specially trained FBI special agents who serve as evaluators. Interestingly enough, however, the evaluators receive no application or background information on the applicants prior to the interviews. Because the evaluators know nothing about the applicants, each applicant is on an equal footing because the evaluators can be completely objective. The evaluators rate each candidate's performance using standardized scoring criteria. All interviews are audiotaped and the recordings are stored at FBI Headquarters in Washington, D.C.

To begin the interview, a panel member reads the following instructions to the applicant:

> *We'd like to spend the next hour getting to know more about you. During the interview, we will ask you to tell us how you've dealt with various kinds of situations in the past. In answering our questions, you can draw on experiences in family, work, school, or social situations and how you handled them. We would like you to describe the situation, tell us what you did in that situation, and how things turned out.*
>
> *We will be asking you 15 questions. Feel free to take a few moments to think about the answer you would like to give for each question. If you would like a question repeated, please ask. You'll be doing most of the talking during the interview. We will be taking notes while you talk to document the interview. The interview will also be tape recorded.*
>
> *Remember, be as specific and detailed as possible in describing the situation, your actions, and the outcome of your actions.*

After instructions have been given, the panel members ask a series of 15 situational response questions over a one-hour period. If a candidate cannot answer a question, the interview continues with the next question on the list. Panel members return to unanswered questions at the end of the interview and the candidate is not penalized for this. Failure to answer any questions during the interview, however, might adversely affect a candidate's score.

The Written Exercise

Phase II testing includes a written exercise that measures the following:

- Ability to communicate in writing
- Attention to detail
- Ability to evaluate and make judgments and decisions

For the written exercise, applicants are asked to evaluate a problem or situation and compose a written response that addresses the issues at hand. Fact situations or theme can change from one written exercise to the next. However, candidates who recently completed the exercise were asked to write a report as if it were being sent to the editor of a newspaper.

The written exercise is assessed by FBI special agents who serve as evaluators. This segment takes 90 minutes to complete.

Scoring of Phase II Testing

Phase II testing is scored on a "pass or fail" basis, using a passing score that is applied uniformly to all candidates. The Structured Interview is weighted as 75 percent of the total score, whereas the Written Exercise is weighted as 25 percent. As with phase I testing, the FBI does not release the passing score and cannot provide individual feedback regarding test performance.

Candidates are notified in writing as to whether they passed or failed. Applicants who pass the exam receive a conditional offer of employment from the FBI, although a final employment decision is contingent upon successful completion of the final screening process.

Phase II Retest Policy

Applicants who fail the phase II testing may be eligible to retest after one year from the test date. Any applicant who has reached the age of 37—or cannot be processed prior to their 37th birthday—is not eligible to be retested. Only those who are most competitive will be offered an opportunity to retest. The FBI determines eligibility for retesting based on qualifications, skills, experience, the needs of the Bureau at the time, and information provided within a newly submitted Application for Employment. Applicants who want to retake the phase II test must contact their applicant coordinator.

Step Five: Final Screening

Candidates who pass phase II testing receive a conditional appointment and must successfully complete drug testing, a Personnel Security Interview, polygraph examination, background investigation, physical examination, timed run, and medical review. A candidate who successfully completes the final screening process is appointed as an FBI special agent and reports for basic training at the FBI Academy soon thereafter. The following sections detail all the steps in the final screening process.

Conditional Letter of Appointment

This letter offers applicants who have passed both phase I and phase II testing a conditional appointment as a special agent, contingent upon budgetary limitations, authorized positions, and successful completion of final screening. In this letter, candidates are provided with information concerning the remainder of the hiring process, including details relating to the nature of the background investigation and issues that might surface in it.

Drug Testing

All applicants participating in the final screening process are required to submit to a urinalysis drug test, which screens for illegal drug use prior to final appointment.

Personnel Security Interview

All applicants are given a Personnel Security Interview prior to appointment. This is a personal interview that encompasses questions concerning foreign travel and contacts, the extent of any drug usage, status of financial obligations, veracity of the information contained in the application, and other security issues. Information provided during the Personnel Security Interview is often verified during the polygraph examination.

Polygraph Examination

A polygraph examination is administered to every FBI applicant who receives a conditional offer of appointment. This examination focuses on national security and counterintelligence issues, whether the applicant has ever sold illegal drugs for profit or violated the FBI guidelines pertaining to the use of illegal drugs, and the veracity of information provided in the Application for Employment. All FBI polygraph activities—including criminal and personnel matters—are coordinated by the Bureau's Polygraph Unit, which is a component of the FBI Laboratory.

The Functions of the Polygraph

The polygraph examination is used to determine whether someone shows the physiological and psychological reactions that are believed to accompany deception. The examination allows the polygraph examiner to render a diagnostic opinion regarding the honesty or dishonesty of an individual.

The basic function of the polygraph is to record signs of internal stress that people are believed to experience when they respond to questions in a deceptive manner.

The polygraph instrument consists of three or more components, including the following:

- A cardiograph, which monitors pulse and changes in blood pressure

- A pneumograph, which records respiration rate by measuring chest expansions and contractions

- A galvanometer that is normally attached to the hand to measure electrical conductivity through perspiration

Some polygraph instruments measure gross muscular movements, also. The polygraph measures changes in cardiovascular activity, respiratory rate, and skin chemistry while the applicant is asked a series of questions. These changes are recorded in graphic form.

The Phases of the Polygraph Examination

The polygraph examination typically is conducted in three phases, including a pretest, data collection, and data analysis. The examination typically begins with a face-to-face interview between the polygraph examiner and the applicant, during which the instrument and the examination are explained. The pretest interview allows the examiner to secure the confidence and cooperation of the applicant and to evaluate the applicant's idiosyncrasies that might affect the examination results.

During the data-collection phase, the examiner asks a series of control questions—typically of the "true or false" and "yes or no" variety. Many of the control questions are simple and straightforward. These questions might focus on the applicant's name, place of birth, residence, and other biographical details. The examiner uses the responses to control questions to establish a baseline to which to compare the applicant's reactions to essential questions later. Control questions are followed by specific questions that explore national security and counterintelligence issues, experience with illegal drugs, and other information provided in application materials.

In the third phase of the polygraph, the examiner analyzes the results to determine whether they are indicative of truthfulness or deception. If any responses appear to be deceptive, the examiner might ask the applicant additional questions or ask them to explain these responses. The expertise of the examiner is very important in assessing truthfulness or deception.

Polygraph Examination Results

Results of the polygraph examination are sent to FBI Headquarters in Washington, D.C. Applicants who do not fall within acceptable parameters for the polygraph examination are disqualified. Polygraph results are not official until they are approved by FBI Headquarters officials. Applicants are not notified in writing as to whether they passed or failed the examination.

Background Investigation

All FBI applicants are subject to a thorough background investigation prior to appointment. The FBI's applicant program manages background investigations on all applicants for FBI employment. The Bureau also conducts background investigations for certain other government entities, such as the White House, Department of Justice, Department of Energy, Nuclear Regulatory Commission, Administrative Office of the United States Courts, and certain Senate and House committees. Background investigations of applicants for FBI special agent positions typically are conducted by special investigators under contract with the FBI.

Scope and Coverage

FBI special agents must hold a top-secret security clearance as a condition of employment. Information gathered during the background investigation allows the FBI to assess whether applicants are suitable for Bureau employment, including access to classified or Top Secret information.

The background investigation routinely encompasses activity beginning at the age of 18, and earlier years if necessary to fully resolve issues that arise. The investigation typically includes credit history and criminal record checks; driving record and license inquiries; verification of employment history, licenses, credentials, and certifications; interviews of associates, personal and business references, past and present employers, and neighbors; verification of educational achievements and medical history; and verification of birth, citizenship, residency, and medical and military records.

In conducting interviews and reviewing records, background investigators place particular emphasis on the following areas in determining the suitability of applicants for FBI employment:

- **Character,** including attributes such as honesty, trustworthiness, judgment, discretion, diplomacy, dependability, punctuality, stability, and temperament.

- **Associates,** with emphasis on the types of people, groups, or organizations the applicant has been involved or affiliated with.

- **Reputation,** relating to the applicant's standing in the community and in their profession or field of work.

- **Loyalty,** in terms of their allegiance toward the United States, employers, and others.

- **Ability,** as far as their level of competency and capacity to perform well in their occupation.

- **Financial responsibility,** meaning the applicant maintains a satisfactory relationship with creditors and has spending habits that are consistent with their means.

- **Biases or prejudice,** which concerns actions and attitude toward people of various racial, ethnic, gender, or religious groups.

- **Alcohol abuse,** which focuses on excessive use of alcoholic beverages and related behavioral issues.

- **Drug abuse,** including the use of any illegal drugs or abuse of prescription medications.

Information of a derogatory nature is forwarded to FBI Headquarters in Washington, D.C., for adjudication. The complete background investigation is assessed before a final decision on employment is rendered.

The Length of the Background Investigation

The background investigation normally takes from one to four months. The length of the investigation depends on a number of variables, such as the following:

- How completely application forms are filled out

- Issues that arise requiring further investigation

- The extent of foreign travel, or whether the applicant has resided in another country

- Ability to locate and interview employers, references, or other persons

- Availability of records

- The number of applicants being processed at any given time

Background Investigation Results

All applicants are informed of the outcome of their background investigation in writing. Applicants can obtain a copy of their background investigation report in accordance with the Freedom of Information Act (FOIA) and the Privacy Act (PA). Written requests should be mailed to the Bureau's Freedom of Information/Privacy Act (FOI/PA) Section at FBI Headquarters in Washington, D.C. The Bureau might black out certain portions of the report, however, in accordance with FOIA and PA laws.

Pre-employment Physical Examination

A pre-employment physical examination is given to applicants to determine their physical suitability for the special agent position. In many cases, the physical examination raises medical issues or conditions that require applicants to obtain additional information or undergo additional examination at the applicant's expense.

Timed Run

Candidates must clear another hurdle prior to reporting to the FBI Academy for New Agent Training: a 1.5-mile timed run. This event is carried out to provide the FBI with some assurance that new agent trainees are likely to succeed in physical fitness activities at the Academy. To achieve a passing score, males must complete the run in 12 minutes and 40 seconds (12:40) or less, and females must finish in 14 minutes and 10 seconds (14:10) or less. Candidates who fail the timed run are eligible to try again after 60 days. The timed run normally is held after applicants have undergone the physical examination.

Medical Reviews

Applicants' medical histories are reviewed thoroughly and a determination is made whether any medical issue or condition could potentially affect their ability to perform the basic functions of the special agent position. Each candidate's situation is reviewed on an individual, case-by-case basis.

A history of certain surgical procedures (for example, radial keratotomy) or preexisting medical conditions (for example, hypertension) require careful review during the physical examination process. Review of medical issues and conditions sometimes results in delay of the final processing for employment. Although an applicant's doctor may provide information about a medical condition, the final decision as to an applicant's physical ability to perform the duties of an FBI special agent rests with the Bureau's chief medical officer.

CHAPTER 5

Professional Support Career Opportunities

No amount of ability is of the slightest avail without honor.

— *Andrew Carnegie*

The FBI offers a broad range of rewarding career opportunities for those who are interested in nonagent positions that contribute significantly to the Bureau's mission. More than one-half of the FBI workforce is employed in professional support positions, including fingerprint specialists, biologists, security specialists, document analysts, evidence technicians, electronics engineers, and many others. These personnel carry out a variety of tasks within their particular areas of expertise, whether analyzing blood samples, taking surveillance photographs, gathering intelligence information, examining handwriting samples or counterfeit documents, maintaining computer systems, or carrying out other vital functions.

As a member of the Bureau's administrative, technical, scientific, or clerical staff, FBI professional support personnel have a ringside seat to events that make news headlines around the world every day. In addition, although the vast majority of professional support employees are content to remain in nonagent positions, many have used their experience with the Bureau as a stepping stone to becoming an FBI special agent.

Requirements and Qualifications for Professional Support Positions

To be eligible for FBI professional support positions, the applicant must be able to show that his or her background has prepared him or her for FBI employment. This section provides an overview of education requirements, experience requirements, and other minimum qualifications that applicants must address in the hiring process to be considered for appointment to professional support positions.

Minimum Qualifications

Each professional support position has a prescribed set of minimum qualifications that applicants must meet. All applicants must be United States citizens, and most jobs require a particular level of education or experience, depending on the nature of the position. Job vacancy announcements issued by the FBI describe minimum qualifications for each position. Candidates for positions that involve exposure to hazardous situations—such as electronics technician and investigative specialist—must pass a physical examination prior to appointment, and FBI police officer applicants must also meet standards relating to eyesight and hearing. Candidates for most positions also are required to submit a statement that describes how their knowledge, skills, and abilities (KSAs) have prepared them to perform the duties and responsibilities of the job. KSA statements must address specific criteria, depending on the salary level for the position. A list of KSAs is included with each vacancy announcement.

Experience Requirements

Qualification standards for professional support positions often require applicants to possess experience that is either general or specialized in nature. Qualifying general and specialized experience varies widely in its degree of specialty from one position to another, and also between salary grades of the same position. For example, whereas some positions might not require knowledge of law enforcement or investigative techniques, others might call for varying levels of knowledge in these areas, with higher salary grades requiring the most. In addition, qualification standards often specify that a certain amount of the experience must be at a level of difficulty and responsibility equivalent to the next lower grade level in the federal service. In other words, a candidate who wants to qualify for appointment to a position at the GS-9 level might need experience equivalent to a GS-8 position to qualify. Job vacancy announcements normally provide descriptions of qualifying general and specialized experience.

General Experience

General experience is usually required at grade levels where the specific knowledge and skills needed to perform the duties of a position are not prerequisites, but where applicants must have demonstrated the *ability* to acquire the particular knowledge and skills. For some occupations, any progressively responsible work experience might qualify. Others require experience that provided a familiarity with the subject matter or processes of the occupation, or of the equipment used on the job, although not to the extent required of specialized experience.

Specialized Experience

In contrast to general experience, specialized experience is that which has equipped an applicant with the particular knowledge, skills, and abilities to successfully perform the duties of the position and which is in or directly related to the line of work of the position. For example, qualifying specialized experience for the FBI police officer position is defined as follows:

> *Experience that provided knowledge of a body of basic laws and regulations, law enforcement operations, practices, and techniques and involved responsibility for maintaining order and protecting life and property. Creditable specialized experience may have been gained in work on a police force; through service as a military police officer; in work providing visitor protection and law enforcement in parks, forests, or other natural resource or recreational environments; in performing criminal investigative duties; or in other work that provided the required knowledge and skills.*

For many positions, candidates who possess a bachelor's degree but no specialized experience in the career field of the position sought may be eligible for appointment at the GS-5 level. Positions at or above the GS-7 level typically require one year of specialized experience equivalent to the next lower grade level. This means, for example, that in order to qualify for a position at GS-12, an applicant must have had at least one year of specialized experience equivalent to at least GS-11.

Many positions allow applicants to substitute graduate-level education for specialized experience in order to qualify for careers at the GS-7 level and above. In lieu of specialized experience, one year of graduate study is normally qualifying for appointment to GS-7. Similarly, a master's degree or two years of graduate study can be substituted for specialized experience when applying for positions at the GS-9 level, and a Ph.D. or three years of graduate-level education can be substituted for specialized experience for positions at the GS-11 level. In addition, applicants without specialized experience who achieved high academic standing during undergraduate studies—also known as Superior Academic Achievement—may qualify for many FBI jobs at the GS-7 level (see the following section).

Education Requirements

Generally speaking, qualifying education for FBI employment includes study at institutions that have been accredited by one of the regional or national accrediting associations recognized by the United States Secretary of Education. However, education completed at foreign colleges or universities may be used to meet educational requirements if the applicant can show that the foreign education is comparable to that received in an accredited educational institution in the United States.

Applicants who achieved high academic standing during undergraduate study may qualify for appointment at the GS-7 level for many FBI jobs under Superior Academic Achievement provisions, even if they lack job-related experience. Qualification is based on class standing, grade-point average, or honor society membership, as follows:

- **Class standing.** Applicants must be in the upper third of their graduating class in the college, university, or major subdivision (such as the College of Liberal Arts or School of Criminal Justice) based on completed courses.

- **Grade-point average.** Applicants must have a grade-point average of 2.95 or higher out of a possible 4.0 for all courses completed at the time of application or during the last two years of the curriculum; or a 3.45 or higher out of a possible 4.0 for all courses completed in the major field of study at the time of application or during the last two years of the curriculum.

- **Honor society membership.** Applicants who have membership in one of the national honor societies (other than freshman or sophomore societies) recognized by the Association of College Honor Societies. Dozens of honor societies are qualifying, such as Phi Beta Kappa, Mortar Board, Alpha Phi Sigma Criminal Justice Honor Society, and Order of the Coif.

For some positions, coursework must have been related to the field of the position applied for in order to be qualifying under Superior Academic Achievement provisions. For example, qualification standards for the Biologist position specify that undergraduate coursework must have been related to biochemistry, biological sciences, or biotechnology to be acceptable.

Qualifying for Salary Grade Levels

Qualification standards for each position also give specific criteria for salary grade levels for which candidates can qualify. Not surprisingly, positions filled at higher grade levels call for a higher level of education or more experience than those filled at lower salary levels. Criteria for each salary level normally are described in vacancy announcements.

Temporary Duty Assignments and Permanent Transfers

Candidates for many FBI jobs, such as financial analyst and police officer, must be willing to accept temporary duty (TDY) assignments in areas that are located away from their permanent duty station. These assignments may last anywhere from a few weeks to several months—or longer under certain circumstances. Other personnel, such as investigative specialists and language specialists, must also be willing to accept permanent transfer to other areas. The majority of professional support employees are in positions that do not require TDY assignments or permanent transfers.

Profiles of Key Professional Support Positions

The remainder of this chapter provides profiles of 17 key professional support positions, including an overview of the responsibilities, minimum qualifications, and requirements for salary grade levels of each position.

Biologist (Forensic Examiner)

FBI biologists provide critical support to criminal investigations conducted by the FBI and other federal, state, and local law enforcement agencies. These personnel are assigned to the FBI Laboratory, which is one of the largest and most comprehensive forensic science facilities in the world, and the only full-service federal forensic laboratory.

Overview of the Position

Biologists plan, coordinate, direct, and perform a wide variety of examinations and comprehensive technical analyses. Their primary responsibilities revolve around the examination and analysis of body tissues, body fluids, and stains recovered as evidence in violent crimes. In doing so, they apply a full range of scientific theories and principles, serological techniques, and biochemical analysis to identify and characterize hair, bones, blood, teeth, semen, saliva, urine, and other body fluids and substances.

On the cutting edge of forensics, FBI biologists perform mitochondrial DNA analysis (mtDNA), a powerful analytical tool that was implemented at the FBI Laboratory in 1996. MtDNA is applied to forensic specimens such as human hair, bone, teeth, blood, and other tissues, and is the most sensitive of all forensic DNA techniques. MtDNA analysis can be used to associate body fluids or a single hair from a crime scene to a suspect, or to identify the skeletal remains of unidentified crime victims. Once a sample is obtained, it is characterized by protein analysis or DNA analysis, and the results are compared to known blood or saliva samples submitted from victims or suspects. Biologists determine whether DNA is present in a variety of samples. For example, cigarette butts, postage stamps, hat bands, shirt collars, and other items that have been in close contact with a person can often yield a genetic profile.

Biologists also analyze samples for use in the Bureau's Federal Convicted Offender Program. Under the program, samples are taken from federal offenders who have been convicted of violent crimes, and the results are entered into a database for potential comparison to unknown DNA samples collected from crime scenes. The FBI Laboratory is currently the only law enforcement forensic laboratory in the United States that is capable of performing mtDNA analysis. At the FBI Laboratory's Forensic Science Research and Training Center, biologists also conduct research to improve and develop the methodology of forensic analyses.

In support of criminal investigations and prosecutions, FBI biologists prepare and present oral briefings and detailed written reports to case agents and supervisory personnel, assistant United States attorneys, and grand juries. Biologists also play a crucial role in the courtroom because they must occasionally provide expert testimony in evidentiary hearings and criminal trials in support of their findings. Their testimony could relate not only to scientific procedures and analytical findings, but also to the preservation and inventory of evidence obtained at crime scenes and turned over to the FBI Laboratory for examination. In order to prevail in the face of scrutiny surrounding the integrity of evidence, biologists must maintain a detailed inventory of items submitted to the laboratory to establish the so-called "chain of evidence."

Minimum Qualifications and Salary Requirements

Basic eligibility requirements for the biologist position include a bachelor's degree in biochemistry, biological sciences, biotechnology, or a related field with at least 24 semester hours in biochemistry or the biological sciences. Biologist applicants are required to submit a KSA statement to address various elements, such as the following:

- Knowledge of biological principles and practices
- Skill in interpreting test results and evaluating data

- Skill in oral and written communication
- Ability to operate various scientific instruments
- Ability to organize, plan, and prioritize testing and analysis activities

Salary Grade Requirements

GS-7   One full year of graduate-level education, or superior academic achievement during undergraduate studies in a curriculum related to biochemistry, biological sciences, biotechnology, or a related discipline; or a bachelor's degree and one year of specialized experience in one of the above-listed disciplines.

GS-9   A master's degree or two years of graduate-level education; or a bachelor's degree and one year of specialized experience equivalent to at least GS-7.

GS-11   A Ph.D. or equivalent doctoral degree, or three years of graduate-level education; or a bachelor's degree and one year of specialized experience equivalent to at least GS-9.

GS-12   A bachelor's degree and one year of specialized experience equivalent to GS-11.

GS-13   A bachelor's degree and one year of specialized experience equivalent to GS-12.

Chemist (Forensic Examiner)

Chemists are assigned to the FBI Laboratory, where they perform highly complex examinations of evidence in support of criminal investigations and foreign counterintelligence matters. The chemistry unit of the FBI Laboratory is divided into four subunits, whose analyses and functions vary substantially. The expertise of FBI chemists is often the basis for prosecutions of criminals for offenses ranging from homicide to bank robbery, drug trafficking, terrorism, product tampering, and financial fraud.

Overview of the Position

FBI chemists investigate, analyze, and interpret the composition, molecular structure, and properties of various substances, the transformations that they undergo, and the amounts of matter and energy included in these transformations. Their work can be hazardous because they are exposed periodically to hazardous materials, toxic substances, and bloodborne pathogens.

FBI chemists assigned to the laboratory's general chemistry subunit identify dyes, chemicals, and marking materials used in bank security devices; controlled substances associated with drug investigations; ink from pens, typewriters, stamp pads, and other sources; as well as other solids and liquids. In the toxicology subunit, they analyze biological specimens of food products for drugs, drug metabolites, pharmaceuticals, poisons, biological tissues and fluids, and substances associated with product tampering investigations. Analyses performed in the paints and polymers subunit include paint chips, plastics, petroleum products, tapes, adhesives, caulks, and sealants. This subunit maintains the National Automotive Paint File, which stores examples of car paints and is used to locate vehicles involved in hit-and-run accidents. Chemists assigned to the instrumentation operation and support subunit are responsible for calibrating and maintaining analytical instruments used to analyze and identify samples, maintaining databases, and evaluating new technologies.

As members of FBI evidence response teams that examine evidence at crime scenes, chemists locate, identify, reconstruct, and preserve pertinent items of evidence for examination and analysis in the laboratory. For example, in support of investigations involving bombing incidents and arson, they conduct comprehensive technical analyses of explosives, explosive residues, and accelerants. FBI chemists played a major role in the investigation of TWA Flight 800, which crashed into the ocean off Long Island Sound in 1996. Many of the one-million-plus pieces of aircraft debris were retrieved from the ocean and examined using sophisticated methods of chemical analysis. During the investigation, traces of high explosive chemicals were found on the wreckage. The FBI later determined that months before the crash, the St. Louis Airport Police conducted explosives training for canine units aboard the aircraft, which left explosive residues on the aircraft. Chemists also tested evidence recovered from the 1995 bombing of the Murrah Federal Building in Oklahoma City, and from the wreckage of EgyptAir Flight 990, which crashed off the Massachusetts coast in 1999.

Because all evidence must be carefully accounted for at all times in order to maintain the legal chain of custody, chemists are required to prepare accurate inventories of evidence under their control and to make these available to FBI special agents, prosecuting attorneys, and grand juries. Their responsibilities also include preparing and presenting written reports and oral briefings that convey their opinions and findings, as well as testifying as expert witnesses during evidentiary hearings and criminal trials. Chemists also provide scientific support to other federal, state, and local law enforcement agencies.

In an ongoing effort to expand the knowledge base in the field, chemists conduct scientific research at the FBI Laboratory's Forensic Science Research and Training Center and present their findings and newly established procedures to the forensic science community. They also conduct training in examination techniques for prosecuting attorneys, judges, police officers, and forensics examiners of other law enforcement agencies.

Minimum Qualifications and Salary Requirements

To qualify for the chemist position, applicants must have one of the following:

A. A bachelor's degree in the physical sciences, life sciences, or engineering that included 30 semester hours in chemistry, supplemented by coursework in mathematics through differential and integral calculus, and at least six semester hours of physics.

B. A combination of education, experience, and coursework equivalent to a college major as outlined in item A, including at least 30 semester hours in chemistry, supplemented by coursework in mathematics through differential and integral calculus, and at least six semester hours of physics. To qualify under item B, the quality of the combination of education and experience must be sufficient to demonstrate that the applicant possesses the knowledge, skills, and abilities required to perform work in the occupation, and must be comparable to that normally acquired through the completion of a four-year course of study with a major in the field.

KSA statements for the chemist position are likely to focus on elements such as the following:

- Knowledge of chemical concepts, theories, and principles
- Skill in written and oral communication
- Skill in operating scientific instruments and interpreting data to analyze evidence
- Ability to organize, plan, and prioritize testing and analysis activities, and to evaluate information

Salary Grade Requirements

GS-7   One full year of graduate-level education, or superior academic achievement during undergraduate studies; or a bachelor's degree and one year of specialized experience.

GS-9   A master's degree or two years of graduate-level education; or a bachelor's degree and one year of specialized experience equivalent to at least GS-7.

GS-11   A Ph.D. or equivalent doctoral degree, or three years of graduate-level education; or a bachelor's degree and one year of specialized experience equivalent to at least GS-9.

GS-12   A bachelor's degree and one year of specialized experience equivalent to GS-11.

GS-13   A bachelor's degree and one year of specialized experience equivalent to GS-12.

Computer Specialist

Few occupations within the FBI cover as broad a range of responsibilities and areas of focus as computer specialists. Personnel working under this position classification range from specialists who maintain computer hardware, to others who perform software engineering tasks, and to those who are directly involved in criminal investigations. To accomplish these and myriad other tasks, FBI computer specialists are employed at FBI Headquarters; at the Bureau's Criminal Justice Information Services (CJIS) Division complex in Clarksburg, West Virginia; and at FBI field offices.

Overview of the Position

Generally speaking, FBI computer specialists are responsible for programming and other tasks associated with the design, development, testing, implementation, and maintenance of the Bureau's information systems. Specialties in the computer specialist classification include areas such as information security, systems analysis, applications software, operating systems, network services, data management, computer support, and systems administration.

A substantial proportion of the Bureau's computer specialists are employed at the CJIS Division, which was established in 1992 to serve as the focal point and central repository for the Bureau's criminal justice information services. CJIS is the largest division within the FBI. Many of the Bureau's information technology programs are consolidated under the CJIS Division, such as the

National Crime Information Center, Uniform Crime Reporting Program, National Instant Criminal Background Check System, Integrated Automated Fingerprint Identification System, and the National Incident-Based Reporting System.

Responsibilities of computer specialists working at the CJIS vary widely depending on the functions of the unit they are assigned to. For example, those assigned to the CJIS software development unit are responsible for tasks such as the installation of commercial off-the-shelf software, applying patches supplied by software vendors, analyzing computer errors attributed to software, and communicating with software vendors to resolve technical problems. They also modify database structures and develop operational software for a variety of needs. In the engineering unit, computer specialists perform systems engineering, hardware and software engineering, and telecommunications engineering, as well as other functions to ensure that modifications to CJIS computer systems meet operational requirements and standards. Computer specialists in the technical maintenance unit provide preventative, corrective, and adaptive hardware maintenance for CJIS computer systems, networks, voice and security systems, and communications systems. Day-to-day monitoring of the CJIS system-of-systems is the responsibility of computer specialists within the operations unit, including database administration, program analysis, system backup and restore functions, and responding to error conditions.

In direct support of criminal investigations, many FBI computer specialists are members of the Bureau's computer analysis and response team (CART). CART computer specialists assist in the search and seizure of computer evidence, and also provide forensic examinations and technical support for FBI investigations involving computer intrusions and other crimes. Using a combination of proprietary tools, commercial off-the-shelf software, and commercial forensic tools, CART conducts computer forensic examinations on evidence seized in virtually all of the FBI's investigative programs. For example, CART computer specialists analyzed and restored data during the Columbine High School shooting investigation and assisted in the investigation of Theodore Kaczynski—known also as the Unabomber. They also were involved in the search and analysis of more than one million computer files in the investigation of Wen Ho Lee, a nuclear weapons engineer at the Los Alamos National Laboratory who was convicted of illegally downloading sensitive data from a classified computer system. CART computer specialists are often hired into the CART program directly.

Because information technology management is an around-the-clock operation, some computer specialist positions require shift work, which may include duty on weekends and holidays, as well as reporting for work during adverse weather conditions or emergency situations—even if federal agencies are closed in the immediate vicinity.

Minimum Qualifications and Salary Requirements

Areas to be addressed in KSA statements for computer specialist positions may vary widely depending on the nature of positions being filled, including elements such as the following:

- Knowledge of network design, data recovery, and software integration
- Skill in database management and in developing and testing information systems

- Skill in writing and debugging code and in troubleshooting techniques
- Ability to analyze system requirements, determine computer system configuration, and analyze automated data-processing system design.

Salary Grade Requirements

GS-7   One full year of graduate-level education; or superior academic achievement during undergraduate studies; or one year of specialized experience equivalent to at least GS-5.

GS-9   A master's degree or two years of graduate-level education; or one year of specialized experience equivalent to at least GS-7.

GS-11   A Ph.D. or equivalent doctoral degree; or three years of graduate-level education; or one year of specialized experience equivalent to at least GS-9.

GS-12   One year of specialized experience equivalent to GS-11.

GS-13   One year of specialized experience equivalent to GS-12.

Qualifying education must include major study in computer science, information science, information systems management, mathematics, statistics, operations research, or engineering; or coursework that required the development or adaptation of computer programs and systems and provided knowledge equivalent to a major in the computer field.

Document Analyst (Forensic Examiner)

The skilled expertise of FBI document analysts is utilized by the Bureau—and other law enforcement agencies—in the investigation of crimes involving fraud against the government, check fraud, forgery, counterfeiting, bank robbery, threats, kidnapping, homicide, and many other offenses. As a result, examinations and opinions of these expert analysts are often the focal point of FBI investigations and prosecutions.

Overview of the Position

The work of FBI document analysts focuses primarily on the examination and comprehensive technical analyses of evidence seized at crime scenes or during the execution of search warrants; or obtained from individuals, government agencies, and private firms in response to subpoenas or through other investigative means. Examinations often focus on identifying common authorship of documents, as well as authenticity, alteration, obliterated writing, erasures, and mechanical impressions. Document analysts also conduct research or development projects on the identification and analysis of document evidence to improve technology and solve evidence problems.

Although physical examinations are performed on many types of surfaces, paper is the most common surface examined. Document analysts examine a wide range of documents, notes, letters, forms, paper, and paper products to identify characteristics of handwriting, hand printing, typewriting, indented writing, watermarks, dry seals, inks, and hidden security features. Depending on the nature of the investigation, these examinations might focus on counterfeit or altered checks, securities, contracts, loan documents, promissory notes, application forms, and a wide range of other documents, typically consisting of handwriting comparisons. These often consist of questioned and known documents submitted for side-by-side comparison. If the evidence submitted includes only writing of unknown origin, however, the examination could include only file searches, preservation of the evidence, and evaluation of the potential for future comparisons. The FBI questioned document unit also maintains a number of databases, including the Anonymous Letter File, Bank Robbery Note File, National Fraudulent Check File, Office Equipment File, Shoeprint File, and Watermark File.

Aside from documents and other paper products, examinations are also performed on typewriter ribbons, printers, photocopiers, facsimiles, and other equipment and devices to identify the source of various writings and impressions. For example, document analysts could examine a typewriter ball to determine whether it was used to type a particular document or a portion of a document. During the investigation of the Unabomber, FBI document analysts performed approximately 400 examinations to compare documents to a typewriter that was seized during the search of Theodore Kaczynski's Montana cabin.

Document analysts perform examinations using a variety of imaging techniques that utilize computers, microscopes, chemical substances, photographic equipment, infrared technology, casts, and sequential morphological analysis. They also use this technology to examine shoeprints and tire-tread impressions to determine the brand name and manufacturer of the shoe or tire that made the impression. For example, an FBI document analyst utilized shoeprint identification techniques following the murders of Nicole Brown Simpson and Ronald Goldman in 1994, and later testified in the civil trial of O.J. Simpson. As a result, evidence presented in court linked impressions in blood outside of Simpson's home to the same brand and size of shoes owned by Simpson.

As with other FBI Laboratory personnel, document analysts prepare written reports that address their findings, and present these along with oral briefings to case agents and supervisors, assistant United States attorneys, grand juries, and law enforcement officers of other agencies. They also prepare court exhibits and testify as expert witnesses during trials and evidentiary hearings to explain forensic procedures that were followed and the results obtained.

Minimum Qualifications and Salary Requirements

Document analyst applicants are required to submit a KSA statement to address elements such as the following:

- Knowledge of microscopic examination of materials, investigative techniques and detection procedures, printing, graphic arts, duplicating processes, and business machines

- Skill in photography and conducting scientific experiments

- Ability to examine and compare handwriting, printing, typewriting, and other mechanical impressions to determine their identity or genuineness

- Ability to analyze inks, papers, and recording instruments and materials by various scientific means

- Ability to write reports

Salary Grade Requirements

GS-7   One full year of graduate-level education, or superior academic achievement during undergraduate studies; or a bachelor's degree and one year of specialized experience.

GS-9   A master's degree or two years of graduate-level education; or a bachelor's degree and one year of specialized experience equivalent to at least GS-7.

GS-11 A Ph.D. or equivalent doctoral degree, or three years of graduate-level education; or a bachelor's degree and one year of specialized experience equivalent to at least GS-9; or certification by the American Board of Forensic Document Examiners.

GS-12 A bachelor's degree and one year of specialized experience equivalent to GS-11.

Electronics Engineer

The work of the FBI—whether it involves catching criminals, providing assistance to other agencies, or developing new technologies—relies heavily on state-of-the-art electronic equipment and systems. The Bureau places a high priority on obtaining and utilizing the most advanced technology available to conduct investigations, maintain sensitive and national security information, and protect its operations and personnel. FBI electronics engineers form the backbone of the Bureau's efforts to sustain its electronic capabilities at the highest level possible.

Overview of the Position

The Bureau's electronics engineers perform research and development engineering studies on an assortment of technical projects that are geared toward the FBI's specialized electronic systems, equipment, investigative aids, and other devices. Their assignments cover a broad range of activities and engineering functions in areas such as telecommunications, security systems, audio and video system design, countermeasures, and covert electronic and physical surveillance system design. Electronics engineers are involved in many phases of applied engineering research and are also responsible for the development of equipment prototypes that are designed for use in criminal investigations and for other purposes. They often specialize in one or more aspects of their broad field of work. The nature of assignments is largely dependent on the grade of the electronics engineer, with particularly difficult projects being assigned to those serving in GS-12 through GS-14 positions.

Their daily activities focus on designing circuits, bread-boarding, performing computer-aided design and modeling tasks, mechanical layout functions, testing and evaluating prototypes, pre-production tasks, and the mass production of electronic equipment. They also determine requirements for special test equipment and perform troubleshooting functions to isolate and define specific engineering problems. Troubleshooting often involves investigating, analyzing, and preparing design layouts to resolve specific problems with equipment and electronic systems. Many assignments involve major problems that require extensive experimentation and the development of new approaches and technology.

To succeed in their day-to-day activities, electronics engineers maintain constant contact with local and national research institutions, associations, and professional organizations to exchange ideas and seek solutions to problems. Although much of their work is performed within FBI facilities, many projects are carried out at contractor facilities.

Electronics engineers prepare engineering drawings and review contractors' drawings for accuracy and adequacy. They also conduct site surveys to determine what must be done to prepare the environment for new equipment, and specify the types of equipment to be used, power requirements, and whether structural modifications are necessary. Their responsibilities also include developing and evaluating the adequacy of maintenance programs, training equipment and materials, operating manuals, and repair procedures.

In furtherance of their mission to develop and improve technology for use by the Bureau and other law enforcement agencies, FBI electronics engineers write reports and author scientific papers for publication in peer-reviewed literature. These may also be presented at training seminars and academic conferences, or distributed for use by law enforcement agencies and others in the intelligence community. Many engineers serve on special agency and interagency committees that address long-range planning and the establishment of future research and development programs. They also maintain continuing liaison with law enforcement agencies, the intelligence community, and scientific groups in the private sector to exchange information and provide technical assistance.

Minimum Qualifications and Salary Requirements

Electronics engineers candidates can meet basic eligibility requirements either by possessing a bachelor's degree in engineering or through a combination of education and experience, as follows:

Bachelor's Degree in Professional Engineering. To be acceptable, the curriculum must: (A) be in a school of engineering that has at least one curriculum in professional engineering that is accredited by the Accreditation Board for Engineering and Technology in professional engineering; or (B) include differential and integral calculus and advanced courses in five of the following seven areas of engineering science or physics: (1) statics, dynamics; (2) strength of materials (stress-strain relationships); (3) fluid mechanics, hydraulics; (4) thermodynamics; (5) electrical fields and circuits; (6) nature and properties of materials (relating particle and aggregate structure to properties); and (7) any other comparable area of fundamental engineering science or physics, such as optics, heat transfer, soil mechanics, or electronics; OR,

A Combination of Education and Experience. This includes college-level education, training, or technical experience that furnished a thorough knowledge of the physical and mathematical sciences underlying professional engineering, and a good understanding (both theoretical and practical) of the engineering sciences and techniques and their applications to one of the branches of engineering. The adequacy of a candidate's background must be demonstrated by one of the following:

- **Professional registration**, including current registration as a professional engineer by any state, the District of Columbia, Guam, or Puerto Rico.

- **A written test,** which requires evidence of achieving a passing score on the Fundamentals of Engineering Examination (formerly known as the Engineering-in-Training Exam), or a written test required for professional registration that was administered by the Boards of Engineering Examiners in the various states, the District of Columbia, Guam, or Puerto Rico.

- **Specified academic courses,** including successful completion of at least 60 semester hours of courses in the physical, mathematical, and engineering sciences that included the courses specified in the basic requirements of a vacancy announcement. The courses must be fully acceptable toward meeting the requirements of a professional engineering curriculum.

- **Related curriculum,** meaning that successful completion of a curriculum leading to a bachelor's degree in engineering technology or in an appropriate professional field (for example, physics, chemistry, architecture, computer science, mathematics, hydrology, or geology) may be accepted in lieu of a degree in engineering, provided that the applicant has had at least one year of professional engineering experience acquired under professional engineering supervision and guidance.

Depending on the area of specialty for the position being filled, KSA statements for the electronics engineer position are likely to focus on elements such as the following:

- Knowledge of audio and video technologies relating to advanced security, surveillance, and sensor systems

- Knowledge of computer technology, computer hardware, and software

- Knowledge of network communications systems, radio frequency systems, and digital signal processing

- Ability to conduct technical analyses and troubleshooting

- Ability to analyze, test, modify, and develop new technology

- Ability to write reports and prepare professional papers, and to communicate orally

Salary Grade Requirements

GS-7   One full year of graduate-level education, or superior academic achievement during undergraduate studies in a professional engineering curriculum; or a bachelor's degree and one year of specialized experience.

GS-9   A master's degree or two years of graduate-level education; or a bachelor's degree and one year of specialized experience equivalent to at least GS-7.

GS-11 A Ph.D. or equivalent doctoral degree, or three years of graduate-level education; or a bachelor's degree and one year of specialized experience equivalent to at least GS-9.

GS-12 A bachelor's degree and one year of specialized experience equivalent to GS-11.

GS-13 A bachelor's degree and one year of specialized experience equivalent to GS-12.

GS-14 A bachelor's degree and one year of specialized experience equivalent to GS-13.

Electronics Technician

Electronics technicians are assigned to FBI field offices, where they perform the installation and maintenance of specified portions of critical systems and sub-systems of the Bureau's communications and intrusion-detection systems. The work of electronics technicians is similar in many ways to electronics engineers. However, whereas personnel in both positions must apply practical knowledge of engineering methods and techniques, electronics technicians are not required to have full professional knowledge of engineering that is required for electronics engineer positions.

Overview of the Position

The primary responsibilities of electronics technicians revolve around the installation and preventative maintenance of transmitters, receivers, antenna systems, fixed-station units, audio amplifiers, and technical investigative equipment and systems. Maintenance of this equipment typically requires replacing or repairing defective components, adjusting transmitter outputs and modulation, realigning and adjusting FM receivers, and related tasks. Once maintenance work has been completed, electronics technicians inspect the work, furnish advice and assistance on maintenance problems, and conduct on-the-job training for various FBI personnel.

Additional responsibilities revolve around troubleshooting and redesigning complex electronic systems and interrelated subsystems. Electronics technicians perform repairs of all systems utilizing regular as well as highly specialized test equipment. They also assist in planning, organizing, and managing the field office preventative and corrective maintenance programs relating to electronic devices, equipment, and systems. Other tasks include the routine inspection and testing of equipment and systems to ensure technical integrity. They must also ensure that operational and standby systems and equipment are available and are in continuous and reliable operating condition for normal daily functions and emergencies.

In direct support of FBI field investigative operations, electronics technicians assist special agents in planning and carrying out a variety of assignments that require the use of mobile and technical investigative equipment. This could include the design, modification, repair, and testing of radio and electronics systems used in FBI vehicles, as well as video equipment, transmitters, and covert electronic surveillance devices. Their support of field operations ensures that technical equipment is maintained and utilized at optimum operational performance levels. In the course of search warrant or arrest warrant operations, or during major incidents, electronics technicians may set up command posts in the field to ensure reliable communication by radio, phone, and facsimile.

In support of the Bureau's administrative operations, electronics technicians install and provide limited maintenance of radio dispatching and computer equipment and systems. They also provide guidance and assistance in the installation and maintenance of active and passive intrusion-detection systems, which include closed-circuit television, infrared and photoelectric sensors, and a variety of system control panels. In addition, electronics technicians conduct training programs to instruct FBI special agents and support personnel on various types of equipment.

Some of the work of electronics technicians includes contact with high-voltage equipment. They may also be required to work irregular hours or to report to work in emergency situations. Other responsibilities include preparing reports, technical documentation, and diagrams, and reviewing technical publications to stay abreast of electronic technological improvements.

Minimum Qualifications and Salary Requirements

KSA statements for the electronics technician position are likely to focus on the following:

- Knowledge of theory, design characteristics, operation, and functions of electronic communications equipment

- Knowledge of electrical systems, electronics, mechanical equipment, security equipment, and telephone facilities

- Knowledge of professional electronic engineering concepts

- Ability to communicate orally and in writing with engineers, technicians, special agents, and professional support personnel

Salary Grade Requirements

GS-7   An associate's degree or equivalent certificate program; or four years of military service in a technical Military Occupational Specialty (MOS) that required in-depth technical training; or one year of specialized experience equivalent to at least GS-5.

GS-9   A bachelor's degree; or an associate's degree, or completion of an equivalent certificate program and two years of specialized experience equivalent to the GS-7 level; or six years of military service in a technical MOS that required in-depth technical training; or one year of specialized experience equivalent to at least GS-7.

GS-10   A bachelor's degree and one year of specialized experience equivalent to the GS-9 level; or an associate's degree or equivalent certificate program and three years of specialized experience equivalent to the GS-9 level; or eight years of military service in a technical MOS that required in-depth technical training; or one year of specialized experience equivalent to at least GS-9.

GS-11   A bachelor's degree and two years specialized experience equivalent to the GS-10 level; or an associate's degree or equivalent certificate program and four years of specialized experience equivalent to the GS-10 level; or 10 years of military service in a technical MOS that required in-depth technical training or one year of specialized experience equivalent to at least GS-10.

GS-12   A bachelor's degree and three years specialized experience equivalent to the GS-11 level; or an associate's degree or equivalent certificate program and four years of specialized experience equivalent to the GS-11 level; or 12 years of military service in a technical MOS that required in-depth technical training; or one year of specialized experience equivalent to at least GS-11.

Education Requirements

For education to be acceptable, degrees and certification must have included major study in electronics engineering, electrical engineering, electronics engineering technology, electronics technology, or telecommunications.

Physical Requirements

Electronics technician candidates are required to have a physical examination because they might be required to lift heavy objects or climb ladders, poles, towers, and other apparatuses to mount or service electronic equipment and devices. Eyesight requirements include uncorrected binocular vision of not less than 20/200 (Snellen), and corrected vision of 20/20 in one eye and 20/40 in the other. Applicants must also pass a color-vision test. A valid driver's license is also required.

Evidence Technician

The accurate and secure storage of evidence is critical to the integrity of FBI investigations, particularly as it relates to presentation during evidentiary hearings, plea negotiations, and trials. Seized evidence must be properly stored and accounted for so that it can be retrieved for examination or other use by laboratory technicians and specialists, special agents, and assistant United States attorneys.

Overview of the Position

The Bureau's evidence technicians perform a variety of functions associated with the receipt, retention, and disposition of evidence in the custody of the FBI. The integrity of evidence depends on evidence technicians and others to maintain a proper chain of custody at all times until final disposition of the case. Establishing the chain of custody requires accurate records and the diligence of skilled personnel to maintain them.

Evidence that is turned over to evidence technicians by special agents is obtained during the course of investigations, the execution of search warrants, seizures from arrested persons, and other circumstances. Once items have been received, evidence technicians first identify their contents and then ensure that numbering, labeling, and inventory procedures are carried out according to legal requirements and Bureau policies. Some items are also measured, weighed, or photographed, although this depends on the type of evidence and nature of the investigation. Certain items are heat-sealed to protect them from air, moisture, or other contamination.

Initial processing also requires evidence technicians to determine whether precautions or safety procedures are necessary for certain types of evidence, such as blood, semen, explosives and other hazardous materials, or other items that require refrigeration, freezing, or any form of special handling. Packaging and storage space requirements are also evaluated. Evidence technicians make appropriate log and computer entries whenever evidence is turned over to or received from special agents, FBI Laboratory personnel, or others. They are also responsible for following specific procedures to ensure the physical security of evidence-storage facilities. Evidence technicians may be called on to testify in court as witnesses or custodians of records concerning the security and chain of custody of evidence under their control.

As members of the Bureau's evidence response teams (ERTs), evidence technicians also respond to FBI operations in the field, where they assist special agents and other personnel with investigations involving white-collar crime, terrorism, drug offenses, homicide and other violent crimes, civil rights violations, and many other offenses. In this capacity, they offer assistance with evidence processing at the scenes of crimes or disasters or during the execution of search warrants. For example, evidence technicians were deployed to the scene of the Alfred P. Murrah Federal Building bombing in Oklahoma City, where they combed the bombing site along with special agents and conducted inventories of items seized. Evidence recovered at the scene was used to link Timothy McVeigh to the bombing, which led to his conviction. The skilled expertise of evidence technicians sometimes requires these personnel to be deployed overseas as well.

Minimum Qualifications and Salary Requirements

The knowledge, skills, and abilities sought by the FBI when filling evidence technician positions include elements such as the following:

- Ability to read and interpret instructions and written information

- Ability to gather, assemble, and analyze information

- Ability to communicate orally, in order to provide information to other FBI personnel regarding evidence in custody, and to testify in court as a custodian of evidence

- Ability to communicate in writing, in order to maintain written accountability records and logs

Experience in following proper procedures for receiving, logging, storing, packaging, and shipping of evidentiary materials is also helpful. Knowledge of proper procedures for the handling and disposal of items such as weapons, narcotics, toxic substances, blood, and contaminated articles is a plus, and computer skills are also valuable.

Salary Grade Requirements

Evidence technicians normally are hired at the GS-5 salary level and progress to GS-7 and GS-9. To qualify for the position, applicants must have completed technical training or possess work experience that has equipped them with the particular knowledge, skills, and abilities to successfully perform the duties of the position. Applicants are rated on their experience, education, training, employment performance evaluations, and awards as they relate to the duties and qualifications of the position. A high school diploma or equivalent is also required.

Financial Analyst

The investigation of criminal activity—especially white-collar crime—often includes the assistance of financial analysts to crack the case. Their expertise is indispensable in making sense of complex financial information and transactions in a large proportion of FBI investigations.

Overview of the Position

FBI financial analysts are assigned to investigative squads, where they perform accounting and analytical tasks to assist special agents with investigations, particularly those requiring review and analysis of voluminous accounting and financial records. This often involves the preparation of financial spreadsheets based on information obtained through subpoenas and during the execution of search warrants.

FBI financial analysts have particular proficiency in following "money trails" to establish unreported income and the flow of assets. Their expertise is especially useful during the investigation of offenses involving money laundering, illegal political campaign contributions, bribery of public officials, illegal tax shelters, banking violations, bankruptcy fraud, health-care and insurance fraud, and embezzlement. In many cases, these investigations focus on organized crime activities, high-level drug-trafficking enterprises, and public corruption. They also search property records, locate assets, and work with financial regulatory agencies in extracting pertinent information for use in bank failure investigations. Financial analyses often revolve around records obtained from domestic and international banks. In addition to assisting with investigations that lead to criminal prosecutions, financial analysts also perform tasks relating to the seizure and forfeiture of assets.

Financial analysts are responsible for developing financial profiles of suspects based on information gathered during investigations, and preparing special agents for interviews with witnesses and suspects. Occasionally, they accompany special agents during interviews to provide the benefit of their expertise. Many financial analysts also serve as members of multi-agency task force operations that focus on fraud against the government, environmental crimes, health-care fraud, bank fraud and embezzlement, and other offenses. They also prepare investigative materials for presentation in court, and testify during criminal and civil trials. These personnel must be available for assignments that occasionally involve working at night or on weekends, and for temporary duty assignments away from their permanent office for anywhere from 30 days to six months.

Minimum Qualifications and Salary Requirements

Financial analyst applicants are required to submit a KSA statement to address elements such as the following:

- Knowledge of accounting and finance principles and financial management organization operations and practices, in order to interpret and analyze financial documents and records

- Knowledge of the operations of banks and other financial institutions

- Knowledge of legal principles pertaining to subpoenas, search warrants, criminal procedure, and court proceedings

- Ability to communicate clearly and concisely in writing, in order to accurately present information and write factual investigative reports

- Ability to communicate orally, in order to deal effectively with employees in other government agencies, business corporations, banks, courts, and other entities

- Ability to research, collate, evaluate, and analyze information

Salary Grade Requirements

GS-5   A high school diploma or its equivalent, three years of general experience, and a minimum of six semester hours of core accounting courses from an accredited college or university; or a bachelor's degree in business administration with a minimum of six semester hours of college accredited accounting courses.

GS-7   One year of graduate-level education, or a bachelor's degree and superior academic achievement, and six semester hours of core accounting courses.

GS-9   Two full years of graduate-level education, either in business administration (with a strong emphasis in accounting or finance), or accounting, finance, economics or a directly related subject; or a master's degree and a minimum of 12 semester hours of core accounting courses.

GS-11   Three years of graduate-level education in one of the fields described in the preceding item, or a Ph.D. and 12 semester hours of core accounting courses.

Coursework and Transcripts

Examples of acceptable core accounting courses generally include Principles of Accounting, Intermediate Accounting, Advanced Accounting, Cost Accounting, Federal Income Tax, Auditing, International Accounting, and Managerial Accounting. Courses in Business Law, Electronic Data Processing, Statistics, and other business administration courses are not acceptable substitutes for required accounting courses. Applicants must submit academic transcripts along with their applications.

Fingerprint Specialist

Identifying criminals by their fingerprints is one of the most potent factors in apprehending those who might otherwise escape arrest and continue their criminal activities. Fingerprint identification consists of identifying the impressions made by the minute ridge formations or patterns found on the fingertips. No two persons have exactly the same arrangement of ridge patterns and—except in cases of injuries or mutilations—the patterns remain unchanged throughout life. By comparing fingerprints at the scene of a crime with those of suspects and on file, FBI personnel can establish absolute proof of the presence or identity of a person. The FBI maintains the world's largest fingerprint repository—including more than 219 million fingerprint cards—as well as sophisticated computer databases.

Overview of the Position

FBI fingerprint specialists are responsible for classifying, searching, verifying, and filing fingerprints and other vestigial prints for identification in support of criminal investigations for the Bureau and other federal, state, and local law enforcement agencies. Their primary responsibilities include the examination of crime scene evidence to detect, develop, analyze, and preserve latent fingerprints, palm prints, footprints, and lip prints. They compare these latent prints with those of known suspects or victims, or those on file in the Bureau's Automated Fingerprint Identification System database. Fingerprint specialists employ a variety of techniques, including the use of chemicals, powders, lasers, alternative light sources, and other scientific methods.

Many fingerprint specialists assigned to the Bureau's Latent Print Unit also are members of the Bureau's disaster squad, which provides assistance in identifying deceased victims of accidents or catastrophes worldwide. When disaster strikes, this squad may be deployed on request from the ranking law enforcement official at the scene, the medical examiner or coroner in charge of victim identification, the ranking official of a public transportation carrier, the National Transportation Safety Board, the Federal Aviation Administration, or the U.S. Department of State in instances of foreign disasters involving U.S. citizens. Since 1940, the disaster squad has responded to more than 200 disasters worldwide and—with the assistance of FBI fingerprint specialists—has identified over one-half of the victims by fingerprints or footprints. As members of the disaster squad, fingerprint specialists have participated in the identification of victims following the space shuttle *Challenger* explosion in 1986, as well as the Mount St. Helens volcano eruption in 1980, and the mass suicide of hundreds of members of the People's Temple cult in Jonestown, Guyana, in 1978. The identification of disaster victims sometimes involves the use of cleaners, tissue builders, formaldehyde, and other substances to prepare the fingers of dead persons for identification work. Depending on the situation, the identification of disaster victims could also include obtaining latent prints from their personal possessions.

Fingerprint specialists are also responsible for preparing detailed reports developed from their examination and analysis of evidence, and maintaining reports and other records. These are often used by special agents and prosecuting attorneys during criminal case preparation and in court. In many cases, fingerprint specialists are called on to testify in evidentiary hearings and criminal trials in support of their findings, for which they prepare and present charts and other exhibits for use in the courtroom. Their duties also include conducting research studies in latent fingerprint identification, which includes conducting experiments in new techniques and testing new equipment and technology. They also provide training in all aspects of latent print work to local, state, federal, and foreign law enforcement personnel.

Minimum Qualifications and Salary Requirements

Areas to be addressed in KSA statements for fingerprint specialist positions may include elements such as the following:

- Knowledge of chemicals, procedures, and equipment used in developing latent prints on a variety of substances and materials, and of techniques used in the preservation of latent prints

- Ability to communicate in writing, in order to prepare written laboratory reports based on interpretation and evaluation of fingerprint evidence, research papers, and instructional guides

- Ability to communicate orally, in order to brief supervisory personnel, special agents, prosecuting attorneys, and others, and to testify as an expert witness in criminal cases and administrative hearings to explain results of examinations

- Ability to use computers, as well as word-processing, database, and video-imaging software

Salary Grade Requirements

GS-7   One year of specialized experience equivalent to at least GS-5 that demonstrated the ability to classify inked fingerprints by the Henry and NCIC systems.

GS-9   One year of specialized experience equivalent to at least GS-7 that provided knowledge of the techniques for comparing and lifting latent fingerprints on evidentiary materials, in photographing latent and inked prints, and in making photographic enlargements for court demonstrations.

GS-11 One year of specialized experience equivalent to at least GS-9 performing complex latent fingerprint examinations, preparing written laboratory reports based on examinations, and testifying as an expert witness in the area of latent fingerprint examinations.

GS-12 One year of specialized experience equivalent to at least GS-11 analyzing complex fingerprint cases and imperfect or partial latent fingerprint impressions that contain only the minimum number of points necessary to make an identification, and conducting methods-development projects to improve latent fingerprint examination capabilities.

Intelligence Operations Specialist

The work of intelligence operations specialists revolves around the collection and processing of intelligence information relating to criminal investigations and matters of national security. Experience that demonstrates the ability to analyze problems, gather pertinent data and recognize solutions, plan and organize projects, and communicate effectively can be particularly helpful in performing tasks carried out by these vital personnel.

Overview of the Position

Intelligence operations specialists participate in intelligence and investigative operations in support of multi-jurisdictional endeavors by collecting, analyzing, evaluating, and disseminating intelligence information. They frequently obtain intelligence data and reports relating to criminal matters and foreign counterintelligence from special agents who are assigned to the Bureau's field offices or headquarters. Intelligence operations specialists also collect information from organizations that make up the U.S. intelligence community, such as the Central Intelligence Agency, Department of Defense, National Security Agency, and Department of State.

Intelligence operations specialists receive data from a variety of sources, including intelligence reports and communications provided by the FBI and other law enforcement agencies, FBI case files, covert sources of information, published materials, and other forms of communication. This data may include details that are up-to-the-minute concerning situations in foreign countries, such as implications of a recent presidential election, revolution, uprising, or coup. The data may also include speculative intelligence that focuses primarily on projecting what future conditions will be. Specialists carefully review and analyze the data to determine its significance and validity— and the reliability of the source—and to discover gaps in information that can be filled to the extent possible. They also summarize their findings into written reports and present verbal briefings to special agents in the field and other

FBI personnel. On a day-to-day basis, intelligence operations specialists work closely with FBI special agents in managing individual investigations.

Carrying out these responsibilities requires specialists to maintain effective working relationships with their counterparts in the intelligence community and with law enforcement officers from other federal, state, and local agencies. To perform these functions efficiently and effectively, specialists exchange information through various intelligence working groups that are dedicated to specific or mutual foreign intelligence, counterintelligence, counterterrorism, or other operational programs. They also determine the distribution of raw intelligence data and finished intelligence reports, and assess the need for and write intelligence collection manuals and guides.

Minimum Qualifications and Salary Requirements

To be competitive, applicants for this position should have a fundamental knowledge of research and intelligence techniques, as well as an understanding of one or more of the natural or social sciences, political science, engineering, law enforcement, or military science. The FBI evaluates applicants for intelligence operations specialist positions on knowledge, skills, and abilities such as the following:

- Knowledge of foreign and domestic affairs as they relate to counterintelligence and counterterrorism, national security issues, law enforcement, and operational security

- Ability to conduct research and to evaluate and analyze raw data

- Ability to communicate clearly and concisely in writing, in order to compose written intelligence reports

- Ability to communicate orally, in order to provide briefings to FBI personnel, members of the intelligence community, and other law enforcement agencies

Salary Grade Requirements

GS-5   Completion of a four-year course of study leading to a bachelor's degree; or three years of general experience, one year of which was equivalent to at least GS-4.

GS-7   One full year of graduate-level education in the intelligence or intelligence-related disciplines (such as history, political science, international affairs, economics, or journalism); or one year of specialized experience equivalent to at least GS-5.

GS-9   A master's degree or two years of graduate-level education in the disciplines described in the preceding item; or one year of specialized experience equivalent to at least GS-7.

GS-11 A Ph.D. or equivalent doctoral degree, or three years of graduate-level education in the disciplines described in the preceding item; or one year of specialized experience equivalent to at least GS-9.

GS-12 One year of specialized experience equivalent to at least GS-11.

GS-13 One year of specialized experience equivalent to at least GS-12.

GS-14 One year of specialized experience equivalent to at least GS-13.

Intelligence Research Specialist

The FBI's intelligence research specialists play a vital role in the Bureau's extensive intelligence operations, although in a different manner than intelligence operations specialists. Although both of these specialists are responsible for examining and interpreting national security or criminal intelligence information, the focus of each position is different. Intelligence operations specialists provide more direct operational support and assistance to FBI special agents in managing individual cases. In other words, they are primarily based in operational units and work on a day-to-day basis with FBI agents in the field. On the other hand, intelligence research specialists are responsible for strategic and operational analyses and are primarily based in analytical units that are further removed from field-level operations. In this capacity, intelligence research specialists produce broader "big picture" analytical reports and briefings. Personnel serving in both positions work closely together at FBI Headquarters.

Overview of the Position

Similarly to intelligence operations specialists, the Bureau's intelligence research specialists are responsible for the examination and interpretation of national security information in support of the criminal intelligence, foreign counterintelligence, counterterrorism, and organized crime missions of the FBI. Intelligence information is utilized for the preparation of strategic and operational analyses, espionage case studies, and threat assessments, which are distributed within the FBI and to other federal, state, and local law enforcement agencies.

Intelligence research specialists receive intelligence data obtained through criminal investigations and sources such as seized documents, financial records, surveillance reports, photographs, witness interviews, cooperating sources, informants, and court-ordered wiretaps. They compile information and assess its importance, validity, and comprehensiveness; and then they apprise FBI personnel of activity that impacts the Bureau's tactical and strategic initiatives. Intelligence information is entered and processed through the use of sophisticated computer databases and various methods of data manipulation. Intelligence research specialists also prepare comprehensive and authoritative written intelligence reports that summarize their findings. These reports typically provide analysis of and detailed information regarding the background and current situation of intelligence or investigative activity, and are used to facilitate a variety of intelligence and operational, investigative endeavors.

Intelligence research specialists belong to interagency working groups, through which they exchange information with other organizations throughout the U.S. intelligence community. They are also responsible for preparing and presenting briefings and training classes to special agents and supervisory personnel, prosecuting attorneys, grand juries, and high-level decision-makers.

Minimum Qualifications and Salary Requirements

Applicants for intelligence research specialist positions are rated on similar criteria to those seeking intelligence operations specialist careers. Accordingly, applicants should have knowledge of research and intelligence techniques and an understanding of one or more of the natural or social sciences, political science, engineering, law enforcement, or military science. Knowledge, skills, and abilities sought for intelligence research specialist positions include elements such as the following:

- Knowledge of principles, concepts, and methodology of intelligence research in political, economic, social, cultural, geographical, and military conditions or trends relating to national security issues, terrorism, violent gangs, organized crime groups, financial crimes, civil rights, drug-trafficking enterprises, and other criminal activity

- Ability to conduct research by analyzing and extracting information from a number of sources and assessing its validity and veracity

- Ability to communicate clearly and concisely in writing, in order to compose written intelligence reports in various formats

- Ability to communicate orally, in order to provide briefings to FBI personnel, members of the intelligence community, and other law enforcement agencies

Salary Grade Requirements

GS-5   Completion of a four-year course of study leading to a bachelor's degree; or three years of general experience, one year of which was equivalent to at least GS-4.

GS-7   One full year of graduate-level education in the intelligence or intelligence-related disciplines (such as history, political science, international affairs, economics, or journalism); or one year of specialized experience equivalent to at least GS-5.

GS-9   A master's degree or two years of graduate-level education in the disciplines described in the preceding item; or one year of specialized experience equivalent to at least GS-7.

GS-11 A Ph.D. or equivalent doctoral degree, or three years of graduate-level education in the disciplines described in the previous item; or one year of specialized experience equivalent to at least GS-9.

GS-12 One year of specialized experience equivalent to at least GS-11.

GS-13 One year of specialized experience equivalent to at least GS-12.

GS-14 One year of specialized experience equivalent to at least GS-13.

Investigative Specialist

FBI personnel who serve as investigative specialists have a unique opportunity to be directly involved in street-level investigative operations without making arrests or performing other law enforcement tasks. Their role is critical to accomplishing the FBI's foreign counterintelligence and national security missions. The theft of U.S. technology and sensitive economic information by foreign intelligence services and competitors has been estimated by the White House and others to be valued up to a hundred billion dollars annually.

Overview of the Position

The FBI is the lead foreign counterintelligence agency within the U.S. intelligence community. The Bureau's National Foreign Intelligence Program is tasked with preventing foreign espionage and economic espionage and with investigating foreign counterintelligence cases. The program is also involved in international terrorism threats, weapons of mass destruction threats, and attacks on the nation's critical infrastructures such as communications, banking operations, and transportation systems. The FBI conducts espionage investigations anywhere in the world when the subject of the investigation is a U.S. citizen and is not under the jurisdiction of the Uniform Code of Military Justice. The primary mission of the FBI in foreign counterintelligence investigations is to identify, penetrate, and neutralize the threat posed—which is where the Bureau's investigative specialists lend their expertise.

Investigative specialists collect, analyze, and utilize intelligence information to assess and respond to the activities of foreign powers and their agents that could adversely affect national security. Specifically, they participate as members of teams that conduct discreet surveillance coverage in foreign counterintelligence and counterterrorism cases. For example, these cases may focus on foreign powers that conduct intelligence activities either to identify and collect national defense information from the U.S. government or American corporations or to obtain or use chemical, biological, or nuclear weapons and delivery systems.

Surveillance missions are performed in a variety of environments and circumstances. The missions may involve observing individuals from static positions for hours or days at a time or following surveillance targets on foot or in vehicles. Investigative specialists document their observations through surveillance logs, which provide a record of the activities of those under surveillance, as well as detailed written reports. They also provide periodic briefings to special agents in the field and other FBI personnel on a need-to-know basis. Investigative specialists draw on a variety of resources and techniques in carrying out surveillance tasks, including the use of sophisticated photographic equipment to document the activities of their surveillance targets, and broadcasting their observations to other Bureau operatives using radio communication equipment. The work of investigative specialists sometimes involves surveillance activities on extended shifts, at night, and on weekends and holidays.

Minimum Qualifications and Salary Requirements

Unlike the majority of professional support positions, investigative specialists are required to be available for permanent transfers or temporary duty assignments wherever the needs of the FBI dictate. Applicants are required to sign an agreement in which they commit to remaining in the position for at least two years. They must also possess a valid driver's license and pass a physical examination.

Applicants are rated on their knowledge, skills, and abilities, which might include elements such as the following:

- Knowledge of surveillance techniques
- Skill in gathering factual and visual information through questioning, observing, analyzing, drawing conclusions, making recommendations, following guidelines, and working independently
- Ability to operate photographic and radio communication equipment
- Written communication skills, in order to maintain surveillance logs and write detailed reports

- Oral communication skills, in order to communicate with other surveillance team members and to provide verbal briefings to FBI special agents and other personnel

Salary Grade Requirements

GS-5   Completion of a four-year course of study leading to a bachelor's degree; or three years of general experience, one year of which was equivalent to at least GS-4. Preference is given to applicants whose major field of study is in the areas of political science, history, journalism, international studies, psychology, sociology, criminology, or certain foreign languages.

GS-7   One full year of graduate-level education, or superior academic achievement during undergraduate studies in the disciplines described in the preceding item; or a bachelor's degree and one year of specialized experience equivalent to at least GS-5.

GS-9   A master's degree or two years of graduate-level education in the disciplines described in the previous item; or a bachelor's degree and one year of specialized experience equivalent to at least GS-7.

GS-11 A Ph.D. or equivalent doctoral degree, or three years of graduate-level education in the disciplines described in the previous item; or a bachelor's degree and one year of specialized experience equivalent to at least GS-9.

GS-12 One year of specialized experience equivalent to at least GS-11.

GS-13 One year of specialized experience equivalent to at least GS-12.

Language Specialist

The FBI has an ongoing and ever-evolving need for personnel who speak foreign languages. Foreign language needs vary from time to time, and from one office to another, depending on the nature of investigations and initiatives that are underway. For example, proficiency in Arabic might be in demand in Detroit and Los Angeles, whereas Spanish usually is at a premium in cities such as Chicago, New York, and McAllen, Texas. The New York Field Office typically requires support in a wide variety of foreign languages, including Cantonese, French, Hebrew, Italian, Japanese, Mandarin, Russian, and Yiddish. Other language proficiencies sought by the Bureau include Dutch, German, Haitian Creole, Hindi, Jamaican patois, Korean, Punjabi, Thai, Turkish, Urdu, and Vietnamese. The need for language specialists with fluency in Arabic, Farsi, and Pashto reached a critical level following the attacks on the World Trade Center and the Pentagon on September 11, 2001.

In addition to language specialists, the FBI also employs contract linguists for foreign language support. These personnel perform essentially the same tasks as language specialists, although they are not full-time FBI employees and do not receive federal benefits. Contract linguists are paid an hourly wage, depending on the language spoken and level of expertise, and are called upon on an as-needed basis. The FBI also meets its foreign language needs with special agent linguists. Overall, more than 1,000 personnel who are fluent in more than 50 languages and dialects provide foreign language support to the FBI.

Overview of the Position

FBI language specialists provide a wide range of linguistic support services to criminal investigations and national security matters under the Bureau's jurisdiction. Their work revolves around the translation of oral and written material from foreign languages into English in a wide range of settings and during all types of investigations. For example, they might assist special agents with interviews of crime victims or witnesses or during interrogations of criminals involved in organized crime, drug trafficking, white-collar crime, public corruption, or violations of other federal statutes. Language specialists also work closely with special agents involved in foreign counterintelligence work.

Language specialists also translate speech from audio and video recordings that were produced during electronic surveillance, wiretapping operations, and undercover transactions. In addition, FBI investigations that end up in court often require language specialists to translate testimony during hearings and trials. Language specialists also participate as members of the Bureau's evidence response teams in field offices nationwide because crime scene investigations often require FBI personnel to communicate with victims and witnesses who speak little or no English. Language specialists also play a crucial role as members of the Bureau's terrorism squads because many terrorist groups are based outside of the United States, as well as in various multi-agency task force operations.

The expertise of language specialists has been useful during a number of high-profile cases, such as the investigation of the crash of EgyptAir flight 990 in 1999. In this case, they worked for 130 hours to translate speech from the aircraft's cockpit voice recorder from Arabic into English. Language specialists also assisted FBI special agents during court hearings in the case against Mohamed Rashed Daoud Al-'Owhali, who—along with Osama Bin Laden—was charged with the 1998 bombings of the U.S. Embassies in Kenya and Tanzania. The indictments accused Bin Laden, Al-'Owhali, and other members of the *al Qaeda* terrorist group of killing a total of 224 people in the bombings. Language specialists also respond to bombings and other crime scenes worldwide as members of the Bureau's rapid deployment teams.

Minimum Qualifications and Salary Requirements

Each candidate's language proficiency is measured by a battery of language tests, which include written translations from the foreign language into English and oral tests in both languages. These tests focus on listening comprehension, reading comprehension, and translation. (Passing an equivalent Defense Language Proficiency test is also acceptable.) The FBI adheres to the Interagency Language Roundtable (ILR) Skill Level Descriptions for listening, reading, writing, speaking, and translation, which serve as the government-wide standard. In lieu of submitting a KSA statement, candidates are required to provide a self-assessment of their expertise, which is based on ILR language proficiency standards (see appendix I for the Language Proficiency Self-Assessment Chart). In addition to language skills, knowledge of law enforcement and street jargon is also a plus.

Language specialist candidates are required to undergo a hearing test because they must have satisfactory hearing to translate live and recorded speech. They must also be willing to accept permanent transfers or temporary duty assignments wherever the needs of the FBI dictate.

Salary Grade Requirements

Whereas contract linguists receive an hourly wage, language specialists are paid according to the General Schedule salary scale. Requirements for various salary grades include the following:

GS-5　Proficiency in a foreign language (and in English) needed by the FBI that is sufficient to attain passing language-test scores.

GS-7　Four years of college-level education; or four years of specialized experience. At the GS-7 level, specialized experience may include life experience from residing in a non–native-language culture. Where English is the applicant's non-native language, residence in the United States qualifies.

GS-9　Five years of college-level education; or five years of specialized experience; or a master's degree in the needed foreign language or a related subject (such as English, foreign affairs, country area studies, and so on).

GS-10　Six years of college-level education; or six years of specialized experience. Advanced education must be related to the needed foreign language or country area studies.

GS-11　Seven years of college-level education; or a Ph.D. related to the needed foreign language or country area studies; or seven years of specialized experience.

Specialized experience for all levels includes any work with a foreign language, such as translating, teaching, interpreting, editing foreign language manuscripts, or experience in positions that require a bilingual capability.

Personnel Security Specialist

The FBI employs personnel security specialists to assess the reliability, loyalty, suitability, and trustworthiness of persons who have access to sensitive or classified information, resources, and material that could adversely affect the national security, public welfare, or efficiency of the FBI.

Overview of the Position

FBI personnel specialists conduct a variety of inquiries to determine whether Bureau personnel—or applicants for employment with the Bureau—meet security standards to the extent that their retention, hiring, or access to classified information or work sites is consistent with FBI standards and policies. Tasks these personnel perform also focus on security clearance determinations for contractors who perform work for the FBI.

The responsibilities of personnel security specialists include reviewing and evaluating investigative reports, personnel files, and other information; determining the degree and extent of investigative inquiry that is required to resolve allegations of adverse information; and conducting interviews and other investigative tasks to obtain information relating to minor derogatory allegations against FBI personnel. They also develop detailed and objective summaries of the information considered and recommend approval or denial of security clearances based on their findings. Although background investigations are performed mostly by special investigators under contract with the

FBI, personnel security specialists are responsible for conducting certain components of background investigations, such as indices checks, criminal record inquiries, and other related tasks.

Their administrative responsibilities include developing and implementing policies and procedures for the FBI's personnel security program, and advising FBI officials on personnel security policies and the impact of personnel security requirements on the Bureau's mission. They also administer programs for continuous security evaluation of FBI personnel and security awareness. Personnel security specialists might be called upon to testify at formal hearings regarding security clearance processes, criteria, and justification for adverse actions. They are also responsible for ensuring the proper storage and safeguarding of classified information under their control.

Minimum Qualifications and Salary Requirements

Applicants for personnel security specialist positions are required to submit KSA statements that address elements such as the following:

- Knowledge of laws, regulations, and precedents governing personnel security programs

- Knowledge of personnel security programs, concepts, and principles; and of investigative procedures

- Knowledge of medical, legal, and law enforcement terminology for analysis of expert opinions

- Ability to develop information and apply the significance of information to adjudicative determinations

- Ability to communicate effectively orally and in writing

Salary Grade Requirements

GS-5   Completion of a four-year course of study leading to a bachelor's degree; or three years of general experience, one year of which was equivalent to at least GS-4.

GS-7   One full year of graduate-level education, or superior academic achievement during undergraduate studies; or one year of specialized experience equivalent to at least GS-5.

GS-9   A master's degree or two years of graduate-level education; or one year of specialized experience equivalent to at least GS-7.

GS-11   A Ph.D. or equivalent doctoral degree, or three years of graduate-level education; or one year of specialized experience equivalent to at least GS-9.

GS-12   One year of specialized experience equivalent to at least GS-11.

GS-13   One year of specialized experience equivalent to at least GS-12.

Photographer

Photography plays a significant role in the FBI's mission to investigate violations of criminal law and conduct foreign counterintelligence operations. The Bureau employs skilled photographers who capture, process, analyze, and disseminate images relating to crime scenes, forensics, surveillance, tactical operations, courtroom testimony, and training purposes.

Overview of the Position

FBI photographers perform investigative and noninvestigative photographic assignments in a broad range of conditions and environments. Much of their work involves photographing evidence at crime scenes in both indoor and outdoor settings. In this capacity, FBI photographers choose the appropriate equipment and determine the selection, exposure, positioning, angle, background, and lighting sources for each item to be photographed. They are also responsible for marking items of photographed evidence, such as jewelry, furs, oil paintings, motor vehicles, equipment, weapons, documents, notes, damaged property, drugs and contraband, cash, and other goods. Photographers capture images at crime scenes to show the condition and location of evidence, as well as its position relative to other evidence or objects. They work closely with special agents and other FBI specialists to photograph latent fingerprints, footprints, shoe prints, tire prints, grease prints, and other evidence susceptible to photographic enhancement. Photographers apply a range of specialized technical methods to bring up fine details, sharpen images, or eliminate certain colors or features when processing photographic renditions that can be used in court. They must also prepare a log that records all photographs taken and a description and location of evidence. Depending on the nature of the case, photographers might also photograph victims at crime scenes or at offsite locations.

The Bureau's photographers also perform a wide range of static and moving surveillance photography during the course of criminal investigations, which sometimes involves the use of concealed cameras. These activities often include covert photography of crime suspects who are engaged in criminal activity or interacting with criminal associates. In some cases, photographers are called upon to take photographs from aircraft, including aerial mapping and surveillance applications, and during the execution of search warrants. FBI photographers use an assortment of equipment in accomplishing their missions, such as medium-format cameras, zoom lenses, image intensifiers, 2X and 3X extenders, cable and electronic release mechanisms, remote tripping devices, tripods, infrared flash equipment, high- and low-contrast films, infrared films, and various lens filters. They also adapt standard and special techniques in processing black and white film to meet the requirements of specific photographic projects.

As members of the Bureau's evidence response teams, FBI photographers have responded to many incidents around the world to provide their expertise. For example, photographers were deployed to Yemen following the bombing of the *USS Cole* guided-missile destroyer in October 2000, where they photographed the impact of the explosion and assisted in identifying the victims. In the attack, two suicide bombers in a small fiberglass boat blew a 40-by-40–foot hole in the side of the destroyer, killing 17 American sailors and wounding 39. In 1983, FBI photographers traveled to Grenada, where they produced approximately 1,000 images of skeletal remains that were buried in U.S. military body bags found in unmarked graves. In this case, the government of Grenada wanted to determine whether the bags contained the remains of Maurice Bishop, the former prime minister of Grenada, who was assassinated along with 18 government officials. Laboratory examinations disclosed that none of the exhumed bodies included remains of Maurice Bishop. In 1993, photographers were deployed to massacre sites in Kosovo, where they photographed bodies and other evidence in support of war-crimes prosecutions of Slobodan Milosevic. FBI photographers also photographed important evidence in the

1995 bombing of the Murrah Federal Building in Oklahoma City and during the 1993 siege of the Branch Davidian complex in Waco, Texas.

FBI photographers must also testify in court and present photographic exhibits during evidentiary hearings and trials to explain their photographs as well as the photographic and film-processing techniques they applied.

Minimum Qualifications and Salary Requirements

When applying for FBI photographer positions, candidates are required to address KSAs such as the following:

- Ability to photograph moving and stationary objects

- Ability to operate photographic processing equipment, to process photographic films and prints, and to enhance photographic images

- Ability to use equipment developed or adapted for use at crime scenes and in surveillance situations, including flash devices, telephoto lenses, tripods, concealed cameras, and other equipment

- Ability to take aerial photographs

Salary Grade Requirements

GS-8   One year of specialized experience equivalent to at least GS-7.

GS-9   One year of specialized experience equivalent to at least GS-8.

GS-10   One year of specialized experience equivalent to at least GS-9.

GS-11   One year of specialized experience equivalent to at least GS-10.

Physical Security Specialist

Physical security is concerned primarily with preventative measures designed to safeguard sensitive or classified information, facilities, equipment, personnel, visitors, and materials from criminal, terrorist, or hostile intelligence activities. With national security and the integrity of FBI investigations and other operations at stake, it is crucial for the Bureau to protect FBI Headquarters, field offices, resident agencies, legal attaché offices, off-site locations, and its personnel through its extensive physical security program.

Overview of the Position

The FBI's physical security specialists develop security policy and procedures; they also design, develop, evaluate, and maintain intrusion prevention and detection systems to ensure that sensitive information, equipment, and other material is not compromised, sabotaged, stolen, misused, or damaged. Physical security specialists provide technical expertise and hands-on support in the areas of physical security, fire safety, and chemical, biological, and radiological (CBR) countermeasures.

Their responsibilities include conducting physical security surveys; determining the need for safes, alarms, locking devices, and markings needed to effectively secure various sites; and defining restricted, controlled, or secure areas. They also establish procedures for the movement, handling, storage, and

protection of national security information, sensitive compartmented information, and other sensitive documents or materials, and inspect facilities where
national security data and equipment will be located.

To protect FBI employees and visitors, physical security specialists conduct fire
safety surveys, evaluate fire protection systems, implement personnel evacua-
tion plans, and develop countermeasures to explosive and CBR threats against
FBI personnel and facilities. Security surveys are designed to evaluate elements
such as the use of X-ray and magnetometer devices to screen packages and visitors, the presence and visibility of uniformed officers, personnel access systems, visitor-control procedures, proximity of parking to FBI facilities, building
construction and design, exterior lighting and security barriers, closed-circuit
television monitoring systems, and backup systems for security devices. To protect FBI personnel from explosives and hazardous materials, physical security
specialists develop procedures for screening mail, packages, and cargo that are
delivered to the FBI. They are also responsible for analyzing technical problems
associated with the Bureau's security equipment and systems and for developing appropriate solutions.

To ensure that the physical security program is operating properly, physical
security specialists periodically conduct security compliance reviews to verify
adherence to FBI security regulations and policies and write reports to ensure
the proper application of the Bureau's security requirements. Physical security
specialists conduct risk and threat assessments on a continuous basis in order
to respond to criminal and terrorist threats.

As members of the Bureau's rapid deployment teams, physical security specialists are prepared to respond within four hours to bombings and other high-
profile incidents under the FBI's jurisdiction worldwide. In this capacity, when
they arrive at the crime scene they are responsible for reporting on the threat
level to other responding FBI personnel, as well as the need for additional
physical security at the scene and housing for FBI personnel.

Minimum Qualifications and Salary Requirements

Physical security specialist applicants are required to submit KSA statements to
address elements such as the following:

- Knowledge of physical security programs, concepts, and principles

- Knowledge of access-control systems, locking devices, closed-circuit television systems, fire safety, and other security devices and systems

- Knowledge of laws and regulations relating to physical security

- Knowledge of procedures regarding the safeguarding and handling of
  sensitive compartmented information and other classified or sensitive
  information

- Ability to conduct security surveys

- Ability to communicate effectively orally and in writing

Salary Grade Requirements

GS-5   Completion of a four-year course of study leading to a bachelor's
        degree; or three years of general experience, one year of which was
        equivalent to at least GS-4.

GS-7   One full year of graduate-level education, or superior academic achievement during undergraduate studies; or one year of specialized experience equivalent to at least GS-5.

GS-9   A master's degree or two years of graduate-level education; or one year of specialized experience equivalent to at least GS-7.

GS-11   A Ph.D. or equivalent doctoral degree, or three years of graduate-level education; or one year of specialized experience equivalent to at least GS-9.

GS-12   One year of specialized experience equivalent to at least GS-11.

GS-13   One year of specialized experience equivalent to at least GS-12.

Police Officer

In addition to maintaining a professional staff of physical security specialists, the FBI also has uniformed officers who are committed to protecting Bureau personnel, property, and national security information from acts of assault, terrorism, sabotage, espionage, trespass, theft, fire, and accidental damage or malicious destruction.

Overview of the Position

The FBI maintains a force of uniformed police officers whose primary mission is to maintain law and order and to protect life, property, and the civil rights of Bureau employees and visitors. FBI police officers are stationed at the Bureau's Headquarters building in Washington, D.C.; the Washington, D.C., Field Office; the FBI Training Academy in Quantico, Virginia; two buildings occupied by the New York City Field Office; and at the Bureau's Criminal Justice Information Services Division complex in Clarksburg, West Virginia. They are assigned to fixed posts, roving patrols, and control-desk duties on rotating shifts around the clock.

FBI police officers conduct patrols on foot and in vehicles to check for unsecured windows and doors, detect and prevent illegal entry, identify suspicious persons and vehicles, and respond to other conditions. They also answer calls for service, respond to crimes in progress and emergency situations, conduct physical security escorts, and administer first aid and CPR to sick or injured persons. When crimes are detected, officers secure crime scenes, collect and preserve evidence, interview victims and witnesses, and process prisoners. Fixed-post duty revolves around access-control tasks, such as checking the identification of FBI employees and screening visitors seeking access to secure areas. Officers are also assigned to a control desk where they monitor electronic intrusion-detection systems and communications systems. FBI police officers are authorized to carry firearms and make arrests.

Many officers have the opportunity to participate in special operations, such as providing security at the 2002 Winter Olympic Games in Salt Lake City, Utah. FBI police officers also provided on-site security during the investigation of TWA Flight 800, which crashed near Long Island in 1996. Occasionally, the Bureau's police officers assist the Metropolitan Police of the District of Columbia (MPDC) with calls for service, arrest situations, and other law enforcement matters. Officers must be willing to accept temporary duty assignments away from their permanent office, at locations wherever the needs of the FBI dictate.

FBI police officers also are eligible to participate in the Bureau's canine (K-9) program, which provides support to criminal investigations and response to disaster situations. The K-9 program affords FBI police officers, special agents, and special agent bomb technicians the opportunity to serve as dog handlers on the Bureau's evidence response teams or to assist FBI field offices nation-wide with situations that require the expertise of K-9 teams. Each handler works with a dog that is specially trained to detect narcotics, explosives and the components used in explosives, firearms, currency, or people. K-9 teams carry out assignments such as searching for victims under rubble at the scenes of explosions, or detecting bombs or illegal drugs in cars, trucks, buses, boats, aircraft, houses and apartments, or commercial buildings. The teams also provide support at major events such as the Super Bowl, the Olympic Games, and the Goodwill Games.

Minimum Qualifications and Salary Requirements

Applicants must be a high school graduate, at least 21 years of age, and possess a valid driver's license. Candidates must past a physical examination, including eyesight and hearing tests.

Eyesight Requirements

Eyesight standards for police officer applicants are the same as for candidates seeking special agent positions. These include uncorrected vision not worse than 20/200 (Snellen), and corrected vision not worse than 20/20 in one eye and 20/40 in the other eye. All candidates must also pass a color-vision test. Applicants who have undergone surgical vision correction are evaluated on a case-by-case basis by the FBI's Health Care Programs Unit. The Bureau has accepted applicants who have had LASIK laser vision correction in the past, although these candidates must wait one year from the time of surgery to be considered.

Hearing Requirements

Hearing requirements also mirror those for the special agent position. Hearing loss must not exceed: (a) average hearing loss of 25 decibels (ANSI) at 1000, 2000, and 3000 Hertz; (b) a single reading of 35 decibels at 1000, 2000, and 3000 Hertz; (c) a single reading of 35 decibels at 500 Hertz; and (d) a single reading of 45 decibels at 4000 Hertz. An audiometer test is used to determine whether police officer candidates meet minimum hearing requirements.

Salary Grade Requirements

GS-5   Completion of four years of undergraduate coursework leading to a bachelor's degree related to law enforcement, criminal investigation, or criminology; or one year of specialized experience equivalent to at least GS-4.

GS-6   One year of specialized experience equivalent to GS-5.

GS-7   One year of specialized experience equivalent to GS-6.

GS-8   One year of specialized experience equivalent to GS-7.

GS-9   One year of specialized experience equivalent to GS-8.

CHAPTER 6

The Hiring Process for Professional Support Positions

Blessed is he who has found his work. Let him ask no other blessedness.

—*Thomas Carlyle*

As discussed in chapter 4, the hiring process for the special agent position is clearly defined, standardized, and systematic for all applicants nationwide. This approach ensures that candidates are evaluated equally, based on the same criteria and according to merit principles. The hiring process for FBI professional support personnel is also designed to provide equal opportunity to all applicants, although with less uniformity. Although support personnel candidates must clear many of the same hurdles as special agent candidates, applicant processing for support positions varies from one position to another, depending on the type and location of positions being filled. Nonetheless, there are more similarities than differences. After all, every Bureau employee must qualify for a top-secret security clearance, and standards relating to loyalty, integrity, drug use, and other criteria are also the same.

This chapter provides an overview of applicant processing for administrative, professional, technical, clerical, and other FBI careers. Specific strategies that applicants can use to describe their knowledge, skills, and abilities in application materials are presented in chapter 7, "Standing Out from the Crowd." Qualification requirements for various positions are reviewed in chapter 5, "Professional Support Career Opportunities."

FBI Hiring Policies

It is widely known that the FBI has established employment policies to safeguard the rights of applicants and ensure that the Bureau recruits, hires, and retains the most qualified special agents. These principles and practices also apply to professional support applicants and employees. The FBI Employment Drug Policy, for example, applies to all Bureau personnel—from special agents to automotive workers. Truthfulness during the hiring process is also required of applicants for professional support positions. Applicants with disabilities are provided all protections afforded under the Rehabilitation Act of 1973, including entitlement to reasonable accommodation in the hiring process. Applicants for professional support positions are provided equal employment opportunity also, free from discrimination based on their color, race, religion, national origin, political affiliation, marital status, disability, age, sex, sexual orientation, membership or non-membership in an employee organization, or on the basis of personal favoritism.

An Overview of Applicant Processing

Hiring processes for FBI professional support positions are similar to special agent applicant processing, although there are notable differences. For example, there are slight variations in application processes for certain technical careers, depending on the positions' qualification requirements. In addition, whereas written examinations are given to applicants for clerical positions, such as clerk and typist candidates, written exams are not given to applicants for most other positions.

Final screening of candidates for support positions is similar to the special agent hiring process and includes a security interview, background investigation, polygraph examination, and urinalysis drug screening. Applicants for certain other positions must also undergo a physical examination.

The remainder of this chapter provides a step-by-step breakdown of applicant processing for support positions.

Step One: Initial Application

To begin the hiring process, you must conduct research, gather information about your background, submit a great deal of paperwork, and wait for the Bureau to screen your application. The following sections discuss the components of the first step in the application process.

The FBI Vacancy Announcement

The first step toward landing a support job with the FBI is to obtain information about the position you seek and the application procedures. The FBI generates a detailed vacancy announcement for every professional support position it needs to fill. These announcements provide details about the duties and responsibilities of each job, as well as information concerning qualification requirements, selection criteria, and how to apply. Most FBI vacancy announcements consist of the same components, although some include additional elements to facilitate hiring for certain positions. Vacancy announcements typically provide the following information:

- Position title and announcement number
- Salary range and promotion potential
- Opening and closing dates
- Duty location
- Area of consideration

- Statement of position duties
- Qualification requirements
- Ranking factors and basis for rating
- Application instructions

Each type of information is discussed in the following sections.

Position Title and Announcement Number

The top portion of the vacancy announcement lists the position title, followed by a posting number. The posting number is used to facilitate the processing of application materials and record-keeping functions. FBI vacancy announcements sometimes use the term announcement number in place of the posting number.

Salary Range and Promotion Potential

The position title and posting number typically are followed by the salary range, the General Schedule (GS) grade at which the position is being filled. When only one salary grade is indicated, such as GS-7, applicants must meet the minimum qualifications for the specified grade level and cannot be hired at any other grade. Some vacancy announcements specify a range of salary grades, such as GS-07/09/11, which allows the agency to fill positions at the highest grade level for which appointees are qualified—in this case, GS-7, GS-9, or GS-11. See chapter 2 for an explanation of the GS pay scale and a listing of 2002 salaries for each grade level.

The promotion potential is the highest grade to which an employee could expect to advance, provided that his or her job performance is satisfactory. In some cases, personnel might be able to advance to supervisory and management positions above the highest grade specified in the vacancy announcement.

Opening and Closing Dates

The period in which applications are accepted is marked by the opening and closing dates specified in the vacancy announcement. The opening date is the first day in which candidates are permitted to submit application materials. Applications must be received by the closing date in order to receive consideration. FBI vacancy announcements normally remain open for about three weeks, although announcements for some hard-to-fill positions remain open indefinitely.

Duty Location

The location where the job will be performed is included under this heading. When vacancies exist in more than one field office or resident agency, including those that are being filled nationwide, applicants must specify where they are willing to work.

Area of Consideration

This item specifies who is eligible to apply for a particular vacancy, such as FBI personnel only, current federal personnel, former federal employees with reinstatement privileges, those who reside in a particular geographic area, or other qualified candidates.

Statement of Position Duties

A summary of the duties and responsibilities is provided in this item. This statement typically includes examples of the assignments and tasks required of the job, and it sometimes provides an overview of the division, branch, or unit where the selectee will serve.

Qualification Requirements

An outline of the eligibility standards for each position is incorporated under this heading. This section provides a description of basic qualifications, including required specialized experience, education, training, and other qualifications. Applicants must meet minimum requirements to be given further consideration in the application process. Personnel management specialists use minimum qualification standards to evaluate candidates' eligibility for positions and to eliminate those who do not qualify. Positions advertised under multiple salary grades usually include a breakdown of minimum requirements for each grade.

Ranking Factors and Basis for Rating

Applicants who meet basic eligibility requirements are rated on the basis of whether they possess specific attributes needed for the positions being filled. Ratings are based on particular knowledge, skills, and abilities (KSAs) that are required to perform the position. The number of KSAs applicants must address varies from one vacancy announcement to the next. Some applications require candidates to respond to only three or four KSAs, whereas others might ask for eight to ten responses. Applicants must write a narrative statement indicating how their experience, education, and training have provided them with the required KSAs. (Detailed guidance for completing KSA statements is included in chapter 7, "Standing Out from the Crowd.")

Application Instructions

The "How to Apply" section provides detailed instructions about application forms and supporting documentation to be submitted, as well as addresses to which materials should be sent and other information concerning application procedures. This section usually includes the telephone number of a particular person whom applicants can contact with questions or other inquiries.

Submitting Application Materials

Although job application processes in the private sector often require candidates to submit little more than basic information about their education and experience, this is only the tip of the iceberg in the FBI hiring process. In addition to biographical information, applicants for FBI professional support positions must submit a narrative statement that addresses their qualifications and suitability for employment, a resume, military and security clearance information, details about citizenship, and sometimes college transcripts and a variety of other forms.

Completing the Online Application Form

In the past, the FBI has permitted candidates for professional support positions to submit a typewritten application form or resume when applying for employment. Although these options are still available, the Bureau strongly encourages candidates to apply for employment on the Internet, using the FBI's online application system. This process provides a measure of uniformity and facilitates the efficient collection of information needed to evaluate applicants. Although there are minor differences in the information requested in the online application for some positions, the application generally requires candidates to submit the following:

- **Biographical information,** which consists of the applicant's name, address, home and work telephone numbers, e-mail address, the lowest grade an applicant is willing to accept, and whether veterans' preference is claimed.

- **Employment history,** such as the name of current and most recent employers, current and most recent job titles, dates of employment, years of full-time work experience in the field, and details on special skills or certificates related to the position applied for.

- **Educational background,** including the level of education attained and college major.

- **Assignment location,** which includes the location of the field office or resident agency where the applicant is seeking employment, as well as whether the applicant is willing to relocate to the office at his or her own expense if the FBI is unwilling to pay for relocation.

- **Citizenship status,** which requires applicants to indicate whether they are U.S. citizens. (U.S. citizenship is required for FBI employment.)

- **Military background,** indicating whether the applicant has served on active duty in the U.S. military, the branch of service and dates of active duty, and military school attendance.

- **Security clearance information,** including information relating to the agency that previously issued a security clearance to the applicant.

Submitting a Resume

Applicants are required to type or paste a text copy of their resumes into a box provided in the online application form. The resume should include information relating to previous employment, such as the following:

- Job titles
- Series and grade of federal employment
- Names, addresses, and telephone numbers of current and previous employers
- Starting and ending dates of employment
- A description of duties and accomplishments

- The average number of hours worked for each position
- The number of people supervised
- Salary details

Submitting a KSA Statement

Applicants are also required to submit a detailed statement of their knowledge, skills, and abilities relating to the selection criteria for the position. Like the resume, this statement can be typed or pasted into the appropriate block of the online application. (Also see chapter 7, "Standing Out from the Crowd," for guidance on composing a KSA statement.)

Submitting College Transcripts

Many professional support positions, particularly those that involve technical or scientific work, require applicants to submit copies of their college transcripts along with their application form and resume. For example, applicants who apply for financial analyst, intelligence operations specialist, electronics technician, or computer specialist positions online are required to submit their college transcripts to the FBI. Candidates who mail their application to the Bureau must include college transcripts with their application package. Those who submit an application online are required to fax their transcripts to FBI Headquarters. Vacancy announcements indicate the telephone number to which faxed transcripts and other documents must be sent.

Submitting Other Documents

Some applicants, such as federal employees and certain veterans, must submit additional materials with their application packages. Federal employees, for example, are required to submit their latest SF-50 Notification of Personnel Action and their most recent Performance Appraisal. In addition, candidates seeking veterans' preference must also submit supporting documentation for their claim. Vacancy announcements specify the names and form numbers of documents that must be included in application materials. As with college transcripts, applicants who send their application packages through the mail must include all required documents in the package, whereas candidates who apply online must fax supporting documentation.

Selection of Candidates for Further Processing

To conclude the initial application phase, the FBI reviews all application materials and excludes those candidates who do not meet basic requirements. Of those remaining, only candidates whom the Bureau determines to be most competitive will be invited to continue in the hiring process.

Step Two: Written Examinations

The application process for some FBI professional support positions includes either a written or practical skills examination. Many candidates are required to take the Clerical and Administrative Support Examination, whereas other exams are administered to applicants seeking certain technical positions.

The Clerical and Administrative Support Examination

The U.S. Office of Personnel Management (OPM) administers the Clerical and Administrative Support Examination to candidates for many positions, such as clerk, typist, secretary, and office automation clerk. The exam takes about two and a half hours to complete and covers grammar, spelling, alphabetizing, vocabulary, reading comprehension, name and number comparisons, and arithmetic. OPM notifies test-takers of their results by mail.

Other Examinations

Some candidates for FBI professional support employment must take other examinations that are geared specifically to the nature of the positions sought. Candidates for clerk positions, for example, must take a typing proficiency test in addition to the Clerical and Administrative Support Examination, and word processor applicants are required to take a data-transcription test. Although electronics engineer candidates are not given the Clerical and Administrative Support Examination, they must have passed the Fundamentals of Engineering Examination (formerly known as the Engineering-in-Training Exam) or a written test required for professional registration administered by the boards of engineering examiners in the various states. Language specialist and contract linguist candidates must achieve passing scores on a hearing test, as well as a battery of language tests that focus on listening comprehension, reading comprehension, and translation. Applicants should carefully review vacancy announcements to determine whether testing is required.

Step Three: The Long-Form Application for Employment

After the FBI reviews application forms, resumes, and test results, only the most competitive candidates are asked to take the next step in the selection process. Competitiveness is based not only on applicants' background, but also on the hiring needs of the FBI at the time.

Those selected to continue will be asked to submit the FD-140 Application for Employment, a 15-page form that is used to gather additional information relating to applicants' qualifications and background. Information provided by applicants on the FD-140 is also used to conduct the background investigation and for security clearance determinations.

The FD-140 requests information relating to availability for employment, birth and citizenship, places of residence, employment history, educational background, association membership, references and social acquaintances, relatives, roommates, military service, foreign travel, financial status, civil and criminal court record, and drug use. A recent full-face photograph of the applicant must be attached to the form. A copy of the FD-140 is provided in appendix E.

Step Four: The Personal Interview

The personal interview phase of the professional support personnel selection process differs in many ways from special agent hiring procedures. Unlike the special agent hiring process, during which interviewers follow a standard list of questions, interviews of professional support candidates tend to vary from one position to another, both in style and the level of formality.

A variety of interviewing formats is utilized, involving personnel from various operational divisions or units. Techniques also range from structured panel interviews to less-formal one-on-one discussions. Depending on the position being filled, panel interviews could include peers from the field of expertise, whereas other interviews might be conducted by a single supervisor or manager representing the division or unit where the selectee will serve.

Structured Interviews

Candidates for certain FBI positions must undergo a structured interview in this phase of the hiring process. During structured interviews, the interviewers ask all candidates a standard set of questions. This method allows interviewers to compare and evaluate candidates on a level playing field and to determine which candidates possess the knowledge, skills, and abilities that are required of the position being filled. The FBI conducts structured interviews when filling clerical vacancies—including jobs such as clerk, secretary, and typist—and other positions.

Semi-Structured Interviews

Other interviews for professional support positions tend to be semi-structured in nature, meaning that they are less formal than structured interviews. These often include a combination of standard questions—similar to the format of a structured interview—and questions that have not been predetermined. Semi-structured interviews are effective in the selection of technical and scientific personnel, where detailed answers are often required. The semi-structured approach allows interviewers to probe, explore, and revisit applicants' responses to a variety of open-ended questions that are tailored to each position.

Step Five: Final Screening

The final screening phase includes procedures that are similar to those followed during special agent applicant processing. Tentative appointees receive a conditional letter of appointment, and must also pass a polygraph examination, personnel security interview, drug test, and background investigation, and submit to fingerprinting. In addition, some candidates must pass a physical examination.

Conditional Letter of Appointment

To begin this phase, successful candidates receive a letter from the FBI notifying them that they will be hired if the outcome of the final screening process is satisfactory. Final appointment is contingent on budgetary limitations, authorized positions, and the results of a background investigation, polygraph exam, and urinalysis drug screening. The letter provides tentative appointees with details concerning the background investigation, and other information relating to final screening.

SF-86 Questionnaire for National Security Positions

Applicants for FBI employment are asked to complete the SF-86 Questionnaire for National Security Positions. This 11-page form allows the Bureau to collect information that is used in making security clearance determinations. Information provided by the applicant is confirmed during the background investigation. The SF-86 also includes an Authorization for Release of Medical Information that permits the Bureau to obtain limited information from health practitioners relating to an applicant's mental health.

Personnel Security Interview

Professional support candidates must complete a personnel security interview prior to appointment. The interview focuses on the veracity of the information contained in employment application forms, the SF-86 Questionnaire for National Security Positions, drug use by the applicant, foreign travel and contacts, financial status and obligations, and various national security issues. Applicants must bring photo identification to the interview and might be asked to bring their Social Security card, birth certificate, or other documents.

Polygraph Exam and Drug Testing

All tentative appointees are administered a polygraph exam, during which information provided during the Personnel Security Interview is verified and other areas are explored. The exam includes questions relating to national security and counterintelligence issues, illegal drug use and activity, and the truthfulness of information provided during the hiring process. (Details concerning functions and phases of the polygraph exam are discussed in chapter 4, "The Special Agent Hiring Process.") Prior to appointment, all FBI applicants are required to submit to a urinalysis drug test, which screens for illegal drug use.

Background Investigation

All FBI professional support personnel must hold a top-secret security clearance as a condition of employment. Therefore, the background of all tentative appointees is thoroughly investigated by the FBI prior to appointment. Background investigations normally are conducted by special investigators under contract with the Bureau.

During the background investigation, the FBI verifies employment, credentials, educational background, citizenship and birth records, residency, military service, and medical history; interviews friends, neighbors, references, and employers; and inquires into an applicant's credit history and criminal record. The background investigation is used to explore a number of issues relating to suitability for employment and a top-secret security clearance. These include an applicant's character, associates, reputation, loyalty, ability, financial responsibility, biases or prejudice, and alcohol or drug abuse. (Further discussion of these issues is provided in chapter 4, "The Special Agent Hiring Process.")

Applicants are provided written notification of the outcome of their background investigation. Those who would like to obtain a copy of their background investigation report should send a written request to the FBI's Freedom of Information/Privacy Act Section at FBI Headquarters in Washington, D.C.

Pre-employment Physical Examinations

Most professional support personnel candidates are not given a pre-employment physical examination. Considering the physical demands and hazardous work conditions of some positions, however, the FBI must ensure that certain personnel are physically fit for duty. Physical exams are performed to rule out any medical issue or condition that could potentially affect applicants' abilities to perform the basic functions of the position for which they have applied.

For example, electronics technician candidates must have a physical exam because they might be required to lift heavy objects or climb ladders, poles, towers, and other apparatuses to mount or service electronic equipment and devices. Due to the strenuous nature of law enforcement work, FBI police officer applicants also must pass a physical exam. Language specialist candidates are required to undergo a hearing test because these personnel must have adequate hearing in order to translate live and recorded speech.

Physical examinations sometimes reveal medical issues or conditions that require applicants to undergo additional examination. Applicants who are required to have a physical examination are also subject to a review of their medical history. Each candidate's health and fitness is reviewed on an individual, case-by-case basis. These reviews sometimes result in delay of the final processing for employment. Although input or copies of medical records might be requested from an applicant's doctor, the final decision as to an applicant's physical ability rests with the FBI's chief medical officer.

Sources of Job Vacancy Information

Information relating to professional support position vacancies is available on the Internet and in published materials from the FBI, the U.S. Office of Personnel Management, and a number of private sources.

FBI Resources

FBI vacancy announcements and other professional support position recruiting details are posted online at the Bureau's employment Internet Web site. The address is www.fbijobs.com. Information concerning vacancies and position details can also be obtained over the telephone by contacting the recruiter or applicant coordinator for professional support positions at any FBI field office. In addition, vacancy announcements are available for viewing at some field offices.

U.S. Office of Personnel Management (OPM) Resources

The U.S. Office of Personnel Management oversees human resources management for the federal government. OPM disseminates employment information and job vacancy announcements for many government agencies—including the FBI—and establishes basic qualification standards for federal occupations. The public can access information about employment with the FBI and other agencies online and at OPM offices nationwide.

USA Jobs Web Site

The USA Jobs Web site, which is maintained by OPM, posts information relating to current job openings not only with the FBI, but also with other federal agencies. This Web site displays full-text vacancy announcements that you can print. The USA Jobs address is www.usajobs.opm.gov/.

Career America Connection

OPM's Career America Connection is a telephone-based system that provides instant access to current information on federal job opportunities worldwide, including positions with the FBI. Users are guided through a series of prompts that allow searches for position vacancies by occupational category, job series, or position title. Requested information is normally mailed or faxed within 24 hours. Career America Connection can be reached by telephone at 912-757-3000, 24 hours a day, 7 days a week.

Federal Job Opportunities Bulletin Board

This electronic bulletin board posts want ads for the FBI and other federal agencies. The board, which is maintained by OPM, features job vacancy information, job search tips, salary information, details on job fairs, and other information. You can access the bulletin board via a Telnet connection at fjob.opm.gov.

Federal Job Information Touch-Screen Computers

OPM also maintains a network of computers that utilize touch-screen technology to disseminate job vacancy information. These kiosks are located at OPM Federal Employment Information Centers in major cities nationwide, at many state employment service centers and social service agencies, and within job placement offices at some colleges and universities.

Federal Job Publications

Many printed and online publications provide information about federal job vacancies worldwide. Two popular publications, *Federal Career Opportunities* and *Federal Jobs Digest,* are discussed in the following sections.

Federal Career Opportunities

The *Federal Career Opportunities* newspaper is a biweekly publication that contains details on federal job vacancies, including professional support positions with the FBI. *Federal Career Opportunities* is published every two weeks and is available from Federal Research Service, 370 Maple Avenue West—Suite 5, P.O. Box 1059; Vienna, VA 22183. Federal Research Service can be reached by phone at 800-822-5027. An online version is also accessible by subscription at www.fedjobs.com/.

Federal Jobs Digest

Another publication that contains details on vacancies with the FBI and other agencies is *Federal Jobs Digest.* This publication is available in bookstores or from Breakthrough Publications, 310 North Highland Avenue; Ossining, NY 10562. *Federal Jobs Digest* can be reached by telephone at 800-824-5000. The *Federal Jobs Digest* Web site is located at www.jobsfed.com/.

CHAPTER 7

Standing Out from the Crowd

Genius is one percent inspiration and
ninety-nine percent perspiration.

—*Thomas Edison*

T he FBI workforce is diverse, talented, and well trained. To maintain excellence and prepare for future challenges, the Bureau recruits special agents and support personnel with a variety of skills and experience. Given its broad mission and commitment to diversity, the Bureau does not maintain a single "profile" of the ideal special agent or professional support employee. Instead, criteria for the selection of FBI personnel are based on the knowledge, skills, and abilities needed for the specific jobs being filled, while taking into consideration the Bureau's particular needs at any given time. Although there is no secret formula for landing a position as one of America's finest, there are things you can do to stand out from the crowd. This chapter presents a number of strategies you can apply before and during the application process to increase your chances of getting hired.

Are You Right for the FBI?

One of the most common questions those who are interested in working for the FBI ask is "What sort of background is the FBI looking for?" To begin to answer this question, it is important to note that your background encompasses far more than employment experience and education. In other words, your background also is concerned with your character, reputation, training, abilities, involvement in civic and community activities, military service, financial matters, criminal history, and many other aspects of your life. Although the requirements for employment vary from one position to another, the Bureau is always looking for bright individuals who possess "Fidelity, Bravery, and Integrity," which is the motto and motivating force behind the men and women of the FBI.

Character Issues

The most important thing you can do prior to applying for employment with the FBI is to carry out your personal affairs and professional business in a responsible manner. Character, honesty, integrity, and loyalty are far more important to the Bureau than any amount of experience, education, or skill that applicants may have. In fact, many applicants who otherwise meet basic qualification standards for FBI jobs either fail the drug test or polygraph examination or are disqualified for other reasons. In addition to unlawful drug use, the FBI disqualifies applicants who have been convicted of felony or major misdemeanor offenses, have defaulted on student loans, or have failed to pay income taxes. Candidates with bad credit also face an uphill battle, and those who show a lack of candor or falsify information during the hiring process are routinely disqualified. Lying, cheating, or stealing are wholly inconsistent with everything the FBI stands for. In other words, the best way to prepare for a career with the FBI is to "keep it clean" before requesting an application.

Experience and Education

The Bureau's personnel needs change from time to time depending on the expertise on staff and projected needs for the future. For example, in 2002 the FBI announced that special agent applicants with knowledge, skills, and abilities in nine critical skill areas would be given special consideration. These areas include the following:

- Foreign language proficiency, especially in Arabic, Farsi, Pashto, Urdu, Chinese, Japanese, Korean, Russian, Spanish, and Vietnamese

- Computer science and other information technology specialties

- Engineering

- Physical sciences (physics, chemistry, and biology)

- Law enforcement or other investigative work

- Foreign counterintelligence

- Counterterrorism

- Military intelligence experience

- Fixed-wing pilots

Of course, those with education, training, and experience in other areas should not hesitate to apply, because a substantial proportion of special agent recruits will not have expertise in these areas. For example, the Bureau will always place a premium on applicants with accounting experience and education, because a significant percentage of the Bureau's criminal investigations revolve around white-collar crime. Similarly, the FBI is likely to continue seeking law school graduates, because lawyers tend to be proficient at problem-solving and sorting out legal issues during investigations. Indeed, two of the Bureau's four entry programs are geared to recruiting candidates with accounting and legal skills. Language proficiency will always be helpful, although language needs vary from time to time and from one office to another. Finally, through its diversified entry program, the Bureau recruits talented individuals who have expertise in many other areas or who otherwise show great potential to succeed as special agents. These candidates range from store managers to school teachers, dental hygienists, real estate agents, paramedics, journalists, stock brokers, and many others.

As far as college education is concerned, the FBI does not have a preference for certain college courses or diplomas earned from any particular schools. Instead, the Bureau prefers candidates who have completed a course of study that develops communication, research, and analytical skills. Some of the college majors that develop these skills include psychology, sociology, criminal justice, nursing, medicine, business, journalism, and political science. In a nutshell, although the criteria for determining the most qualified candidates are constantly evolving, certain skills and experience will always be in demand.

Volunteer Work and Community Service

The FBI recognizes that volunteer work and community service provide valuable experience that is unavailable in most traditional employment settings. These activities demonstrate a commitment to the community and important causes, while also providing an opportunity to develop skills in communication, leadership, planning, administrative tasks, and decision-making, among other skills. In fact, a 1997 article in the *Wall Street Journal* pointed out that five years of volunteer work provides management experience most corporations couldn't provide in 20 years. Volunteer work with hospitals, churches, synagogues, animal shelters, public broadcasting stations, the American Red Cross, and other nonprofit organizations provides a sense of accomplishment and builds character. Community service as a volunteer firefighter, coach, scout leader, police reserve officer, Parent-Teacher Association board member, or in other positions is rewarding—and worthy of recognition. Volunteer work and community service also provide additional employment references. You should not overlook this experience on FBI application forms or during interviews.

Military Service

Service in the military is a definite plus. Experience in the armed forces provides structure, discipline, exceptional training, skill development, and technical knowledge that are transferable to many careers in the FBI. In addition, military service builds responsibility, leadership skills, camaraderie, and other traits the FBI looks for in its employees. Many of the Bureau's intelligence specialists, electronics technicians, electronics engineers, language specialists, special agents, and others developed their skills in the armed forces prior to hiring on with the FBI.

Internships

Anyone who is serious about making a career in the FBI should take full advantage of internship opportunities that become available during college. These provide an opportunity for students to enhance their education and make practical application of classroom theory. They also enable students to explore their career interests under actual working conditions and to make informed choices before moving into the workforce. The FBI and many other federal law enforcement agencies offer internships that allow students to perform some of the primary duties that special agents and professional support personnel carry out. For example, many agencies allow interns to participate in interviews, review financial records and create spreadsheets, conduct surveillance, operate technical investigative equipment, assist with the execution of search warrants, recover and process evidence, and meet with assistant United States attorneys, among other tasks. In many instances, interns also participate in training exercises alongside full-time personnel. These experiences are valuable in demonstrating your skills and potential when you are seeking employment with the FBI.

Filling Out the Application for Employment (FD-140)

Many applicants underestimate the importance of filling out the FD-140 Application for Employment accurately and completely. Unfortunately, submitting an incomplete application might delay the processing of your application or cause the FBI to eliminate you from the applicant pool. In other words, it is critical that you include Social Security numbers, middle names, maiden names, employment information, previous addresses, and other requested information so that you will receive full consideration for employment. The following areas deserve special attention when you're completing the FD-140 application form.

Using Continuation Sheets or Attachments

It is important to note that many sections of the FD-140 application do not provide adequate space for the information requested. For example, the Employment section affords enough space for only two jobs, even though you are required to list all jobs you have held since age 16. The FBI has a continuation sheet for the FD-140 form that you can use to furnish additional information on employment and residences. However, no such form exists for other information. The continuation sheet is adequate for residence information, and you should use it for this purpose.

However, the Employment section of both the FD-140 application and continuation sheet provides less than one inch of space for a description of "...your specific duties and all supervisory, managerial, scientific, and professional experience." Unless your job involved only licking envelopes, you'll need more space to list your responsibilities and receive full credit for your accomplishments. The best approach is to use attachments when listing employment information or when responding to any other items (except for residence information) where the space provided on the form is insufficient. Attachments should reiterate the form title, item number, section and subsection names, and your name and Social Security number on a plain sheet of letter-size (8½" × 11") paper, as shown in figure 7.1.

Edward R. Applicant, Jr.
123-45-6789

ATTACHMENT TO FD-140 APPLICATION FOR EMPLOYMENT

IV. Employment

Continuation of Item 1:

SAFETY OPTIONS, INC
BRIGHTON, MICHIGAN

Work Description: _____

_____

_____

_____

_____

Figure 7.1: Suggested format for extra attachments to the application.

Residence Information

Residence information is among the most common omissions on the FD-140 application form. The FBI requires applicants to provide details on all residences for the past 10 years or since high school, whichever is longer. Many applicants fail to provide information on campus and summer housing and on- and off-base addresses during military service. List your residence information in chronological order, with all time periods accounted for. Leaving gaps in time periods could cause a delay in application processing.

Educational Achievements and Transcripts

The Education section of the application asks for academic information going back to high school. Do not make the mistake of overlooking Item 3, "Specialized Schools," if you have completed any specialized education or training programs, especially if you earned a license, degree, or certificate. Many applicants with experience in law enforcement, the physical sciences, or technical fields have completed an abundance of programs that should be listed in this block. Considering that Item 3 allows enough space for only two entries, indicate "see attachment" if you have attended more than two programs. Create an attachment according to the sample in figure 7.1.

Applicants for certain FBI positions, such as electronics technician, financial analyst, and intelligence operations specialist, are required to submit copies of college transcripts along with their applications. If you mail your application to the Bureau, you must include transcripts with your application package. If you submit an application online, you are required to fax your transcripts to FBI Headquarters. Fax numbers are indicated in vacancy announcements.

Employment Information

The Employment block requires a listing of all full- and part-time jobs you have held since age 16. The fastest way to raise a "red flag" in this section is to leave unexplained gaps in employment, even if you omit part-time jobs. If you were unemployed while attending college or for any other reason, indicate this by filling out an employment block, indicating the appropriate code, and listing the name of someone who can provide verification. Also, do not omit entries relating to jobs you held with companies that are no longer in business. For these positions, the FBI requires you to list as much information as possible. Failure to do so may also create a gap in employment. As discussed earlier in this section, you probably will need to fill out continuation sheets or attachments to adequately account for your employment history.

Volunteer work, community service, and internship experience are among the most commonly overlooked entries on the application form. You should list these and describe them as employment in the same manner as you do for paid positions. Do not include volunteer work and internships in a list of extracurricular activities. This approach does not provide an adequate accounting of your accomplishments or responsibilities. Instead, under separate headings for each position, provide complete details of your activities and place emphasis on the specific tasks you performed and your achievements, especially those that are in any way related to the position you are applying for.

When describing internships, it is critical that you identify exactly what you did rather than what you observed. In most cases, volunteer, community service, and internships provide valuable hands-on experience that is directly related to the career you are seeking.

Military Record

Be careful not to skip over this section if you have not served in the military, because you must verify that you have registered with the Selective Service System (if required) and list your registration number. Those who have served in the armed forces are required to provide quite a bit of information, including a copy of your DD-214 discharge papers. As with other sections, failure to provide requested information could cause processing delays or rejection of your application.

References and Social Acquaintances

In this section, you must list three references and three social acquaintances who know you well and live in the United States. Common omissions include middle names, birth dates or approximate age, complete addresses, and phone numbers. You should not list relatives, coworkers, or your teachers in this section. Also, do not list past or present employers. They should already be included in the Employment section.

Foreign Travel

Make no mistake about it—this section is not intended to determine whether you are a well-rounded world traveler with extraordinary life experiences. The Bureau is interested primarily in your contacts with people and places that might be relevant to national security issues. You should not be concerned if you have taken a family vacation to Sweden. On the other hand, if you spent six months in Afghanistan attending tactical training, you should be prepared to answer all sorts of questions later in the hiring process.

Court Records

The FBI is interested in any criminal or civil actions you have been a part of, including the results. Note that the Bureau wants to know whether you have been arrested or charged with a criminal offense. Do not make the mistake of omitting information relating to arrests or criminal charges just because you were not convicted. Withholding this information could result in disqualification—even if you were innocent.

Financial Status

There are nine questions in this section that are concerned with your financial and credit history. The FBI will review your credit report during the background investigation. Although bad credit can be cause for disqualification, these determinations are made on a case-by-case basis and perfect credit is not required. You should attach an explanation and supporting documentation concerning any loan defaults, serious delinquencies, liens, judgments, or failure to pay taxes.

Relatives

Many applicants are concerned that they will automatically be disqualified from consideration for FBI employment if one of their relatives has an arrest record. This is not true. Do not throw in the towel if your brother-in-law was arrested for tax evasion or your mother was convicted of drunk driving. The Bureau looks very carefully at each situation, including your relationship to the person and any involvement you might have had, and makes determinations on a case-by-case basis. In this section, be sure to include all middle names, maiden names, complete addresses, birth dates, and places of birth. Attach an explanation if you are unable to determine information about relatives with whom you have had no contact for several years.

False Statements

Applicants should be aware that providing any false statements to the FBI during the hiring process not only will be cause for disqualification from consideration for employment, but may also result in criminal prosecution. Title 18 of the United States Code, Section 1001, provides that knowingly falsifying or concealing a material fact is a felony that may result in fines of up to $10,000 or five years in prison, or both. In addition, if false statements are discovered after you are hired, your employment can be terminated. The FBI verifies information you provide on application materials through your associates, your former employers, criminal record checks, fingerprint records, a drug test, a polygraph examination, and other means.

Strategies for Special Agent Phase I Testing

Three examinations are given to special agent applicants during phase I of the hiring process, including the Biodata Inventory Test, Situational Judgment Test, and three-part Cognitive Ability Test. Applicant coordinators or staffing assistants from FBI field offices coordinate the testing, which is administered nationwide. The relevant field office contacts candidates about 30 days prior to testing and gives them the date, time, and location of the testing session. The FBI advises applicants to wear casual, comfortable clothing that would be suitable for an office environment.

Phase I tests are of the paper-and-pencil variety and are machine-scored. The tests are graded on a "pass or fail" basis, and the FBI does not disclose numerical scores. Applicants are notified in writing within 30 days whether they passed or failed. In some cases, those who fail can repeat phase I testing one year later (see chapter 4 for more information on the retest process).

General Test-Taking Tips

The special agent phase I hiring process includes multiple-choice tests that are designed to test your ability to recognize and sort out information and to apply facts and concepts. Here are some strategies for succeeding on these tests:

- **Follow directions.** Read and listen to all directions carefully before starting the test. One of the most important test-taking skills is the ability to follow directions. Some candidates are so anxious to get the test over with that they skip the directions, which is often a costly mistake.

- **Read the questions and choices carefully.** As much as multiple-choice questions examine your knowledge and problem-solving skills, they are also designed to test your ability to review information carefully and thoroughly. Failure to read questions carefully is a common cause for selecting incorrect answers on multiple-choice tests. Read difficult or confusing questions more than once, if necessary, and resist the temptation to jump to conclusions about what you think the questions ask. Instead, rely only on the information presented and decide which answers are best. Also, read all of the answers before making a selection, even if the first or second choice appears correct. The best answer might be listed last. In other words, keep in mind that more than one correct answer may be presented and that you must choose the best answer from among the choices.

- **Make educated guesses.** The FBI phase I tests are scored on the total number of correct answers. Therefore, because there is no penalty for guessing, you should answer every question—even if you have to guess. If you do not know the answer, keep in mind that eliminating only one or two of the choices will increase the probability of selecting the correct answer.

- **Pace yourself.** Work through questions quickly but also carefully. If you come to a question that you can't answer or are unsure about, it is best to skip the question for the time being and to return to it after answering the other questions. Tackling difficult questions is often easier when you are more relaxed after answering easier questions. In addition, your answers to easier questions may provide clues to those that are more difficult.

- **Fill in answers carefully.** The FBI tests are administered using test booklets and separate answer sheets. Therefore, it is critical that you make sure that the number you are answering corresponds to the number of the question. If you skip a question, be sure to leave the space for that question blank. Although this is a matter of common sense, many test takers have been thrown off by one question in a sequence and marked one incorrect answer after another. Also be sure to fill in the answer ovals completely so that the machine that grades the test can easily record your responses.

Managing Test Anxiety

Many special agent applicants experience what is commonly known as test anxiety prior to phase I and phase II testing. After all, it's not every day that they voluntarily subject themselves to intense examination by the world's best-known law enforcement agency. Test anxiety is merely a reaction to stress that accompanies test taking. Some applicants experience symptoms such as nervousness, muscle tension, headaches, stomach discomfort, rapid heartbeat, or sweating. The most detrimental of symptoms is mental blocking, which can affect memory, reasoning skills, perception, and the ability to focus.

Test anxiety is not necessarily bad news. According to many prominent research studies, a moderate amount of pretest stress actually boosts performance, although either too little or excessive amounts can diminish performance. In other words, applicants who are able to recognize, manage, and channel test anxiety can actually use it to their advantage. To accomplish this, consider the techniques in the following sections.

Confront Your Fears

For most people, test anxiety ultimately boils down to a fear of failure. Recognizing that fear is the culprit and confronting your fear are the primary challenges in conquering test anxiety. Although it is easier said than done, many test-takers succeed in overcoming pretest fear simply by putting the outcome of the FBI hiring process into perspective. It is important to keep in mind that, in the worst-case scenario, failure to be selected by the FBI will not bring an end to the world. If you fail the phase I test, nobody will take away your college degree, you will not lose your job, and your pets will still worship you. In addition, considering that you were among the few that the FBI selected to take the test, you might have an opportunity to retest at a later date. So, although you should do everything within reason to ensure your success in the hiring process, be sure to maintain proper perspective overall.

Be Fully Prepared

Perhaps the most important tool for conquering test anxiety is to have a firm understanding of what lies ahead. Oftentimes the most stressful part of an event—whether you're going out on a blind date or moving your family across the country—boils down to fear of the unknown. After the event is over, you often find that the stress was for naught. Adequate preparation also leads to an increase in confidence. It is far easier to have confidence going into a situation if you understand the challenges you're facing and expect to succeed.

You can best prepare for phase I and phase II tests by studying this book, brushing up on your math skills, and gaining insights from others who have completed the FBI hiring process or similar employment application experiences. Also, study with someone else periodically. Discussing the material with others is not only an effective tool for reinforcing the information, it also reduces test anxiety. In addition, review the strategies for mastering multiple-choice exams discussed in the preceding section, as well as test-taking tips offered in the remainder of this chapter. Following these strategies can lead to higher scores also.

Avoid Cramming for the Tests

It is very important to space studying over a period of weeks or months instead of cramming for the test the night before. Cramming is most often the result of procrastination. Unfortunately, cramming increases anxiety, which interferes with clear thinking. Procrastination itself also increases stress—and excessive stress reduces test scores. On the other hand, studies have repeatedly shown that students absorb more information when studying takes place over a period of time.

Reduce Stress Prior to the Tests

To the greatest extent possible, try to reduce stress in your life for the days and weeks leading up to testing. This could include tactics such as getting organized, working fewer hours, following a nutritious diet, exercising, and getting plenty of rest. It is also important to get enough sleep the night before and to eat breakfast on the day of the tests. Visualizing success and maintaining a positive attitude can also be very helpful. Of course, all of these should be part of your everyday routines, but that's a topic for another discussion.

Use Relaxation Techniques

Many people find that relaxation techniques are useful in reducing test anxiety and other forms of stress. A common method of relaxing tense muscles is known as the Progressive Muscular Relaxation (PMR) technique. The PMR technique involves tightening a group of muscles for a few seconds at a time, holding them in a state of tension for a few seconds, and then relaxing them completely. You can achieve this best by working head to toe and waiting about 30 seconds between muscle groups. You can use PMR in conjunction with slow, deep breathing, which also aids in relaxation.

The Biodata Inventory Test

The FBI administers a Biodata Inventory Test during phase I of the hiring process as a supplement to cognitive testing. Biodata tests are useful for predicting aspects of job performance—such as interpersonal relationships with coworkers, communicating with the public, personality, and motivation—that cannot be predicted by cognitive measures. These tests have been used in many fields to predict everything from salesmanship of life insurance agents to productivity of research scientists, turnover of bank clerks, proficiency of naval personnel in diver training, and many other performance issues.

Biodata questions may ask about academic achievements, leisure activities, hobbies, interests, community service, goals, preferences for working in groups or alone, or other variables. Research has demonstrated that biodata inventory tests are reliable predictors of job performance in groups ranging from unskilled workers to office clerks, service station workers, chemists, engineers, and high-level executives. The underlying assumption of biodata is that past behavior is a valid predictor of future behavior. More specifically, these tests have shown that information obtained from job applicants about their backgrounds, previous work experience, education, and interests can be used to predict job performance.

The Biodata Inventory Test consists of 47 questions that measure motivation and initiative, ability to prioritize and adapt to changing situations, organization and planning skills, and judgment abilities. The questions must be answered within 45 minutes, which provides plenty of time for most applicants. All responses are recorded on answer sheets that are read by a computer.

Sample Biodata Inventory Questions

The following are examples of the types of biodata questions that you might encounter on the test:

1. In connection with your work, in which of the following have you taken the most pride?

   (A) Having been able to avoid any major controversies.

   (B) Having gotten where you are on your own.

   (C) Having been able to work smoothly with people.

   (D) Having provided a lot of new ideas, good or bad.

   (E) Having been able to do well whatever management has requested.

2. Which has provided your greatest source of motivation on the job?

   (A) Praise from your supervisors.

   (B) Receiving good scores on performance evaluations.

   (C) Satisfaction accompanied by assisting others with their problems.

   (D) Devising new ways to accomplish various tasks.

   (E) Allowing enough free time to concentrate on personal interests.

3. When carrying out your work assignments, would you prefer:

   (A) To work alone.

   (B) To work in small groups.

   (C) To lead small groups.

   (D) To work in large groups.

   (E) To lead large groups.

Tips for the Biodata Inventory Test

As you can see from the sample questions, there are no correct or incorrect answers. Instead, responses to these questions provide an indication of whether the respondent will fit in with the FBI. Keep in mind that the hiring process is geared to identify candidates who are well adjusted, well rounded, and likely to succeed. When taking the Biodata Inventory Test, resist the temptation to outsmart the exam by marking answers you believe the FBI considers correct. This could spell disaster. Instead, selecting the answers you believe are best will provide the most accurate characterization of yourself.

If the biodata inventory was designed to test knowledge of mathematics or grammar, or even law enforcement practices or investigative techniques, applicants could take a fairly straightforward approach to preparing for the test. However, the Biodata Inventory Test evaluates nonacademic elements, for which it is virtually impossible to study. After all, the Bureau administers the test to determine which applicants have the motivation, attitude, and personal characteristics that are best suited for the work of FBI special agents—qualities that are difficult to hone through study guides. In other words, there is no magic formula for success with this test. The best approach you can take is to answer biodata questions honestly, based on common sense and a genuine assessment of the problems, situations, or issues presented.

The Situational Judgment Test

Situational judgment tests are commonly used for selecting law enforcement officers and other workers—from school principals to military personnel—to evaluate critical thinking, decision-making skills, integrity, and other attributes. In these tests, brief descriptions of realistic scenarios are followed by a number of options for handling various situations. These types of questions enable employers to assess candidates' abilities to evaluate information, prioritize, adapt, and decide on a course of action. The FBI uses a situational judgment test to forecast the likelihood of applicants' job success by evaluating their behavior in various situations.

The Situational Judgment Test is a 90-minute examination that is given during the phase I testing process. It consists of 33 questions that present a range of problem scenarios. After carefully evaluating the facts, respondents must choose both their *most likely* and *least likely* courses of action from among a number of alternatives. Most applicants can finish this test within the time allotted.

Sample Situational Judgment Questions

The Situational Judgment Test includes questions that are similar to the following examples:

1. You are standing in line at a bank when a man approaches a teller and announces a robbery. You are armed and wearing business attire. What would you do?

   (A) Nothing, as you do not want to get involved in the incident.

   (B) Remain in line and observe the robber until he leaves, then call the police.

   (C) Rush out of the bank and call the police.

(D) Wait until the robber leaves, then follow him until he settles somewhere.

(E) Try to apprehend the robber.

2. While you are interviewing a fraud suspect at his residence, the suspect offers you a $500 cash bribe to "make the investigation go away." You and the suspect are alone in the residence. What would you do?

(A) Decline the suspect's offer, complete the interview, and continue the investigation as if the bribery attempt had not occurred.

(B) Decline the suspect's offer, complete the interview, and contact your supervisor immediately after you leave the residence.

(C) Accept the $500 payment, terminate the interview, and contact your supervisor immediately after you leave the residence.

(D) Decline the offer, complete the interview, arrest the suspect as soon as the interview has been completed, and contact your supervisor immediately.

(E) Arrest the suspect when the bribe is offered and contact your supervisor immediately.

3. While you are off duty and driving through a grocery store parking lot, you observe a vehicle in front of you strike a man who was loading groceries into a car. The driver speeds away, leaving the man lying injured on the pavement. What would you do?

(A) Observe what you can about the vehicle and immediately give aid to the injured man.

(B) Run into the store to call the police and then return to the parking lot and give aid to the injured man.

(C) Catch up to the vehicle, get a good look at the driver, then return to the scene to aid the injured man.

(D) Pull in front of the vehicle to prevent the driver from escaping and then arrest the driver.

(E) Follow the vehicle and arrest the driver when he stops somewhere.

Tips for the Situational Judgment Test

Responses to situational judgment questions depend on the unique perspectives and priorities of each applicant. Although the questions typically are straightforward, the answers require intense analysis of problems and the underlying issues. The best strategy involves *carefully* reading each question, imagining yourself in the situation, recognizing signs of danger or ethical issues, analyzing the problem overall, and applying common sense. Many experts suggest deciding on a course of action before reading the answers, and then seeking the chosen response among the answers. This approach makes sense, although its effectiveness varies from one person to another.

As a rule of thumb, officer safety and providing emergency aid take precedence over enforcing the law. Therefore, making an arrest probably would not be the best approach in either of the preceding scenarios. Ultimately, if your chosen actions are professional, free from emotional or biased behavior, and based on commonly accepted protocols, they probably will be correct.

The Cognitive Ability Test

The Cognitive Ability Test is divided into three segments that focus on mathematical reasoning, data interpretation, and mathematical relationships. Many applicants find this test to be the most demanding part of the phase I process.

Mathematical Reasoning Segment

The first segment of the Cognitive Ability Test measures mathematical reasoning, which is used to assess your ability to sort out information and apply basic mathematical concepts to solve problems. Questions in this section require candidates to sort through, organize, and interpret information presented in mathematical terms. Mathematical abilities required in this section, as well as in other parts of the Cognitive Ability Test, do not extend beyond the high school level. Candidates are given 29 minutes to answer 25 multiple-choice questions in this part of the test.

Sample Mathematical Reasoning Questions

1. The nine poker chips shown below are placed in a sock and then mixed up. Debi will draw one chip from this sock. What is the probability that Debi will draw a chip with an even number?

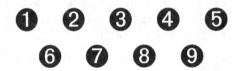

   (A) $1/9$

   (B) $2/9$

   (C) $4/9$

   (D) $1/2$

   (E) $4/5$

2. A contractor is building 5 different styles of houses on 5 adjacent lots. If one house is to be built on each lot, how many different arrangements of the 5 houses are possible?

   (A) 5

   (B) 10

   (C) 25

   (D) 60

   (E) 120

3. A savings account earns 1 percent interest per month on the sum of the initial amount deposited plus any accumulated interest. If a savings account is opened with an initial deposit of $1,000 and no other deposits or withdrawals are made, what will be the amount in this account at the end of 6 months?

(A) $1,060.00

(B) $1,061.52

(C) $1,072.14

(D) $1,600.00

(E) $6,000.00

4. A rectangular pool 24 feet long, 8 feet wide, and 4 feet deep is filled with water. Water is leaking from the pool at a rate of 0.4 cubic feet per minute. At this rate, how many hours will it take for the water level to drop 1 foot?

(A) 4

(B) 8

(C) 12

(D) 16

(E) 32

5. It takes 30 minutes for a certain bacteria population to double. If there are 5,248,763 bacteria in this population at 1pm, about how many bacteria will there be at 3pm on the same day?

(A) 42 million

(B) 64 million

(C) 80 million

(D) 84 million

(E) 90 million

6. It takes 64 identical cubes to half-fill a rectangular box. If each cube has a volume of 8 cubic centimeters, what is the volume of the box in cubic centimeters?

(A) 8

(B) 16

(C) 128

(D) 512

(E) 1,024

Answers to Mathematical Reasoning Questions

1. C
2. E
3. B
4. B
5. D
6. E

Data Interpretation Segment

The next segment of the Cognitive Ability Test requires you to interpret data presented in various pie charts, bar graphs, line graphs, and tables. In this segment, each table or graph is followed by up to four questions pertaining only to that table or graph. The questions require you to interpret and analyze the data, identify relevant information, and solve problems based on the data. This segment of the test is designed not only to measure your mathematical knowledge, but also your analytical skills, attention to detail, and ability to evaluate information and make decisions. You will have 24 minutes to answer 25 questions in the Data Interpretation segment.

Sample Data Interpretation Questions

1. According to the table below, what is the average wage for Thursday's earnings if the total earnings for the five days was $307.00?

Time Card for Harvey Martenfeld				
Day of Week	Time of Day	Number of Hours	Average Hourly Wage	Total Daily Earnings
Monday	9:00am–2:00pm	5	$11.00	$55.00
Tuesday	9:00am–4:00pm	7	$11.00	$77.00
Wednesday	3:00pm–7:00pm	4	$11.50	$46.00
Thursday	2:00pm–8:00pm	6		
Friday	4:00pm–9:00pm	5	$12.00	$60.00

   (A) $11.00

   (B) $11.25

   (C) $11.50

   (D) $11.75

   (E) $12.00

2. Dr. Komyathy treated 11,821 patients from 1998 through 2001. According to the pie chart below, how many patients did Dr. Komyathy treat in 2001?

Percentage of Patients 1998 through 2001

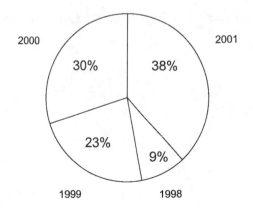

(A) 4,492

(B) 4,787

(C) 4,937

(D) 5,014

(E) 5,326

3. Four litters of five Labrador Retriever puppies each were fed a commercial ration from birth until six months of age. Each puppy was weighed at birth and at six months. The weight of the puppies at birth was subtracted from their weight at six months. These differences, in pounds, are shown below for each puppy:

Litter 1 Ration A	Litter 2 Ration B	Litter 3 Ration C	Litter 4 Ration D
45	28	35	62
65	36	76	46
33	49	53	52
49	71	55	61
58	37	41	70
250 Total	221 Total	260 Total	291 Total

What was the average difference in weight gain between the group of puppies who gained the most weight and the group who gained the least?

(A) 7

(B) 14

(C) 25

(D) 35

(E) None of the above

4. The following graph shows proposed spending for police department programs:

Police Department Budget
Fiscal Year 2002

Patrol Operations	$ 175,990
Support Services	$ 155,441
Investigations	$ 114,614
Community Policing	$ 95,032
Traffic Enforcement	$ 70,067
Administration	$ 44,224

What is the ratio of funding for investigations to community policing?

(A) 3 to 2

(B) 4 to 3

(C) 6 to 5

(D) 5 to 6

(E) 3 to 4

Answers to Data Interpretation Questions

1. C

2. A

3. B

4. C

Mathematical Relationships Segment

The mathematical relationships segment of the test focuses on the basic principles of arithmetic, algebra, and geometry to test your mathematical knowledge and reasoning skills. This segment measures your ability to work with numbers and apply mathematical concepts to solve quantitative problems. The questions require knowledge in areas such as addition and subtraction, multiplication and division, fractions, decimals, positive and negative numbers, percentages, divisors, factors, integers, probabilities, and other mathematical concepts and symbols used in algebra, geometry, and arithmetic. Candidates have 22 minutes to answer 25 questions in this segment.

Sample Mathematical Relationships Questions

1. Which of the following figures best illustrates the statement:

    $5 \times (6 + 2) = (5 \times 6) + (5 \times 2)$?

    (A)

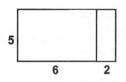

    (B)

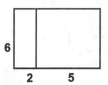

    (C)

    2 [   ]
        6   5

(D)

5	6	2

(E)

5	6	5	2

2. If $d = 110$ and $a = 20$ in the formula $d = \frac{a}{2}(2t - 1)$, then $t =$

   (A) $^{15}/_{22}$

   (B) $^{15}/_{8}$

   (C) $^{111}/_{20}$

   (D) 5

   (E) 6

3. If $x = -4$, the value of $-4x$ is:

   (A) -16

   (B) -8

   (C) 8

   (D) 16

   (E) 64

4. Which of the following is both a multiple of 3 and a multiple of 7?

   (A) 7,007

   (B) 8,192

   (C) 21,567

   (D) 22,287

   (E) 40,040

5. In the figure below, *ABDG* is a parallelogram and *CDEF* is a rectangle. If *EF* = 9 and *CG* = 10, what is *AB*?

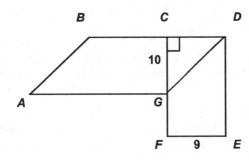

   (A) 11.75

   (B) 13.45

   (C) 14.05

   (D) 14.70

   (E) 15.10

6. *ABCD* is a rectangle. What is the area of *ABCD* if the length of *AC* is 10 and the length of *CD* is 6?

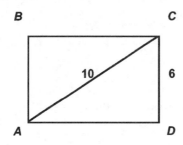

(A) 12

(B) 24

(C) 48

(D) 60

(E) 64

Answers to Mathematical Relationships Questions

1. A
2. E
3. D
4. C
5. B
6. C

Tips for the Cognitive Ability Test

To prepare for the Cognitive Ability Test, your best bet is to brush up on basic arithmetic, algebra, and geometry. This test does not require any knowledge of advanced mathematics, such as trigonometry or calculus. The following tips should be helpful with all segments of the Cognitive Ability Test:

- **Answer the question that is asked.** One of the most common mistakes you can make on the test is failing to read the questions carefully. Many problems in the Cognitive Ability Test include choices that appear correct if you misinterpret the meaning of the questions. Although time limits are demanding, you must be sure that you understand what is being asked.

- **Read all of the choices before answering.** Many questions are easier to answer by examining the choices and skipping the calculations. This technique often allows you to immediately eliminate choices that are obviously incorrect. In addition, many questions can be answered through approximations rather than performing time-consuming calculations. For example, if you estimate that the answer is 50 percent and the choices are 16 percent, 25 percent, 53 percent, 86 percent, and 92 percent, you should select 53 percent and move on to the next question instead of performing the calculations.

- **Don't get stuck on a question.** Cognitive Ability Test questions are designed to be answered without lengthy or complicated calculations. If you cannot answer a question by performing a few rough calculations or estimates, you probably will be better off guessing than spending an excessive amount of time on the question.

- **Review graphs and tables carefully.** Pie charts, bar graphs, line graphs, and simple tables are commonly used in the Data Interpretation segment of the Cognitive Ability Test. Data interpretation questions are designed to test your ability to identify and use relevant information to solve problems, and they rarely require difficult calculations. Be sure to pay close attention to legends, labels, units of measurement, and other indicators of how the data is presented, because these are crucial to arriving at the correct answer.

- **Use the process of elimination.** In many cases you can systematically discard incorrect choices and narrow your options down to one or two by following the process of elimination. This technique is useful when certain choices are obviously incorrect. For example, if you determine that the correct answer will be a positive number and three of the five choices are negative numbers, you can narrow the number of choices to two. In fact, even eliminating only one choice increases your odds of selecting the correct answer.

- **Use a study guide.** Study guides that are geared to the Graduate Management Admission Test (GMAT) are very useful in preparing for the math portions of the FBI phase I test because the math questions are similar on these tests. GMAT preparation guides include full-length practice tests, answers, analyses, and other useful features. *How to Prepare for the GMAT,* which is published by Barron's Educational Series, is one of the best.

Strategies for Special Agent Phase II Testing

The most competitive applicants who passed phase I testing are invited to compete in the phase II process, which consists of a structured personal interview and a written exercise. The following sections discuss strategies for performing well during these segments of the process.

The Structured Interview

Structured interviews are used by the FBI, other law enforcement agencies, and firms in the private sector to evaluate job candidates by asking each of them identical questions under the same conditions. During phase II of the special agent hiring process, structured interviews provide the FBI with an assessment of candidates' communications skills, judgment, integrity, priorities, initiative, and other attributes that special agents must have to meet FBI standards and succeed in federal law enforcement.

About the Interview

The structured interview takes place at an FBI field office on the same day as the written exercise. The interview is designed to evaluate each candidate's previous behavior in a variety of actual situations to predict their potential for success as an FBI special agent. This approach is commonly known as *behavioral interviewing*. During the interview, which lasts about one hour, a panel of three FBI special agents asks each applicant a series of 15 questions and rates the responses based on predetermined criteria. To ensure objectiveness in scoring, the panel is not provided with any information about applicants' backgrounds, such as their phase I test scores, work history, education, skills, or other qualifications.

Preparing for the Interview

In preparation for the phase II interview, keep in mind that you will be asked to discuss your life experiences in a wide range of situations. These could involve not only your employment, but also your experiences in grade school, college, family and social settings, athletic competition, travel, emergencies, or other situations. A very effective method of preparing for behavioral interview questions is to recall incidents that required you to evaluate a situation and choose a course of action while you were under stress, in difficult or emotional circumstances, responding to emergencies, or faced with moral or ethical dilemmas.

An excellent method you can use to prepare for and answer phase II interview questions is the STAR technique. The acronym STAR stands for

- Situation

- Task

- Action

- Result

To apply the STAR technique, follow these steps:

1. First describe the **situation** or **task** you encountered. For example, you could discuss a conflict between two of your coworkers and how you helped them to resolve it. Be sure to provide sufficient detail so that the interviewers understand the circumstances completely.

2. Next, explain the specific **action** you took toward resolving the situation. The focus of the action should be on what you actually did or suggested. In the scenario involving your coworkers, you could describe a compromise that you suggested.

3. Finally, describe the **result** of the situation. In this case, you could discuss the terms of the compromise and how each worker accepted the outcome, as well as what you accomplished or learned from the incident. In a nutshell, the STAR technique allows you to frame your responses to behavioral questions in a straightforward, organized, and informative manner.

The following example illustrates the STAR technique in action:

Interviewer's Question:

"Describe a situation in which you exercised good judgment and integrity."

Situation or Task:

"Last month, I participated in the execution of a search warrant at a conven-ience store in Chicago that was involved in food stamp trafficking. I was assigned to search a small office at the rear of the store. While I was alone in the office, I opened a desk drawer and discovered a cigar box that contained more than $100,000 in cash."

Action:

"As soon as I noticed that the cigar box contained cash, I placed it back in the drawer, stood in the doorway leading into the office, and notified the team leader of my discovery. I remained in the doorway until he arrived, and then pointed out the box. After I photographed it, we counted the cash together and seized it according to our agency's written policy manual."

Result:

"Considering that I didn't handle, count, or seize the cash until a witness was present, it is unlikely that anyone will question whether I pocketed any of the money. Not only did I maintain my integrity in the situation, the integrity of the evidence—including the chain of custody—was also maintained at all times. In other words, I acted within the law and agency policies, and the prosecutor intends to use the cash as evidence."

In this example, the STAR technique allows the candidate to respond to the question clearly, concisely, and in an organized manner. In addition to address-ing judgment and integrity, the response also focuses on other traits the FBI looks for during the interview, such as oral communication skills, ability to evaluate and adapt to changing situations, and maintaining a positive image.

Although some of the questions could focus on your successes in evaluating, responding, and adapting to various circumstances, you might also be asked about experiences that resulted in negative outcomes. In other words, be pre-pared to discuss situations in which your actions brought results that were somehow unsatisfactory, and any shortcomings that might have caused nega-tive results. The interviewers realize that no applicant has led a life of perfec-tion, and they might be interested in how you address negative outcomes. If you are asked these types of questions, it is best to readily admit to your fail-ures and to explain what you learned from your mistakes.

To take full advantage of the STAR technique, prior to the interview you must think carefully about several scenarios in which you have been involved, including the action you took and the outcome, and write down the details. Writing about the incidents will help you to collect and organize the details. The STAR technique should pay big dividends during the interview, because you will already have a number of situations in mind when you are asked to discuss your experiences. This exercise might seem like a lot of work, but the rewards are well worth it.

Presenting a Positive and Professional Image

A considerable amount of research has shown that job interviewers evaluate applicants not only on their responses to questions, but also on their appearance and demeanor. The saying, "you never get a second chance to make a good first impression," is quite true. It is very important to wear professional business attire to the interview, such as a suit and tie for males and a suit, dress, or pantsuit for females. You must be aware that every aspect of your performance will be judged, including the manner in which you present yourself. Be sure to greet the interviewers with confidence and a firm handshake and to maintain good posture throughout the interview. You should also maintain eye contact with every member of the interview panel in an alternating manner while you are answering questions.

Listening Skills

Many candidates are so anxious to respond to questions during the interview that they overlook the importance of good listening skills. You must listen carefully to each question to understand the meaning and context presented. Do not hesitate to ask the interviewers to repeat questions, if necessary. Also, it is often wise to take a few seconds to think things over before responding to questions instead of blurting out answers you might regret later.

Be Yourself

One of the most common mistakes that applicants make during phase II interviews is to anticipate what the interviewers would like to hear rather than answering questions with sincerity and candor. As a result, attempting to outguess the interview panel is often the fastest way to fail the interview. Keep in mind that there are no "right" and "wrong" answers to the questions and that every candidate is evaluated on whether they possess critical skills and abilities that FBI special agents must have. In other words, if you have what it takes, you will be much better off providing a true snapshot of yourself than putting on an act.

The Written Exercise

The other portion of phase II testing consists of a written exercise that applicants complete in the presence of FBI test administrators. Unlike the multiple-choice tests administered during phase I, the written exercise is an open-ended essay examination that gives applicants considerable latitude in formulating their responses. The examination is administered to measure skills and abilities that are crucial to carrying out the duties of special agents, such as written communication skills, attention to detail, the ability to evaluate the complexities of an issue, judgment, critical thinking, and decision-making skills.

To begin this 90-minute examination, the FBI provides applicants with materials that describe a problem or scenario. You must carefully review the information provided and write a response that addresses the issues presented. For example, a previous written exercise instructed applicants to write a report to the editor of a newspaper to persuade her that an emerging situation should be investigated. Although the Bureau changes the situations or themes from time to time, the format of the written exercise still boils down to analyzing and reporting on a problem or scenario. There are no "correct" answers or positions you can take in this examination. Completed essays are scored by special agents who evaluate how well you analyze the facts and develop an articulate and compelling case in support of your position.

A Sample Written Exercise Question

You are a member of your local school board. The school board is studying ways to reduce vandalism at the buildings within the school district. You have been appointed to write a report to the school superintendent about the problem of vandalism and how to solve it.

To help you get started, the school board has given you the chart shown below, which provides information about the extent of vandalism within the school district over the last seven years. Common acts of vandalism have included damaged furniture, broken windows, graffiti, damaged trees and athletic fields, slashed vehicle tires, and damaged fences. Sixty-five percent of those arrested and convicted of committing the vandalism have been members of local teen gangs within the school district. According to the United States Department of Justice, community policing and police-school liaison programs have been very effective in reducing vandalism and other crimes at schools nationwide.

The school board wants you to discuss ways to prevent some of the different types of vandalism in the school district. In your report, describe the extent of vandalism and discuss what you think are the primary causes. Then present the board with a plan to stop these crimes and solve the problem.

Number of Vandalism Incidents: 1995–2001

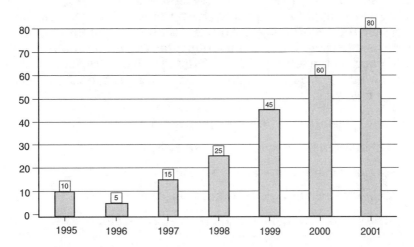

Tips for the Written Exercise

Before beginning the exercise, read the situation and instructions very carefully —more than once, if necessary—to ensure that you understand the exercise. If you have any questions about the examination, ask the test administrator for information or clarification.

Although your approach to the written exercise is clearly a matter of personal preference and style, well-written essays are likely to share a number of common qualities. After you have read the introductory materials, do not rush into writing the essay immediately. Instead, take some time to prepare and outline an organized and logical presentation. If it is practical to do so, give prime consideration to summarizing your position in the first paragraph, and then carefully develop your position over the remainder of the essay. Your essay should provide a thorough and detailed argument for your strategy or course of action based on common sense and accurate analysis of the issues. Whenever possible, support your position with specific examples or discussion of expected outcomes. Most importantly, remember to stay focused and articulate your ideas clearly using standard English.

Strategies for Professional Support Position Applicants

As discussed in chapter 6, the hiring process for professional support positions differs in many ways from the special agent hiring process. Among the primary differences, professional support applicants must submit written statements that outline their knowledge, skills, and abilities, known as KSA statements. They must also participate in job interviews that could differ widely from one position to another. In addition to the tips discussed at the beginning of this chapter relating to application forms, professional support candidates can apply the following strategies when tackling the most critical components of the hiring process: the KSA statement and the interview.

Tips for Preparing a KSA Statement

The most significant difference between hiring processes carried out by the federal government and those of private-sector firms is the use of KSA statements to evaluate applicants' qualifications. In these statements, applicants must describe their education, experience, training, accomplishments, and awards as they relate to the selection criteria for various positions. For example, depending on the setting of the position, FBI biologist (forensic examiner) applicants would be required to submit a KSA statement to address elements such as the following:

- Knowledge of biological principles and practices

- Skill in interpreting test results and evaluating data

- Skill in oral and written communication

- Ability to operate various scientific instruments

- Ability to organize, plan, and prioritize testing and analysis activities

We cannot overstate the importance of composing a high-quality KSA statement. The bottom line is that, although the job interview often serves as the deciding factor in hiring decisions, you are not likely to make it to the interview stage if your KSA statement does not set you apart as one of the most competitive applicants in the pool. Whether you are applying for employment with the FBI or any other federal agency, you can actually outshine more-qualified competition if you have a better feel for preparing your KSA statement.

Evaluating Your Knowledge, Skills, and Abilities

Before writing your KSA statement, you must carefully evaluate your background and experience to determine what career skills you have to offer. It is critical that you carefully analyze the tasks you performed and your accomplishments at each job you held.

The next step is to create an exhaustive list of the skills you developed. Do not limit the list to full-time employment experience. Also include any part-time or volunteer work, internship experience, and co-op positions. Make a list of all professional memberships, achievements, awards, certificates, licenses, leadership activities, proficiency in foreign languages, special skills, public-speaking experience, and other relevant activities. Examine each item on the list and think about the skills or talents they require. Virtually all jobs, internships, extracurricular activities, hobbies, and other pursuits require particular knowledge, skills, and abilities, many of which might be transferable to the position you are seeking. Write them all down. Also list the schools, training seminars, and workshops you attended (including dates and locations) and any degrees, honors, fellowships, and certificates you have received. The quality of your KSA statement depends mostly on the depth and thoroughness of your effort in this step. Don't skimp here.

Matching Your KSAs to the Position

After you have prepared a list of your knowledge, skills, and abilities, you must match them to the KSAs listed in the vacancy announcements of the positions for which you are applying. It is critical that you tailor every KSA statement to the specific requirements of each targeted position, highlighting all of your education, training, experience, talents, and accomplishments that demonstrate your ability to perform the job skills. Do not make the mistake of providing generic job descriptions that present little or no information about your individual accomplishments. Instead, clearly describe your specific responsibilities and achievements. Also, do not overlook any experience and accomplishments that are related in any way to the career you are pursuing. These could include interacting with the public, gathering and organizing information, resolving complaints, troubleshooting, solving problems, writing reports, making oral presentations, using computers, establishing and attaining goals, following organizational policies and procedures, and coordinating projects with other people or organizations. Also highlight any experience that demonstrates communication skills, initiative, leadership, dependability, persistence, innovation, and the ability to perform in stressful situations.

Tips for Professional Support Interviews

As discussed in chapter 6, the most competitive professional support applicants must participate in either structured or semi-structured interviews toward the end of the application process. Considering that most FBI careers require confidence and interpersonal skills, interviewers will evaluate these attributes carefully, in addition to other criteria. Personal interviews provide knowledgeable and well-prepared applicants with a golden opportunity to showcase their qualifications. The following strategies are useful in making a positive impression.

Interview Preparation

The first step in preparing for the personal interview is to learn about the FBI and the position being filled. If you are knowledgeable in these areas, you will be far more likely to adequately articulate what you have to offer, while also sending the message that you are serious about a career with the Bureau. Some applicants conduct no more than minimal research about the careers they are seeking, and it shows. It is best to present yourself in the most positive light by showing that you have done your homework.

Be sure to review your resume and application prior to the interview, because many interview questions are likely to be based on information you provided in these documents. Interviewers often start off by confirming information that applicants provided months prior to the interview. Brush up on the details so as not to provide contradictory information.

Also be prepared to ask questions during the interview. A one-way job interview that consists only of questions asked by the employer and none by the applicant is more of an interrogation than an interview. An exchange of information is appropriate for virtually all job interviews, and applicants should be prepared to ask meaningful questions about the FBI, the division, and the position.

During the Interview

One of the most effective strategies you can apply is to focus on the positive during the interview. In other words, answer questions in a direct and positive manner and speak positively of present and former employers whenever possible. You can express a positive attitude and interest in the position using information you gathered to prepare for the interview. Explain how your experience, education, and training will make you productive in the shortest time with minimal supervision. Sell yourself with specific examples of your skills and accomplishments.

Candidates who perform well during job interviews owe much of their success to good listening skills. Those who make an effort to listen attentively for information about the position and the agency tend to ask better questions, which sets them apart from others. Always listen carefully and take a brief moment to think about each question before responding.

Considering that job interviews are designed to provide an exchange of information, feel free to ask questions during the interview. The interviewers will expect you to ask questions about the FBI, working conditions, training programs, advancement opportunities, job performance measures, and other issues. Having the confidence to ask appropriate questions during an interview will not only make a positive impression, but will also allow you to become more informed about the Bureau and the position.

After the Interview

It is possible that the interviewers will ask you to provide copies of references, certificates, diplomas, transcripts, or any other credentials that were not requested prior to the interview. Be sure to provide these documents or any other requested information as soon as possible after an interview; otherwise, you might lose consideration for the position. Also send a brief letter of appreciation to thank the participants for their time and reiterate your interest in the position. Finally, in an effort to make each interview a learning experience, evaluate your performance by asking yourself whether you prepared adequately, presented your qualifications effectively, listened well, asked appropriate questions, and learned all that you needed to know about the position. By answering these questions as objectively as possible, you will be able to identify specific ways you can improve your interviewing skills.

Strategies for Internship Applicants

For many full-time FBI personnel, the road to the Bureau began with an FBI internship. Whether you pursue an FBI Honors Internship, Presidential Management Internship, National Center for the Analysis of Violent Crime Internship, or FBI Academy Internship, you must put your best foot forward to be competitive in the selection process. Consider the following strategies to increase your chances of landing an internship with the world's best-known law enforcement agency.

Information Is Power

Unfortunately, many college students who are interested in landing a full-time career with the FBI or another law enforcement agency are unaware of FBI internship opportunities that are available to graduate and undergraduate students. This can be good news for you, however, because you are holding the information in your hands. Chapter 9 provides an overview of each FBI internship program, including eligibility, application procedures, selection processes, intern assignments, and training. You can also learn about FBI internship opportunities by visiting career fairs that the Bureau attends or by contacting applicant coordinators at FBI field offices. (A list of field offices is in appendix J.) When you know what is available and how to take the steps to land an internship, you are halfway there.

Make Your Own Opportunities

The second step to landing an FBI internship—or any internship—is to realize that you must get the ball rolling on your own. Countless college students who are close to graduation approach professors and expect to obtain an internship on the way out the door. As a result, these students almost always graduate with no internship or practical experience under their belts, and often with little direction in their career search. Similar to internships with other agencies, the application process for FBI internships starts 10 to 12 months prior to the starting date. You must meet specific deadlines. You must also realize that college professors and internship coordinators typically are swamped with myriad responsibilities; internships most often go to students who are persistent and willing to do much of the legwork themselves. Although academic transcripts, letters of recommendation, or other documents must be submitted by the college, FBI internship application processes must be initiated by the student.

Application Materials

As discussed at the beginning of this chapter, it is important to provide truthful and accurate information in all application materials; otherwise, your application might be delayed or rejected. In addition, be sure to meet all application deadlines, including those for the submission of forms, transcripts, and recommendation letters that others have been asked to submit on your behalf. In other words, stay abreast of things throughout the application process.

Describing Your Experience

Similar to applying for full-time positions with the FBI, you must submit a resume or a detailed application form (or both) to begin the selection process. Carefully evaluate your experience and education before completing these materials, including all full-time and any part-time employment, volunteer work, community service you have performed, and your involvement in professional organizations. Also be sure to provide details of any achievements, awards, leadership activities, licenses or certificates, or special skills you possess. (For additional tips on what to include, see "Strategies for Professional Support Position Applicants," earlier in this chapter.)

Describing Previous Internships

Many applicants for FBI internships have already completed internships with other agencies, firms, or organizations. Always list internships as separate positions on your application or resume, similar to regular employment, so that you will have adequate space to describe your experiences in detail. In doing so, it is critical that you describe exactly what you did rather than what you observed. Under separate headings for each internship, provide complete details of your activities and place emphasis on the specific tasks you performed and any accomplishments. These often provide valuable hands-on experience that could place you ahead of other applicants.

Submitting Application Materials

After you have spent hours putting together your application package, it would be unfortunate if it was misdirected or lost. One of the most important aspects of the application process is to be sure that you send the package to the right address. Mail that is misdirected—either at the FBI or on the way there—could be delayed for days or weeks before it ends up in the right hands. Also, submit all of your application materials via first-class mail or through a major package courier service, such as UPS or FedEx. Mailed packages should be sent either certified with "return receipt" service or by Priority Mail with "delivery confirmation" service. UPS and FedEx provide both tracking and delivery confirmation automatically. Spending a few extra pennies will give you assurance (and supporting details) that your materials were received by the FBI, as well as peace of mind.

Tips for Internship Interviews

The next step in the process involves a personal interview at the FBI field office that processes your application for the Honors Internship; at FBI Headquarters for PMI candidates; or in the Quantico, Virginia, area for NCAVC and FBI Academy Internships. In some cases, the FBI conducts interactive tele-vised interviews with candidates who would otherwise be required to travel to Washington or Quantico. For these interviews, candidates report to a local television station and the interview is broadcast live via satellite.

Interview Questions

The nature of interview questions depends mostly on the type of internship for which you are applying. For example, interviews for PMI candidates are likely to be more elaborate than those conducted for FBI Academy, Honors, and NCAVC applicants, because PMI internships lead directly to full-time positions with the FBI. Therefore, PMI candidates are likely to be asked more detailed questions that focus on their career interests and qualifications. On the other hand, interviews for FBI Academy, Honors, and NCAVC internships are similar to job interviews for many entry-level positions. In other words, the FBI does not expect these internship applicants to have extensive experience. In addition to answering questions that are targeted specifically to the intern-ship they are seeking, candidates should be prepared to answer a number of general questions, such as the following:

- What can you tell me about yourself?
- What can you tell me about this division?
- What would you like to accomplish during the internship?
- Do you have any particular qualities that will be helpful during your internship?
- What are your major strengths and weaknesses?
- What accomplishment are you most proud of?
- What kinds of tasks, assignments, or projects motivate you the most?
- Why have you chosen to pursue a career in this field?
- What are your career goals?
- What can you tell me about yourself that is not on your resume or application?
- Do you have any questions about the internship?

Questions You Should Ask

Regardless of the internship you have applied for, you will be given an oppor-tunity toward the end of the interview to ask questions. Asking questions serves not only as a means of gathering information, but also demonstrates your interest in the internship. Be careful, however, not to ask questions that have already been answered during the interview or questions with obvious answers. Interviewers can assess your maturity, communication skills, and pro-fessionalism based on your questions, so it is important to be prepared and to ask questions that you truly would like answered. Also, have several questions in mind, because the interviewer might answer some of them during the inter-view. Generally speaking, your questions should be geared toward learning more about the internship and the division to which you will be assigned. Here are a few examples of questions you could ask:

- Could you describe a typical day for interns in this division?

- What sort of assignments or projects do interns work on?

- Are interns rotated to other divisions?

- Do interns have an opportunity to participate in training or seminars?

- What have interns found to be most satisfying or rewarding in their internships?

- How do you measure the performance of interns?

Other Interviewing Tips

Preparation, eye contact, listening skills, and a positive attitude are crucial to your success during internship interviews. For guidance on these and other aspects of the interview process, see "Tips for Professional Support Interviews," under "Strategies for Professional Support Position Applicants," earlier in this chapter.

CHAPTER 8

FBI Training

*Anyone can shoot a gun. What counts is how well you stand up
when someone is shooting back at you.*
—Louis L'Amour

One of the Bureau's most important functions is training FBI special agents, support employees, and personnel from other law enforcement agencies. The FBI is widely recognized as one of the finest providers of law enforcement training in the world. The Bureau's training functions are managed by its training division, which is based at the FBI Academy in Quantico, Virginia. This division is responsible for training all new employees and continuing education for the existing FBI workforce. The division conducts advanced training for state and local law enforcement personnel at every level and in many disciplines and also manages the FBI Academy. In recognition of the growth of international crime and terrorism, many of the Bureau's training programs are also offered in foreign countries to our international law enforcement allies. To maintain a skilled and professional workforce, and to meet the needs of other law enforcement agencies, training will continue to be one of the FBI's most urgent priorities.

The FBI Academy

Since its opening in 1972, the FBI Academy has remained on the cutting edge of law enforcement training, assistance, and research as one of the world's most highly regarded law enforcement training centers. The Academy trains three primary groups of students, including newly hired FBI and Drug Enforcement Administration (DEA) special agents participating in basic training programs, Bureau personnel who attend professional development courses and seminars throughout their careers, and representatives of other law enforcement agencies who attend a variety of specialized programs.

FBI Academy Facilities

The FBI Academy is located about 40 miles southwest of Washington, D.C., on the United States Marine Corps base at Quantico, Virginia. The Academy grounds encompass nearly 400 wooded acres of land and more than 20 buildings. The primary training complex includes a classroom building, audiovisual facilities, administrative offices, three dormitory buildings, a dining hall, a library, research facilities, a 1,000-seat auditorium, a chapel, a gymnasium, and an outside track. In addition to the main complex, there is a mock city known as "Hogan's Alley" that is used for practical training, as well as indoor and outdoor firearms ranges, a 1.1-mile pursuit and defensive driving track, and a fully equipped garage. The DEA training academy is also on site and shares the FBI's facilities.

Operational Units at the FBI Academy

More than a dozen units are based at the FBI Academy, where they provide support to a variety of Academy training functions and operations in the field. The following sections summarize the primary functions of these units.

The New Agents' Training Unit

The New Agents' Training Unit coordinates the 16-week New Agent Training program. The training curriculum is broken down into investigative and tactical, noninvestigative, and administrative training components. Staff from this unit oversee the program, which consists of academics, firearms instruction, physical training, defensive tactics, and practical exercises. They are also responsible for evaluating trainees as to their suitability to be FBI special agents.

The Practical Applications Unit

The Practical Applications Unit manages practical training events and problem exercises that the FBI Academy carries out. This unit provides instruction in areas such as surveillance, arrest procedures, and tactical street survival techniques. This unit presents a variety of programs to new agent trainees, veteran FBI agents, and law enforcement officers from other agencies, such as the Bureau's Law Enforcement Training for Safety and Survival Program and the Tactical Emergency Vehicle Operators Course.

The Firearms Training Unit

Firearms training at the FBI Academy is carried out by the Firearms Training Unit, which is also responsible for administering training programs for special agents in the field and conducting a variety of firearms-related research projects. This unit is also responsible for the procurement of handguns, shotguns, submachine guns, other weapons, ammunition, and related equipment, and the maintenance and inventory of the FBI's firearms.

The Physical Training Unit

The Physical Training Unit at Quantico manages the Bureau's fitness and defensive tactics programs. This unit conducts training for the New Agent Training program, the FBI National Academy, in-service personnel, and state and local law enforcement agencies. This unit's instructional staff consists of permanently assigned nutrition advisors, fitness advisors, and defensive tactics instructors.

The Behavioral Science Unit

Training programs, research, and consultation in the behavioral and social sciences for the FBI and law enforcement community are carried out by the Behavioral Science Unit. This unit conducts research and presents instruction relating to criminal and forensic psychology, crime analysis, death investigation, community policing and problem-solving strategies, gangs and gang behavior, interpersonal violence, law enforcement officers killed and assaulted in the line of duty, and stress management in law enforcement.

The Field Police Training Unit

The Field Police Training Unit carries out comprehensive training assistance to local, county, and state law enforcement agencies in the areas of investigative, managerial, technical, and administrative aspects of law enforcement. Instructors in this unit provide training and education programs at the Academy and nationwide. These programs provide agencies with state-of-the-art training while also enhancing the FBI's relationship with state and local law enforcement agencies.

The Technology Services Unit

The Technology Services Unit (TSU) provides a wide range of instructional and communications technology services at the FBI Academy. This unit ensures that audiovisual systems are maintained and available for use in the classrooms, provides technological support to allow the use of computers in Academy courses, and also produces training videos, photographs, slides, and training aids for use at the Academy and in the field. TSU is also home to the FBI Training Network, which offers multimedia-based instruction, satellite broadcasts, distance learning, teleconferencing, and videotape instruction services to the FBI and other agencies.

The Investigative Training Unit

The FBI Academy's Investigative Training Unit offers instruction on the subjects of white-collar crime, organized crime, drug trafficking, and other topics, which better prepares FBI special agents to conduct criminal investigations in these areas. Members of the Investigative Training Unit also teach courses attended by police commanders at the FBI National Academy, by Bureau personnel during in-service training programs, and off-site by law enforcement personnel throughout the United States and internationally.

The Law Enforcement Communication Unit

The Law Enforcement Communication Unit teaches courses concerned with oral and written communication. In the New Agent Training program, instruction is geared to interviewing, informant development, and field office communications. Courses presented for the National Academy include interviewing and interrogation, instructor development, public speaking, media relations, contemporary issues in law enforcement, and effective writing. This unit presents in-service training to FBI personnel and instruction in various police training programs. It also publishes the *FBI Law Enforcement Bulletin,* which is distributed to domestic and foreign law enforcement agencies and professionals in the criminal justice field.

The Leadership and Management Science Unit

This unit designs and administers programs for FBI personnel and law enforcement agencies relating to creative leadership and management practices, including the National Executive Institute for executives of major jurisdictions and the Law Enforcement Executive Development Seminar for heads of mid-sized and smaller agencies. Its instructional staff is accredited by the University of Virginia to teach undergraduate and graduate courses at the FBI National Academy.

The Public Affairs Unit

The Public Affairs Unit of the FBI Academy is responsible for all media and public relations for the training division of the FBI. The Public Affairs Unit coordinates events such as briefings, on-location filming, interviews with Academy staff, dignitary visits, and other public relations matters. This unit also provides media and public relations support to other FBI divisions represented at the Academy, including the Critical Incident Response Group, the Engineering Research Facility, and the Forensic Science Research and Training Center.

The Investigative Computer Training Unit

The Investigative Computer Training Unit presents investigative computer training to new agent trainees, other FBI employees, and law enforcement personnel throughout the world. This training focuses on a variety of computer topics, including how to use the computer as an investigative tool, a communications device, a research platform, and a tool for examining and analyzing digital evidence. The staff also provides instruction on subjects such as Internet investigations, computer intrusion investigations, search and seizure of computers, and cyber crime. This unit provides training to the FBI's regional computer crime squads, evidence response teams, undercover investigators working crimes against children cases, National Infrastructure Protection Center personnel, and National Security Division agents.

The Forensic Science Research and Training Center

The Forensic Science Research and Training Center provides forensic training to FBI and DEA recruits, the FBI National Academy, FBI laboratory examiners and technicians, other FBI in-service students, and personnel from federal, state, and local law enforcement agencies. It also supports the FBI Laboratory with forensic science research and quality-assurance functions. Training programs that this center offers to crime laboratory personnel provide hands-on instruction to enhance their basic skills and procedures. The programs also introduce them to advanced techniques used in examining physical evidence.

The FBI National Academy

Since 1935, the FBI National Academy has provided leadership and management training for mid- and upper-level police commanders from around the world. FBI National Academy classes are offered on a quarterly basis and consist of 11 weeks of intensive multidisciplinary training for which graduates can earn undergraduate and graduate credits from the University of Virginia. The program focuses on six academic disciplines, including Management Science, Behavioral Science, Law, Education, Health and Fitness, and Forensic Science. Among these disciplines, attendees can take courses in white-collar crime, youth and gang crime, hate crimes, racial profiling, community policing, computer crime, communication skills, abnormal psychology, budgeting and finance, stress management, ethics, and other subjects. Instructors in the program include permanent staff of the FBI Academy, personnel from various FBI field offices, and visiting scholars who are recognized experts in their fields. More than 30,000 law enforcement officers from the United States and more than 100 countries have graduated from the program since its inception in 1935.

Training for FBI Special Agents

The FBI Academy is responsible for training special agent recruits, veteran agents, and professional support personnel through instructional programs that are presented to people all at levels of the Bureau's workforce. These programs range from the 16-week New Agent Training program, which provides basic training in a multitude of disciplines, to a variety of courses and seminars that are geared to specific tasks. This section provides an overview of training programs for the Bureau's special agents.

The New Agent Training Program

All newly appointed special agent candidates are required to complete basic training at the FBI Academy in Quantico, Virginia, regardless of their previous experience, education, or training. Although the trainees are considered full-time FBI employees, their basic training effectively serves as the final stage of the special agent hiring process. The training atmosphere is similar to that of a college campus. A maximum of 50 trainees are assigned to each new agent training class. FBI Academy staff carefully evaluate every aspect of trainees' performance—from their test scores to character and attitude—before they are permitted to graduate from the program. The New Agent Training program is designed to push trainees' minds and bodies to their limits, leaving them with new tools, a few dozen close friends, and a keen sense of accomplishment and pride.

The graduation ceremony serves as their final assignment at the Academy, during which they are issued their badges and credentials and are sworn in as FBI special agents. During the ceremony, an award is given to each trainee who achieved the highest score in academics, weapons proficiency, and physical fitness. In addition, each graduating class selects a member of the class to receive the Fidelity, Bravery, and Integrity (FBI) Award. This is the highest award for a new special agent and recognizes the recipient's commitment to law enforcement ethics, professionalism, and the FBI's core values.

Overview of the Training Curriculum

The FBI New Agent Training program includes 16 weeks of intensive instruction involving three components, including investigative and tactical training, noninvestigative training, and administrative matters. The program is designed to provide trainees with the basic knowledge and skills they will need to effectively carry out their responsibilities after they are assigned to one of the FBI's field offices. New agent training consists of classroom and practical instruction that is spread over four major concentrations, including academics, firearms, physical training and defensive tactics, and practical applications. The program uses a building-block approach, in which lessons and practical exercise are presented in a carefully planned sequence. Table 8.1 provides a breakdown of the curriculum and the number of hours for each subject.

Table 8.1: New agent training curriculum, including number of hours for each subject area.

Investigative and Tactical Subjects	**588.5**
Firearms	(114.0)
Practical Applications	(80.0)
Physical Training, Defensive Tactics, Arrest Techniques	(74.0)
Legal Subjects	(66.5)
Law Enforcement Communication	(51.0)
Forensic Sciences	(32.0)
Computers	(30.0)
White-Collar Crime	(25.0)
National Security Programs, Counterterrorism	(23.0)
Organized Crime, Drugs, Violent Crimes, Major Offenders	(21.0)
Tactical Emergency Vehicle Operators Course	(20.0)
Informants and Cooperating Witnesses	(14.0)
Management of Integrated Case Scenario	(10.0)
Behavioral Sciences	(7.0)
National Crime Information Center	(3.0)
Case Management	(2.0)
Polygraph	(2.0)
Drug Identification	(2.0)
Civil Rights	(2.0)
Background Investigations	(2.0)
Technical Investigative Program	(1.5)
Undercover Operations	(1.5)
Command Post Operations & Rapid Start Program	(1.0)
Information Security	(1.0)
Security Awareness	(1.0)
FM Radio	(1.0)
International Investigations	(1.0)
Noninvestigative Subjects	**41.0**
Ethics	(12.0)
Leadership	(7.0)
First Aid, CPR, Bloodborne Pathogens	(6.5)
Cultural Diversity	(4.0)
History of the FBI	(2.0)
Employee Assistance Program	(2.0)
Equal Employment Opportunity	(1.0)

Freedom of Information Act, Privacy Act	(1.0)
Drug Enforcement Administration Briefing	(1.0)
Assistant Director Briefing	(1.0)
Office of Professional Responsibility Adjudication	(1.0)
Victim and Witness Assistance	(1.0)
FBI National Academy Briefing	(.5)
New Agent Training Unit Chief Briefing	(.5)
Ombudsman	(.5)
Administrative Subjects	**14.0**
Graduation Ceremony	(4.0)
Personnel Matters	(1.5)
FBI Vouchers	(1.5)
Credential Photos	(1.0)
Relocation Management	(1.0)
Insurance Matters	(1.0)
Oath of Office	(1.0)
Transfer Policy	(1.0)
Federal Employees Retirement System	(1.0)
Fingerprinting	(1.0)
TOTAL CURRICULUM HOURS	**643.5**

Academics

Academics in the New Agent Training program consist of a wide range of subject areas that provide a foundation for trainees to build upon throughout their careers. The largest academic block revolves around legal instruction, including 66.5 hours of training on topics such as criminal law, civil law, constitutional law, laws of arrest, admissions and confessions, and civil liability. Trainees also receive 48 hours of training in law enforcement communications, which is concerned primarily with interviewing and interrogation, informant development, effective writing, and field office communications. Other large training blocks focus on computers (54 hours); forensic sciences (32 hours); white-collar crime (25 hours); national security programs (23 hours); organized crime, violent crimes and major offenders, and drugs (21 hours); the Tactical Emergency Vehicle Operators Course (20 hours); and informants and cooperating witnesses (14 hours).

Trainees also participate in an Integrated Case Scenario throughout the program, in which they conduct a criminal investigation based on information they develop throughout the course. The scenario provides trainees with hands-on experience relating to law enforcement computer databases, interviewing, informant development, consensual monitoring, wiretapping operations, surveillance, FBI paperwork, and other material that will prepare them for their responsibilities as special agents. The scenario culminates with a practical exercise toward the end of the course that involves the arrests of multiple suspects in the Hogan's Alley complex.

The remainder of the academic portion of the program covers subjects such as the history of the FBI, behavioral sciences, case management, civil rights, ethics, first aid and CPR, information security, international investigations, and undercover operations. Noninvestigative training is headlined by 12 hours of ethics instruction, which covers FBI ethics standards, the ethical basis of the Constitution, classic philosophy on ethics, and the nature of criminal and noncriminal misconduct. Ethics coursework focuses on corruption, deception, ethical problems unique to law enforcement, and the standards of conduct for executive-branch personnel. This training also includes a lesson concerning the Holocaust, in which six million Jews were exterminated and others were persecuted in Nazi-controlled territory, so that trainees will understand the consequences when law enforcement fails to protect citizens, their civil rights and dignity, and their moral and humane values. The Holocaust lesson includes a guided tour of the United States Holocaust Memorial Museum in Washington, D.C., where trainees learn further about the role the police played during Hitler's reign.

Firearms Training

Firearms training is the largest single block of instruction in the program. Special agent trainees spend more than 100 hours developing their firearms skills at an indoor firing range, eight outdoor firing ranges, four skeet ranges, and a 200-yard rifle range. This training is designed to teach familiarity and confidence with semiautomatic pistols, shotguns, and submachine guns. Instruction is broken into three areas, consisting of fundamental marksmanship, combat survival shooting, and judgmental shooting. Various techniques are taught, including shooting at stationary and moving targets; from behind barricades and other forms of cover or concealment; from standing, kneeling, and prone positions; and when moving into various positions. Each trainee fires about 3,500 rounds of ammunition during the program, and trainees are responsible for maintaining and cleaning their own weapons. Those who either handle weapons in an unsafe manner—regardless of their shooting proficiency or qualifications scores—or fail to qualify in all firearms courses by the 11th week are dismissed.

Firearms training goes beyond skill development and includes instruction in the Bureau's deadly force policy and judgmental shooting exercises. These areas are examined during one of the most important and stressful segments of the training, during which Firearms Automated Training System (FATS) scenarios are introduced. FATS training consists of a full spectrum of realistic scenarios that are projected on a large video screen in front of participants. In these computerized scenarios, trainees are effectively placed in the midst of incidents, requiring them to respond to various threats and situations, many of which require them to draw or fire simulated firearms at the screen to protect themselves or others. The primary purpose of FATS scenarios is to test participants' judgment, including adherence to the Bureau's deadly force policy. FATS equipment also keeps track of shooters' reaction time and accuracy.

Practical Applications

Practical application exercises provide realistic, hands-on application of material covered in the classroom. In addition to focusing on skill development, these multidisciplinary exercises help trainees to build confidence, overcome obstacles, and learn how to work with others as a team. Most of these exercises—known as "practicals"—are conducted in the Hogan's Alley complex, where academics, firearms, defensive tactics, communications skills, and legal knowledge are collectively put to the test. Hogan's Alley consists of facades and buildings replicating a small town, including a bank, movie theater, drug store, post office, courthouse, used car lot, and other facilities. Behind the facades are fully functioning classrooms, audiovisual facilities, storage areas, and administrative and maintenance offices. The Practical Applications Unit presents 80 hours of practical instruction throughout the program.

Practical scenarios carried out in the Hogan's Alley complex focus primarily on surveillance techniques, arrest procedures, and tactical street survival skills. In these exercises, trainees are taken through realistic scenarios revolving around bank robberies, assaults, hostage situations, illegal drug transactions, kidnapping incidents, daytime and nighttime surveillance of criminal suspects, felony traffic stops, the execution of search and arrest warrants, and other situations. Through the Integrated Case Scenario, trainees conduct a criminal investigation throughout the program that culminates with the arrest of a number of suspects in Hogan's Alley. Some of these exercises require trainees to use guns that fire artificial bullets (containing soap or paint) in order to test their tactical skills. Bureau vehicles, two-way radios, surveillance devices, and other equipment are provided to scenario participants. To increase the level of realism, professional role-players confront the trainees with a variety of problems and situations.

Other practical exercises carried out within and beyond the Hogan's Alley complex focus on surveillance, driving, interviewing techniques, defensive tactics, firearms proficiency, and other law enforcement skills. For example, surveillance training is conducted on public streets and highways in cities such as Washington, D.C.; Richmond, Virginia; and in other areas. These daytime and nighttime scenarios require trainees to keep sight of suspects who are involved in various activities in vehicles and on foot, and to maintain proper radio communications with one another as a team. Trainees also complete the FBI's Tactical Emergency Vehicle Operators Course (TEVOC), in which they navigate obstacles, demonstrate defensive and evasive driving techniques, practice skid control, and display other emergency driving skills in different types of vehicles. Interviewing scenarios are carried out in a variety of settings, including rooms that are outfitted with video cameras. Instructors use videotapes of interviews to evaluate and discuss trainees' questioning and listening skills. Practical training also includes testifying on the witness stand during moot court exercises, during which actual lawyers question trainees about their roles during other training exercises.

Physical Training, Defensive Tactics, and Arrest Techniques

The physical training (PT), defensive tactics (DT), and arrest techniques segment is the third-largest block of instruction—and one of the most popular—accounting for 74 hours of the New Agent Training program. Fitness advisors, defensive tactics instructors, and nutrition experts from the Academy's Physical Training Unit present instruction in this unit. Health and fitness training focuses primarily on proper nutrition and the development of muscular strength, flexibility, endurance, agility, and aerobic capacity. Height, weight, and body fat levels are checked at the beginning, middle, and end of the program.

Physical training includes plenty of running, including the grueling "Yellow Brick Road" endurance and obstacle course that was depicted in the movie *The Silence of the Lambs*. To complete this challenging course, informally known as the "Hell Run," trainees must navigate a wooded trail and overcome log hurdles, a tall rope net structure, walls, roped cliffs, barbed wire, rough terrain, and other obstacles. Inspirational signs posted along the route—which is more than six miles long—include messages such as "hurt," "agony," "pain," "pride," "attitude," and "loyalty." The course got its name from the yellow bricks, inscribed with the class numbers from FBI National Academy, that serve as markers along the way.

Defensive tactics and arrest techniques training revolves around various kicks and strikes, arrest procedures, handcuffing techniques, subject control holds, pressure-point tactics, boxing, ground fighting, weapon retention and disarming techniques, searching of subjects, building entry principles, and other DT techniques. The use of oleoresin capsicum (OC) "pepper" spray is also covered; during practical exercises, the trainees must be able to make an arrest after being sprayed in the face with OC. Trainees must demonstrate their proficiency in these areas during two DT tests.

Supervision and Evaluation of New Agent Trainees

The New Agent Training program is overseen by supervisory special agents who serve as class supervisors, as well as special agents who serve as field counselors. Class supervisors are permanently assigned to the FBI Academy, whereas field counselors are detailed temporarily to the Academy from FBI field offices for 16 weeks. Field counselors play an important role by providing leadership and serving as mentors to trainees during their early development as special agents. Class supervisors and field counselors also carefully observe and evaluate trainees throughout the program to determine their suitability to perform as FBI special agents.

Requirements for Graduation

To graduate from the program, new agent trainees must pass academic and physical fitness tests, qualify with firearms, pass physical fitness and defensive tactics examinations, and otherwise demonstrate their suitability to serve as FBI special agents. Trainees must pass eight academic examinations (with a score of 85 percent or better) in the following disciplines:

- Law (two exams)

- Ethics

- White-collar crime

- National security matters

- Forensic evidence techniques

- Drugs, organized crime, and violent crime

- Communications

Trainees are given a physical training (PT) test during the first, seventh, and 14th weeks of training. This test consists of five events including push-ups, pull-ups, sit-ups, a 120-yard shuttle run, and a two-mile run. PT events are scored on a point system, with up to 10 points possible in each event. To pass the PT test, trainees must score at least one point in each event and at least 15 points total (out of a possible 50) on the test. The PT test not only measures physical fitness, but also provides an indication of trainees' commitment to improve their scores, which demonstrates attributes such as character, initiative, judgment, and maturity. To pass the firearms segment, you must qualify twice with a semiautomatic pistol and once with a shotgun and also demonstrate familiarity with a submachine gun. You must also pass two defensive tactics tests by demonstrating proficiency in various DT skills.

In addition to achieving passing scores in academics, physical fitness, firearms, and defensive tactics, trainees must also demonstrate adherence to the FBI's core values throughout the training program in order to graduate. In other words, test scores alone will not be sufficient if a trainee does not meet the Bureau's standards relating to character, integrity, fairness, and other related criteria. Character and suitability issues are evaluated constantly by class supervisors and field counselors, and also by the Academy's New Agent Review Board in cases where corrective action—including dismissal—is possible.

Professional Development Training for Special Agents

FBI special agents receive periodic professional development training, also known as *in-service training,* to acquire new skills and enhance their knowledge and capabilities throughout their careers. The nature of in-service training depends largely on the needs of individual agents, their responsibilities and special assignments, and the needs of the Bureau at any given time. In-service courses focus on topics such as leadership, management, supervision, ethics, counterterrorism, driving, information technology, and critical-incident stress counseling, among others. Many special agents who serve on special response teams and joint task forces also attend the Bureau's Law Enforcement Safety and Survival Course, which is commonly known as "street survival training."

Training for Special Response Teams

The Bureau's special response teams require specialized training to develop the particular knowledge and skills they need to succeed in their respective operations. Much of the training attended by team members is held at the FBI Academy, although other sources of training are utilized nationwide and in other countries. This section includes a brief overview of training that is provided to special response teams.

Scuba Team Training

Members of the FBI's scuba team are highly trained and experienced special agents who must maintain stringent physical fitness and watercraft skills that far exceed recreational diving standards. Many team members are scuba instructors. Ongoing training focuses on skills relating to underwater crime scene investigation, evidence collection, search and recovery operations, photography, searching for explosives, diving in varying degrees of currents, night diving, under-ice operations, deep-water diving, helicopter water entries, and diving in zero-visibility conditions. Scuba team members are also trained to use specialized equipment such as scuba regulators, dive computers, underwater scooters, metal detectors, sonar units, global positioning system (GPS) satellite navigation units, underwater communications systems, hand-held underwater video and still cameras, dive watches, wet and dry suits, and surface-supplied air systems.

Evidence Response Team Training

All members of the Bureau's evidence response teams (ERTs), which include special agents and support personnel, attend an 80-hour basic course that provides instruction in crime scene photography, evidence photography, latent fingerprint subjects, crime scene management and documentation, and general physical evidence recovery matters. After they have completed the basic course, ERT members are eligible to attend advanced courses covering topics such as recovery of human remains, blood-spatter analysis, and post-blast investigation techniques at bombing crime scenes. ERT training is presented by the FBI and other forensic experts.

Hazardous Materials Response Unit Training

Personnel assigned to the Hazardous Materials Response Unit are trained to safely and effectively respond to criminal acts and other incidents involving hazardous materials, including chemical, biological, and radiological materials. The Hazardous Materials Response Unit trains its personnel in areas such as terrorism, weapons of mass destruction, chemical agents, biological agents, nuclear devices and radiological weapons, hazardous materials regulations, hazardous materials labels, personal protective equipment, breathing devices, decontamination procedures, crime scene preservation and evidence collection, conventional explosives as weapons of mass destruction, downwind hazard analysis, planning for hazardous materials incidents, and the role of first responders. Training in these areas typically includes lectures, multimedia presentations, and practical exercises.

Hostage Rescue Team Training

FBI Hostage Rescue Team training begins with a rigorous two-week selection course, in which prospective team members are carefully evaluated to determine whether they possess the knowledge, skills, and abilities necessary for hostage rescue assignments. Once selected, team members attend a four-month initial training program at the FBI Academy that consists of highly specialized tactical law enforcement instruction. The primary subjects covered during this program and ongoing in-service training include hostage rescue fundamentals and planning, barricaded subject incidents, execution of high-risk arrest and search operations, firearms and defensive tactics, rappelling, weapons of mass destruction, maritime operations, helicopter operations, mobile assaults, and cold weather operations. When team members are not engaged in hostage rescue operations, they participate in full-time training at the FBI Academy and other locations. In order to be prepared for deployment to a wide range of climates and conditions, they also attend training at sites throughout the United States and its territories year-round.

Crisis Negotiation Unit Training

The FBI Crisis Negotiation Unit must be prepared and trained to respond immediately to crisis situations anywhere in the world, 24 hours a day, seven days a week. Initial training for the Bureau's negotiators includes a two-week negotiation course at the FBI Academy. Negotiators also participate in advanced and periodic update training at the FBI Academy, at other sites nationwide, and worldwide in cooperation with foreign law enforcement agencies. The Crisis Negotiation Unit has exchange programs in place through which it conducts training with British, Canadian, Australian, Israeli, German, and South African law enforcement agencies. Crisis negotiation training includes instruction in areas such as incident management, negotiation concepts and techniques, communication skills, behavioral sciences, abnormal psychology, crisis assessment and intervention, suicide intervention, active listening skills, coordination with tactical teams, terrorism, case studies in crisis negotiation, post-incident debriefing, and role-playing scenarios. FBI negotiators are also trained through computer-based simulation training programs that present realistic scenarios involving real-time negotiation dialogue and decision-making applications.

Special Weapons and Tactics Team Training

Special weapons and tactics (SWAT) training prepares FBI SWAT team members for the execution of high-risk arrest and search operations, drug raids, barricaded suspect incidents, sniper assaults, dignitary protection details, and other crisis situations and tactical operations. This training is conducted at the FBI Academy, in various FBI field offices, at law enforcement academies and agencies, and in other locations. To prepare for these incidents, FBI SWAT teams nationwide are trained in intelligence gathering, operational planning, command and control operations, communications, threat assessment methods, strength and conditioning, and legal issues. The teams also participate in ongoing practical training in areas such as building-entry and room-clearing techniques, containment techniques, arrest and subject-control tactics, diversionary techniques, rappelling, vehicle stops and assaults, weapons of mass destruction incidents, and tactical first aid. Weapons training carried out by SWAT team members includes subjects such as tactical firearms skills, low-light shooting techniques, cover and concealment principles, impact weapons, weapon retention, use of chemical agents, and countersniper issues.

Canine Team Training

FBI canine teams train year-round to develop and maintain the skills required of the dogs and dog handlers to perform their invaluable service for the Bureau. Canine teams attend training provided by state and local police departments; other federal law enforcement agencies; the U.S. Customs Canine Enforcement Training Center in Front Royal, Virginia; and organizations such as the North American Police Work Dog Association and the United States Police Canine Association. Training focuses primarily on the teams' particular areas of expertise, including the detection of explosives, explosives residues, firearms, marijuana, hashish, cocaine, methamphetamine, and heroin, as well as tracking fleeing criminals and locating missing persons and cadavers. Their training also is concentrated in areas such as animal obedience and behavior, search sequences and techniques, and the recovery and preservation of evidence.

Training for Professional Support Personnel

The FBI ensures that professional support personnel stay abreast of trends and developments in their respective areas of expertise through a variety of training programs. Unlike training for special agents, the majority of FBI personnel who serve in professional support positions do not attend lengthy introductory basic-training programs. Instead, those who are hired into entry-level jobs receive on-the-job training. Experienced employees attend periodic professional-development training.

Courses for support personnel are offered at the FBI Academy and various facilities nationwide, within mobile classrooms, through distance-learning applications such as Web-based programs and satellite teleconferences, through interactive video programs, and on CD-ROM. Many of the Bureau's distance-learning programs are created and produced by the FBI Training Network at the FBI Academy, which offers training to FBI personnel and law enforcement officers worldwide. The FBI Training Network is a component of the Academy's Technology Services Unit, which carries out broadcast and studio production operations from a television studio located in Hogan's Alley. The remainder of this chapter provides examples of training that is offered to the Bureau's professional support employees.

Biologist (Forensic Examiner) Training

Biologists/forensic examiners in the FBI Laboratory must successfully complete a combination of on-the-job and in-service training to be certified as FBI forensic examiners. Training for biologists is designed to expand their knowledge and skills relating to various scientific theories and principles, serological techniques, biochemical analysis, mitochondrial DNA analysis, preserving evidence, courtroom testimony, and other areas. Training topics might revolve around the identification of hair, bones, blood, saliva, and other biological samples. They also receive training that prepares them to use the latest technology, instruments, and equipment in the laboratory. Training might be presented by FBI staff, colleges and universities, and other organizations.

Chemist (Forensic Examiner) Training

Similar to that of FBI biologists, chemists/forensic examiners assigned to the FBI Laboratory attend a variety of professional seminars, workshops, and courses throughout their careers that focus on laboratory techniques and procedures utilized in the examination and analysis of evidence. These personnel must also complete training to be certified as FBI forensic examiners. In-service training for chemists/forensic examiners could focus on scientific techniques used to identify various chemicals, poisons, controlled substances, explosives residues, paints, petroleum products, and many other substances. They are also trained in the use and maintenance of scientific instruments, and also in various computer hardware and software that is used in chemical analyses.

Computer Specialist Training

The nature of training for FBI computer specialists depends mostly on their area of expertise. For example, members of the Bureau's Computer Analysis and Response teams could receive a wide range of specialized training concerning computer crimes and the search and seizure of computers, data recovery, information linking, and other computer forensic techniques. Depending on their responsibilities and areas of focus, computer specialists could also complete training relating to commercial and proprietary forensic tools, Internet investigations, software development, Web design, data networks, computer security, computer system maintenance and repair, and data management. Training for computer specialists is conducted by staff of the Computer Training Unit at the FBI Academy and also by various computer hardware and software manufacturers, private firms that specialize in various facets of information technology, colleges and universities, and law enforcement training academies.

Document Analyst (Forensic Examiner) Training

Newly hired FBI document analysts complete a two-year apprenticeship program that includes classroom training and actual document examinations under the guidance and evaluation of experienced FBI document analysts. Some of the classroom portions of the program can be shortened or modified for trainees who have prior experience in the field. In addition to subjects relating to the examination and analysis of handwriting, typewriting, shoeprints, and tire treads, document analyst trainees also participate in moot court exercises to qualify for certification as FBI forensic examiners. In-service training for these personnel includes courses and professional seminars that are presented by FBI staff, academic institutions, firms associated with the ink and paper industry, and related professional organizations. Instruction focuses on subjects such as ink and paper chemistry and dating procedures, various printing processes, laboratory techniques, and other aspects of forensic document examination.

Electronics Engineer Training

Professional development for electronics engineers covers a wide range of technologies. Depending on their expertise and area of specialty, electronics engineers receive ongoing in-service training that is geared to areas such as covert electronic and physical surveillance system design, countermeasures, telecommunications, audio and video system design, security systems, and other areas. Material covered in these training programs focuses on topics such as circuit configurations, alternating current and direct current, electronic circuit applications, circuit protection, switches and relays, semiconductors, project management, signal processing, and troubleshooting. Although the FBI conducts formal and on-the-job training in these and other areas for its personnel, electronics engineers can also take advantage of training that is offered by academic institutions and organizations such as the Institute of Electrical and Electronics Engineers.

Electronics Technician Training

FBI electronics technicians attend a variety of courses, seminars, and conferences throughout their careers that focus on the assembly, installation, disguising, application, maintenance, and repair of technical investigative equipment and other electronic devices the FBI uses. These programs are often geared to the design, modification, repair, testing, and troubleshooting of transmitters, audio and video equipment, radio and electronics systems used in FBI vehicles, as well as video equipment, transmitters, and covert electronic surveillance devices. Instruction could also focus on the development and advancement of new technical surveillance techniques, electronic audio and video surveillance devices, and other technical investigative equipment. Training is presented by the FBI, colleges and universities, and organizations that manufacture, sell, or service electronic devices and other equipment. Some of the training for electronics technicians is similar to programs attended by electronics engineers.

Evidence Technician Training

Most of the career development for FBI evidence technicians is provided by the FBI through on-the-job training in the areas of evidence handling and tracking procedures, chain-of-custody requirements, computer system hardware and software, Bureau policies and regulations, and other related topics. These personnel could also attend training offered by organizations such as the International Association of Chiefs of Police and the International Association for Property and Evidence. Material covered during formal classroom training could focus on evidence handling, documentation, inventory control, record-keeping, chain-of-custody issues, legal guidelines, civil liability, evidence packaging and shipping, evidence destruction, security practices, biohazards, and safety procedures. Evidence technicians who are members of the Bureau's evidence response teams also receive 80 hours of training to prepare them for their responsibilities with the team, such as instruction concerning evidence-collection techniques and preparing crime scene diagrams.

Financial Analyst Training

To enhance their knowledge and skills pertaining to white-collar crime and criminal investigations, FBI financial analysts might attend conferences and seminars that are conducted by organizations such as the Association of Certified Fraud Examiners, the International Association of Financial Crimes Investigators, and the United States Attorney's Office. Training these organizations present could focus on subjects such as forensic accounting and auditing techniques, criminal law, rules of evidence, white-collar crime investigation, health-care and insurance fraud, financial institution and securities fraud, interviewing techniques, fraud schemes, locating hidden assets, asset forfeiture, computer fraud, sources of information, contract and procurement fraud, and courtroom testimony.

Fingerprint Specialist Training

FBI fingerprint examiners attend an in-house training program that revolves around the examination and classification of fingerprints, fingerprint identification procedures, and FBI policies and procedures relating to fingerprint classification. They also complete a period of supervised on-the-job training and can attend courses, seminars, and conferences conducted by organizations such as the International Association for Identification or the American Academy of Forensic Sciences, academic institutions, and the FBI Academy. Fingerprint specialists assigned to the FBI disaster squad or evidence response teams also attend training programs to enhance their fingerprint identification skills and assist them in carrying out other responsibilities relating to these special assignments. For example, this training could focus on methods for obtaining fingerprints, palm prints, and footprints from deceased victims.

Intelligence Operations Specialist Training

Training for FBI intelligence operations specialists varies widely depending on the unit of assignment. For example, those who are assigned to the National Domestic Preparedness Office are likely to receive ongoing training concerning counterterrorism, weapons of mass destruction, and emergency preparedness. Similarly, intelligence research specialists who serve in the FBI National Security Division may receive training in areas such as counterintelligence, counterterrorism, theft of U.S. technology and sensitive economic information by foreign intelligence services, the Economic Espionage Act of 1996 and other pertinent laws, weapons of mass destruction, the national information infrastructure, and other national security issues. On the other hand, intelligence operations specialists assigned to the Bureau's Jewelry and Gem program could receive training relating to gemology, handling jewelry and gems, and other related subjects. As with other professional support personnel, these training programs could be sponsored by the FBI Academy, other government agencies, educational institutions, and various associations.

Intelligence Research Specialist Training

Basic initial training for newly appointed FBI intelligence research specialists includes courses, lectures, and seminars pertaining to criminal intelligence, foreign counterintelligence, counterterrorism, legal issues, basic analytical methodologies, and other related subjects. In-service training for these personnel includes conferences and courses presented by the FBI and organizations such as the International Association of Law Enforcement Intelligence Analysts. This training focuses on subjects such as Arab/Israeli conflict, liaison with foreign law enforcement and government agencies, the role of CIA analysts, hostage rescue operations, firearms and explosives, organized criminal enterprises, team building, behavioral science matters, communication skills, polygraph examination, computer databases, and FBI laboratory operations.

Investigative Specialist Training

Initial basic training for FBI investigative specialists consists of an eight-week course at the FBI Academy that covers fundamentals of surveillance, foreign counterintelligence, and defensive driving techniques. Basic and in-service training for investigative specialists is likely to concentrate on subjects such as foreign counterintelligence operations, national security issues, economic espionage, terrorism, and weapons of mass destruction. Depending on the nature of assignments and expertise of individual investigative specialists, instruction in surveillance methods could focus on surveillance planning, mobile and static surveillance techniques, foot surveillance, countersurveillance, observation skills, daytime and nighttime operations, urban and rural surveillance techniques, covert photography and video techniques, technical investigative equipment, radio communications, law enforcement computer databases, legal subjects, defensive tactics, and report writing.

Language Specialist Training

Training for FBI language specialists could vary widely depending on the languages spoken and level of expertise of individual personnel. In general, this training could focus on skill development relating to the translation of written and oral material from various foreign languages into English, listening skills, reading comprehension, vocabulary, translating testimony during court hearings and trials, and providing testimony in the courtroom concerning their translating activities. Language specialists who are members of the Bureau's evidence response teams also receive 80 hours of training pertaining to the operations of the team and their responsibilities. Similarly, those who are members of the FBI's counterterrorism squads or rapid deployment teams could also receive additional training in these areas.

Personnel Security Specialist Training

To ensure that FBI personnel security specialists have the tools they need to carry out their responsibilities, in-service and on-the-job training for these employees consists of instruction in areas such as agency personnel standards, security clearance eligibility requirements, position sensitivity and security suitability determinations, adverse personnel action and derogatory information, interviewing techniques, report writing, agency policies and procedures, and other subjects. To remain current in applicable laws and regulations, these personnel also receive ongoing legal updates. Personnel security specialists can attend courses presented by FBI staff; by various federal, state, or local law enforcement training programs or academies; by colleges or universities; and by other organizations.

Photographer Training

FBI photographers attend a wide range of training courses, seminars, and workshops throughout their careers to expand their knowledge and hone their skills. These programs focus on subjects such as crime scene and arson photography, flash photography, infrared photography, photographic surveillance equipment and techniques, night-vision photography, darkroom techniques, film processing, camera systems and meters, special films, lenses, photographic equipment maintenance, and other topics. Although the Bureau presents training to photographers at the FBI Academy, these personnel can also take advantage of training programs offered by other law enforcement training academies, colleges and universities, organizations such as the Evidence Photographers International Council, and various firms in the photographic industry. Photographers who are assigned to the Bureau's evidence response teams also receive 80 hours of training to prepare them for tasks they will perform with the team.

Physical Security Specialist Training

FBI physical security specialists attend a variety of in-service training programs depending on their areas of expertise, including nuclear security, explosive operations, security countermeasures, and other specialties. Generally speaking, training for personnel security specialists covers agency policies and directives and subjects such as intrusion-detection systems and devices, security awareness, access-control systems, physical-security surveys, crime prevention, terrorism, applicable laws and regulations, legal updates, investigative techniques, report writing, interviewing techniques, and other training topics that are geared to the responsibilities of individual specialists. Some of these training programs are presented by FBI staff, although others could be presented by law enforcement training programs or academies, academic institutions, and organizations such as the American Society for Industrial Security.

FBI Police Officer Training

Initial basic training for FBI police officers includes the nine-week Basic Police Training Program at the Federal Law Enforcement Training Center in Glynco, Georgia. Topics covered in this program include patrol procedures, emergency-response driving, high-risk vehicle stops, crowd control, hostage situations, critical-incident response, radio communications, legal subjects, crime scene preservation, interviewing techniques, courtroom testimony, report writing, narcotics, terrorism, and criminal intelligence. This program also includes instruction in firearms safety and marksmanship, bombs and explosives, self-defense, nonlethal control techniques, impact weapons control, physical conditioning, first aid and CPR, and many other law enforcement subjects. Ongoing in-service training covers a wide range of topics relating to patrol techniques, vehicle operation, weapons proficiency, response to emergency situations, law, and the development of other law enforcement skills.

CHAPTER 9

FBI Internship Programs

Success only breeds a new goal.

—*Bette Davis*

The FBI offers four internship programs that afford students a unique opportunity to enhance their educations and make practical application of classroom theory. The FBI Honors Internship, Presidential Management Internship, National Center for the Analysis of Violent Crime (NCAVC) Internship, and FBI Academy Internship enable participants to explore their career interests under actual working conditions and to make informed choices before moving into the workforce. FBI internships also provide students with hands-on experience and an exceptional resume builder, as well as an outstanding opportunity to showcase their skills, abilities, and potential to one of the most respected and sophisticated law enforcement agencies in the world. This experience could provide interns with the inside track when seeking employment with the FBI later, as well as a positive reference for those seeking careers with other agencies.

Presidential Management Interns and Honors Interns receive a salary, whereas interns serving the FBI Academy and the NCAVC are not paid. Although the FBI does not pay for housing expenses, Headquarters personnel provide interns with information and assistance in securing housing in the Washington, D.C., area.

The following sections describe each FBI internship in detail.

The FBI Honors Internship Program

Approximately 100 college undergraduate and graduate students are selected to participate each summer in the FBI Honors Internship Program in Washington, D.C. The program was started in 1985 to provide students with an overview of FBI operations and a chance to explore career opportunities within the Bureau. Honors interns work side-by-side with FBI special agents and professional support personnel on important cases and assignments. The program also enhances the FBI's visibility and recruitment efforts at colleges and universities nationwide. The Honors Internship Program, which is conducted only during the summer, begins in early June and ends in mid-August. Undergraduate honors interns are paid at the GS-6 grade level on the federal government pay scale (presently about $540 per week), whereas graduate honors interns are paid at the GS-7 grade level (about $600 per week).

Eligibility

To be considered, applicants must possess strong academic credentials, outstanding character, and a high degree of motivation. Minimum qualifications include the following:

- United States citizenship.

- A cumulative grade-point average of 3.0 or better.

- Undergraduate students should be enrolled in their junior year at the time they apply to the program.

- Graduate students must be attending a college or university on a full-time basis.

- Applicants must plan to return to their school campuses after participating in the program.

- Suitability under the FBI's Employment Drug Policy (see chapter 4).

The Application Process

The application process for honors internships is coordinated through the FBI field office nearest the school the applicant is attending. Interested students must complete and submit an FD-646a application form and other materials to be considered for honors intern positions. Applicants can obtain forms from any FBI field office. They must complete the application and provide the following information:

- An FD-646a Application Form

- An FD-804 Applicant Background Survey

- A current academic transcript

- A resume

- Two recent professional photographs

- A written letter of recommendation from the appropriate dean or department head

- A 500-word essay expressing interest in the program

The application process begins about one year prior to the start of the program. Here are the steps you should follow and the timeframe for doing so:

- **July to August:** Obtain an application package from the FBI field office nearest your campus. Request a letter of recommendation from your dean or department head. Obtain a copy of your current academic transcript.

- **August to September:** Complete your application, prepare your resume, write a 500-word essay, and obtain the letter of recommendation from your dean or department head.

- **September to October:** Review your Honors Internship brochure to ensure that you have obtained and completed all the necessary documents.

- **November:** Ensure that you have completed all application materials. Submit the application package to the FBI field office nearest your school campus by November 1.

The Selection Process

After applications have been received at each field office, FBI representatives from that field office will arrange interviews with competitive candidates. Not all candidates will be interviewed. Each field office then nominates a designated number of candidates to the Administrative Services Division at FBI Headquarters in Washington, D.C., by December 1. A selection committee at Headquarters then reviews application packages and selects finalists.

Appointments are made in the spring of each year, and are based on academic achievement, area of study, and both life and work experiences. Candidates who possess specific skills and educational backgrounds may be given special consideration, depending on the FBI's specific long-range needs. For example, the FBI is particularly interested in candidates with skills and education in areas such as engineering, computer science, foreign languages, political science, law, accounting, and the physical sciences. The FBI also actively seeks women and minorities for participation in the program. Appointments are contingent on the results of a background investigation, drug-screening test, polygraph examination, and fingerprinting.

Assignment

The Honors Internship Program normally starts on the first Monday in June, beginning with an orientation at FBI Headquarters. Interns are assigned to a Headquarters division based on their academic disciplines, potential contributions to the division, and the needs of the Bureau. Tasks that interns perform vary widely, depending on projects or initiatives underway at the time. The following are examples of tasks:

- Interns whose discipline is in the physical sciences may be assigned to the Forensic Science Research and Training Center at the FBI Laboratory, a component of the Training Division. There they could assist scientists in the development and validation of forensic technologies and procedures.

- In furtherance of the FBI's information technology strategies, the Information Resources Division could assign interns who possess exceptional computer skills to evaluate computer hardware and software or to participate in other projects that focus on the Bureau's collection, management, and use of information.

- Interns with a legal background may be assigned to the Office of General Counsel (OGC). In this office they could participate in legal research regarding law enforcement and national security matters, including the defense of civil litigation and administrative claims involving the FBI, its personnel, and its records.

- Accounting skills and education could land interns an assignment to a unit within the Financial Crimes Section. In this section, they could contribute to the investigation of health care fraud, public corruption, government fraud, environmental fraud, telemarketing fraud, or other offenses.

Interns work alongside special agents and professional support personnel under the supervision of the assistant director of their assigned division. Field trips to the FBI Academy and the Bureau's field offices are also common. The Honors Internship experience provides participants with a thorough understanding of the inner workings of the FBI, as well as an overview of various career opportunities within the Bureau.

Training

Training begins with an orientation at FBI Headquarters that focuses on internship rules and procedures. Interns receive progressive on-the-job training. About once a week, they attend executive briefings conducted by FBI division directors that focus on various aspects of Bureau operations. FBI personnel and representatives of other agencies also provide instruction at Headquarters and the FBI Academy throughout the internship experience. Additional training is provided through field trips to the Washington, D.C., Field Office and other facilities. Interns also receive firearms training, including instruction in safety procedures, familiarization with various firearms, target practice, and other live-fire scenarios. The nature of other training depends on the functions and current activities of the unit to which interns are assigned.

The Presidential Management Internship Program

President Carter established the Presidential Management Intern (PMI) Program in 1977 to attract graduate students from various academic disciplines who are interested in careers in federal government. PMIs receive an initial two-year full-time excepted-service appointment, after which they are eligible for conversion to a permanent federal government position. The PMI program is a government-wide undertaking administered by the U.S. Office of Personnel Management (OPM). Although PMIs are ultimately hired by individual agencies for their two-year appointments, OPM conducts the nomination and selection process.

The FBI has participated in the program since 1990, through which it has hired dozens of interns for placement in various divisions of the Bureau. These interns participate in training provided by the FBI and other government agencies, as well as executive briefings by senior-level FBI and Department of Justice management, including the attorney general. Their duties might also include field trips to the FBI Academy and various FBI field offices, special tours of FBI Headquarters, temporary assignments to other federal agencies, and international travel.

PMIs are hired at the GS-9 grade level, which presently is about $38,000 per year. After successfully completing the first year, PMIs are eligible for promotion to GS-11, which is about $46,000 per year. As employees of the federal government, they also earn annual leave and sick leave, paid federal holidays, and coverage under the Federal Employees Retirement System. They are also eligible to participate in the Thrift Savings Plan and to obtain life insurance and health insurance coverage. As an added benefit, PMIs are also provided full access to the gym and workout facilities at FBI Headquarters.

Many of the permanent positions offered to PMIs who have completed the internship extend to the GS-14 level, providing substantial future promotional potential.

Divisions That Presently Employ PMIs

The FBI has sought PMIs with diverse backgrounds ranging from international relations, to budget and program management, to cyber and computer technology. This diversity has enabled PMIs to contribute to the goals and mission of the FBI and other agencies in the U.S. intelligence community. FBI divisions that presently utilize PMIs include the Counterterrorism Division, the Finance Division, the Investigative Services Division, and the Office of Public and Congressional Affairs. Positions within these divisions are located at FBI Headquarters in Washington, D.C. The following sections provide overviews of each of these divisions.

Counterterrorism Division

All FBI counterterrorism initiatives are consolidated under the Counterterrorism Division, which includes the National Infrastructure Protection Center (NIPC) and the National Domestic Preparedness Office (NDPO). The NIPC serves as the government's focal point for threat assessment, warning, investigation, and response for threats or attacks against the United States. The NDPO coordinates all federal efforts to assist state and local first responders with planning, training, and equipment needs necessary to respond to an incident involving conventional or nonconventional weapons of mass destruction. The FBI shifted additional resources to the Counterterrorism Division following the September 11, 2001, terrorist attacks on the World Trade Center and the Pentagon, which could lead to appointment of additional PMIs in this division.

Finance Division

The Finance Division manages FBI budget and accounting matters, the strategic planning process, voucher and payroll functions, the procurement process, the forfeiture and seized property process, property management, automotive management, and relocation and transportation services. This division also carries out competition advocacy functions to ensure fair and open competition in the Bureau's contracting and procurement processes. Provisions of the Chief Financial Officer Act of 1990 are also overseen by the Finance Division, which includes preparation and auditing of the Bureau's financial statements, overall financial management of FBI operations in accordance with the act, and other responsibilities.

Investigative Services Division

The FBI's analytical capabilities, international programs, language services, and crisis-management functions are coordinated by the Investigative Services Division (ISD). The ISD Intelligence Branch works closely with the National Security, Criminal Investigative, and Counterterrorism Operational Divisions to provide analytical support to FBI investigations and to extract information from case files and other intelligence community sources to identify future trends and means of preventing crime and threats to national security.

Office of Public and Congressional Affairs (OPCA)

The OPCA communicates information on FBI investigations, services, programs, policy, and accomplishments to the public, Congress, and the media. It manages relations with the electronic and print media; prepares FBI speeches, reports, and publications; answers verbal and written inquiries from the general public, scholars, and authors regarding the FBI; oversees the FBI's prepublication review process; manages all liaison with and inquiries from Congress; oversees the FBI's fugitive publicity program, including the "Ten Most Wanted" program; manages the FBI's Web site; and operates the Headquarters tour.

The PMI Career Path

Although PMIs represent only a small segment of the Bureau's professional workforce, their contributions have been substantial. Once appointed, PMIs must serve a two-year probation period, which is the duration of the internship. After two years, PMIs are eligible for conversion to career employment status. Retention of PMIs is high, and the majority of PMIs that convert to permanent positions remain with the Bureau. The FBI encourages career development for PMIs, and several PMIs have achieved management positions within the FBI and other federal agencies. Any PMI who is interested in becoming an FBI special agent must apply through the standard special agent application process.

Eligibility

To be eligible for the PMI Program, you must be a graduate student completing or expecting to complete a master's or doctorate degree from an accredited college or university during the current academic year. No particular grade-point average is required, although school officials establish competitive campus nominating processes to ensure that the best candidates from their programs are nominated. The FBI seeks PMI candidates who have excellent writing skills, critical thinking abilities, and a commitment to public service.

Students from a wide variety of academic disciplines are encouraged to apply, although candidates must have a clear interest in, and a commitment to, a career in the analysis and management of public policies and programs. The majority of previous PMIs have had no prior experience in law enforcement or intelligence. Like all FBI applicants, those applying for PMI positions must meet the criteria of the Bureau's Employment Drug Policy (see chapter 4) and must be U.S. citizens.

The Application and Selection Process

Selection as a PMI finalist is based on nomination, interviews, review of information provided in the written application, and a one-day structured assessment center process that focuses on oral and written communication skills. The length of the application process typically ranges from nine to twelve months from submission of the application to appointment, although it can take up to 14 months. Those who want to apply for PMI positions with more than one FBI unit must contact each unit for instructions because individual units might conduct the hiring process differently.

The basic stages in the PMI hiring process are outlined in the following sections.

Nomination

PMI candidates must be nominated by the appropriate dean, director, or chairperson of their graduate academic program. Nominations from individual professors, advisors, or placement counselors will not be accepted. Once nominated, PMI candidates compete nationwide with other eligible graduate-level students.

PMI Application Materials

Candidates must submit a written application to OPM, along with nomination materials completed by the school. Applications are available from OPM in September and must be postmarked by October 31.

Assessment Center Process

All nominees who meet minimum qualification standards are invited to participate in a one-day assessment center process that is held in January or February. The process is made up of three segments, including a group discussion, an oral presentation by the nominee, and a written exercise. OPM notifies those selected as finalists in March.

Interviews and Initial Selection

After they receive information relating to finalists from OPM, the Bureau invites competitive candidates to personal interviews at FBI Headquarters. Interview format may vary from one section to another. Some sections hiring PMIs might conduct informal interviews with the unit chief or supervisor, whereas others might convene formal panel interviews.

FBI Application Materials

Applicants who pass the initial interview are invited to submit a written application to the FBI. Background screening, which is the next phase in the application process, cannot begin until the applicant has filled out the written application completely and returned it to the Bureau. Each applicant is assigned a local applicant coordinator in his geographic area. Applicant coordinators inform candidates of their status in the application process and describe related personnel procedures.

Initial Background Screening

After applications have been received and processed, candidates are eligible to receive a conditional offer of PMI employment by the FBI, which is contingent on successful completion of a full background investigation. Those who accept the conditional offer of employment are scheduled for a polygraph examination, urinalysis drug screening, and fingerprinting.

Full Background Investigation

During the background investigation, investigators contact former and current employers, references, social acquaintances, and neighbors. They also review school, credit, arrest, medical, and military records, and possibly other records. The completed background investigation is assessed at FBI Headquarters before a final decision is made to offer employment. All applicants are informed of the outcome of their investigation in writing. Like all FBI employees, PMIs receive a Top Secret clearance.

Enter on Duty

Upon successful completion of the full background investigation, candidates are extended a formal offer of employment, or appointment, and are assigned an enter-on-duty (EOD) date. As a general rule, PMIs are appointed about four to six months after submitting their initial applications to the FBI. When they report for duty on their EOD date, newly hired PMIs receive two days of employment processing and orientation before reporting to their assigned units.

Assignment

As with other FBI internships, assignments vary widely according to the skills, education, and career goals of individual interns, as well as the projects or initiatives underway with various Headquarters divisions and units at the time. Here are some examples of possible assignments:

- PMIs with accounting backgrounds could be assigned to the Finance Division, where their responsibilities would revolve around the coordination and administration of the FBI's budgetary and fiscal matters, financial planning, voucher and payroll matters, and property and procurement activities.

- The Counterterrorism Division might utilize PMIs for support of FBI counterterrorism initiatives, which could include activities with the National Infrastructure Protection Center or the National Domestic Preparedness Office. Responsibilities within this division could revolve around terrorism threat assessment and investigation, as well as planning and training relating to incidents involving weapons of mass destruction.

- PMIs assigned to the National Security Division might have responsibilities associated with foreign counterintelligence, including tasks in support of investigations involving espionage, overseas homicide, protection of foreign officials and guests, domestic security, and nuclear extortion. Interns might also be involved in activities relating to the FBI Security Countermeasures Program, which focuses on background investigations and physical security issues.

In the past, many PMIs have visited other FBI field offices, and some have traveled internationally. Many PMIs have also had opportunities to participate in projects at agencies and departments such as the Central Intelligence Agency, Defense Intelligence Agency, Department of Energy, and Department of State, among others.

Training

Training and career development are fundamental components of the PMI Program, and the FBI is committed to assisting and training PMIs to develop the skills necessary to perform at the highest level of competence. The FBI offers its PMI employees at least 80 hours of training each year. Training begins with a three-day Orientation Training Program, conducted by OPM, which provides an overall perspective on how the federal government operates.

Throughout the internship, PMIs attend courses at the FBI Academy, as well as training conducted by other agencies in the U.S. intelligence community, various law enforcement organizations, the U.S. Department of State, other federal agencies, and commercial vendors. PMIs also receive continuous on-the-job training and participate in other developmental opportunities such as seminars, briefings, and conferences. The content of the training is tailored to the specific learning objectives that will qualify the PMI for the target position at the end of the internship. The FBI works with each intern to develop a written outline of core competencies and technical skills the intern must gain before conversion to a target position.

The NCAVC Internship Program

The FBI's National Center for the Analysis of Violent Crime (NCAVC) offers full-time unpaid internships to undergraduate and graduate students. These are offered twice each year, starting either the last week in August or the second week in January. These internships last 14 to 16 weeks.

The NCAVC was established in 1984 at the FBI National Academy in Quantico, Virginia, and originally concentrated on unsolved murder cases. Four years later, although the NCAVC already had an outstanding reputation in the law enforcement community, the Thomas Harris book *Silence of the Lambs* brought worldwide attention to the unit. As a component of the FBI's Critical Incident Response Group, the NCAVC provides investigative support to law enforcement agencies around the world in crimes such as serial murder, child abduction or exploitation, bombing, arson, threats, serial rape, and public corruption. Services the NCAVC provides include profiles of unknown offenders, crime analysis, investigative strategies, interview and interrogation strategies, trial preparation and prosecutive strategies, expert testimony, and coordination of other resources. The NCAVC also conducts research and provides training regarding high-risk, bizarre, or repetitive violent crimes.

Eligibility

Undergraduate applicants must be at least a college junior with a minimum grade-point average of 3.0 and must have student status during the internship. Undergraduate seniors and graduate students are preferred. Students may be studying any discipline, although the most relevant majors are psychology, sociology, criminology, criminal justice, forensic science, and law. Additional requirements include excellent writing skills, analytical abilities, computer skills, and U.S. citizenship.

The Application and Selection Process

As with other FBI internships, the NCAVC requires applicants to submit forms and other documents prior to established deadlines, to participate in a personal interview, and to undergo a background investigation. This section provides a list of application materials you must submit to be considered for an NCAVC internship position and an overview of the application process.

Application Materials

Students who are interested in these internships must submit the following materials directly to the NCAVC:

- A completed SF-86, "Questionnaire for National Security Positions"

- A resume

- An essay indicating background, interests, goals, and reasons for wanting to participate in the internship

- Two letters of recommendation, including at least one from a department faculty member

- Transcripts of credits earned at all colleges attended

- A copy of a college term paper written by the applicant

- A statement from a school official confirming that the applicant is in good standing and identifying a contact person or internship sponsor

Application Deadlines

Application materials for NCAVC internships must be submitted 10 months in advance. Applications for internships starting in September must be submitted by November 1. Applications for internships starting in January must be submitted by March 1.

Interviews

Finalists must participate in a personal interview at the NCAVC offices near Quantico, Virginia, and must travel to the interview at their own expense.

Background Investigation

Selection is contingent on passing a background investigation, which includes a review of school, credit, arrest, medical, and military records, and contact with current and former employers, references, social acquaintances, and neighbors. Applicants must qualify under other FBI employee standards, including policy regarding the use of illegal drugs, and must also pass a polygraph and drug-screening test.

Assignment

Duties vary with the needs of the NCAVC and the skills of the student. Generally assignments involve obtaining criminal case materials, reviewing case files and coding case information, assisting in the analysis and reporting of research data, developing and extending resource materials for the NCAVC, or assisting in the creation of timelines on offenders. Interns also conduct literature reviews; observe case consultations; audit classes taught to FBI special agents, support staff, and other law enforcement personnel; and occasionally perform clerical tasks. Some interns have had the opportunity to author or coauthor articles for publication in the *FBI Law Enforcement Bulletin* and scientific or academic journals.

Training

The NCAVC provides interns with a range of training instruction, including a variety of courses, seminars, and symposia, as well as continuous on-the-job training. About once per week, interns attend two-hour lectures conducted by NCAVC staff, FBI Academy instructors, directors of various FBI divisions, or other trainers. Training typically focuses on the behavioral sciences and subjects such as victimology, threat analysis, stalking, unusual or repetitive violent crimes, child abduction and other crimes against children, sexual assault, serial murder, evidence collection, DNA analysis, and terrorism, among other topics. Training is augmented by field trips to other government agencies and facilities such as hospitals, crime laboratories, and medical examiner offices.

The FBI Academy Internship Program

The Bureau also operates an unpaid internship program at the FBI Academy for college students. These full-time internships are offered twice a year to undergraduate and graduate students and are open to applicants studying a variety of academic disciplines. Like the NCAVC internship program, FBI Academy internships start either the last week in August or the second week in January and last 14 to 16 weeks. These unique internships provide experience with one of the world's premier institutions of higher learning, where FBI personnel and other members of the law enforcement community receive state-of-the-art training.

Eligibility

The FBI Academy seeks interns majoring in accounting, adult education, behavioral sciences, hotel management, human resource management, communications, interviewing and interrogations, and media and television production, among other majors. Academic disciplines sought by the FBI might change periodically depending on the needs of the Bureau at any given time. Undergraduate applicants must be at least a college junior with a minimum grade-point average of 3.0. Undergraduate seniors and graduate students are preferred. Excellent writing skills, analytical abilities, and computer proficiency are also required. Applicants must be U.S. citizens and at least 18 years of age.

The Application and Selection Process

FBI Academy internship application and selection procedures are nearly identical to those of the NCAVC internship. The following section provides a summary of the process.

Application Materials

Internship candidates must submit the following application materials directly to the FBI Academy:

- A completed SF-86, "Questionnaire for National Security Positions"

- A resume

- An essay indicating background, interests, goals, and reasons for wanting to participate in the internship program

- Two letters of recommendation, including at least one from a department faculty member

- Transcripts of credits earned at all colleges attended

- A copy of a college term paper written by the applicant

Application Deadlines

Candidates must submit all application materials about 10 months in advance. Applications for internships starting in August must be submitted by November 1. Applications for internships starting in January must be submitted by March 1.

Interviews

Internship finalists will be interviewed at the FBI Academy in Quantico, Virginia. Applicants must travel at their own expense for the interview.

Background Investigation

Selection is contingent on passing a full background investigation. Applicants must qualify under other FBI employee standards, including policy regarding the use of illegal drugs. They must also pass a polygraph and drug-screening test.

Assignment

Individual training units assign duties and responsibilities depending on the background and education of the intern and the current needs and activities of the unit to which they are assigned. Responsibilities frequently involve research, curriculum development, and updating work projects. The internship experience usually is geared to the student's educational endeavors. Some examples of assignments follow:

- Interns with computer proficiency might be assigned to the Computer Training Unit, where they could be involved in curriculum-development projects relating to computer crime, using computers as an investigative tool, computer fraud, search and seizure of computers, white-collar crime, and Internet investigations. These interns could also perform tasks associated with the creation or improvement of the unit's computer databases.

- The Behavioral Science Unit could assign interns to assist with the development of training programs and research in the behavioral and social sciences, including areas such as criminal psychology, forensic psychology, community policing, crime analysis, death investigation, gangs and gang behavior, interpersonal violence, law enforcement officers killed and assaulted in the line of duty, and stress management in law enforcement.

- Interns in the Technology Services Unit might provide support to the broadcast television studio, where they could assist with the production of video training materials presented in the New Agent and National Academy training programs; to domestic and international law enforcement training programs; and to in-service personnel at FBI field offices.

Interns typically visit other units and groups to observe their activities and gain an overall perspective of academy operations.

Training

Academy interns have many opportunities to participate in formal and on-the-job training. The nature of training provided depends mostly on the unit interns are assigned to. Training might include seminars or conferences at the academy; auditing courses attended by upper and mid-level law enforcement officers in the FBI National Academy Program; observation of firearms, defensive tactics, or other practical training in the New Agent Training program; and on-the-job training geared to the specific functions of individual units and the intern's career aspirations.

PART 3

APPENDIXES

APPENDIX A

Application Checklist for the Special Agent Position (FD-869)

The Application Checklist for the Special Agent Position is a five-page form that lists specific qualifications that applicants must be willing and able to meet. This form also lists "automatic disqualifiers" that will exclude applicants from consideration for FBI employment, several statements about the hiring process that applicants must be aware of, and a long list of job requirements. You must sign and date the application checklist to certify that you are providing truthful information and fill in your Social Security number.

Special agent candidates submit the FD-869 along with the Preliminary Application for Special Agent Position (FD-646), Special Agent Qualifications Questionnaire (FD-843), and Applicant Background Survey (FD-804). The purpose of this form is twofold. First, it provides the FBI with an assurance from applicants that they fully understand the requirements for the special agent position and what is involved in the application and testing process. Second, the form serves as a method of screening out applicants who do not meet minimum qualifications or would be disqualified as a result of their criminal records, drug use, failure to register for selective service, or for other reasons.

It is important to answer the questions truthfully and accurately because misrepresentations can result in disqualification from the hiring process or in termination of employment in cases where misrepresentations are discovered after hiring.

FD-869 (8-26-97)

Application Checklist for the Special Agent Position

Date _____

Name _____   SSAN _____

      (First)   (Middle)   (Last)

FBI Processing Office _____

Listed below are specific qualifications that you must be willing and able to meet, with or without reasonable accommodations in accordance with the Rehabilitation Act of 1973 and Americans with Disabilities Act of 1990 (ADA), in order to be eligible for the Special Agent position. Please read the following minimum qualifications and indicate your response by answering **Yes** or **No** to each item and place your initials next to each response. By initialing, you verify that you have received and understand the information about the Special Agent job and application process. If you do **not** understand **any** of the items listed, or are in need of a reasonable accommodation during this process, please contact your Applicant Coordinator or Special Agent Recruiter and refer to the Applicant Information Booklet for clarification or assistance prior to completing this form.

Section 1 - Minimum Qualifications

I confirm that as a Special Agent candidate:

		Yes	No	Initials
1.	I am a United States citizen.	☐	☐	_____
2.	I am at least age 23. I understand that if I reach age 37 prior to the time of appointment to the FBI Academy I will be disqualified from the applicant process.	☐	☐	_____
3.	I possess a valid driver's license.	☐	☐	_____
4.	I have a four-year degree or an advanced degree from a resident college/university certified by one of the six Regional Accreditation Associations.	☐	☐	_____
5.	**(Those with No degree in Law or Accounting, or No fluency in a foreign language)** Possess a four-year degree plus three years of full-time work experience **Or** possess an advanced degree plus two years of full-time work experience (as defined by my employer), excluding internships, co-operatives, summer or temporary employment.	☐	☐	_____
6.	I am completely available for assignment anywhere in the FBI's jurisdiction (The United States and Puerto Rico) at any time during my tenure with the FBI.	☐	☐	_____
7.	I have discussed my potential transfer with my spouse, significant other, and/or family. They know that I must be willing to relocate as a requirement of the Special Agent position.	☐	☐	_____
8.	I am willing and able to engage in strenuous and potentially dangerous duties to include, but not limited to, the use of **firearms**, participation in raids, arrests and/or the use of defensive tactics.	☐	☐	_____

	Yes	No	Initials
9. I am willing to undergo a comprehensive background investigation, including contacts with all references, employers, co-workers, close personal associates, etc., and review of my driving record, credit history, criminal history, and service in the military, as well as undergo a pre-employment polygraph, physical examination, a urinalysis drug test.	☐	☐	_____

Section 2 - Automatic Disqualifiers

The conditions listed below are **disqualifiers** for the Special Agent position. Please respond honestly to the following questions:

	Yes	No	Initials
10. I am aware that refusal to submit to a FBI urinalysis (drug testing) or polygraph examination is grounds for disqualification from the Special Agent applicant process.	☐	☐	_____

Have you ever:

	Yes	No	Initials
11. Been convicted of a felony charge?	☐	☐	_____
12. Defaulted on a student loan (insured by U.S. Government)?	☐	☐	_____
13. Used marijuana in the past 3 years?	☐	☐	_____
14. Used marijuana more than 15 times in your life?	☐	☐	_____
15. Used any other illegal drug (including the use of anabolic steroids after February 27, 1991) in the past 10 years?	☐	☐	_____
16. Used any other illegal drug (including the use of anabolic steroids after February 27, 1991) more than 5 times in your life?	☐	☐	_____
17. Sold an illegal drug at any time in your life?	☐	☐	_____
18. Engaged in the unauthorized usage of any illegal drug while employed in a position of public trust (e.g., a sworn Law Enforcement Officer, etc.)?	☐	☐	_____
19. Failed to register for selective service, if required?	☐	☐	_____
20. Omitted, mis-stated, or falsely stated any information, in writing or orally, to the FBI during the course of the application process?	☐	☐	_____

Section 3 - Application and Testing Process

	Yes	No	Initials
21. I have received and read the Applicant Information Booklet for the Special Agent position.	☐	☐	_____
22. I understand that I must fully and accurately complete all application forms for employment. Failure to do so will result in the delay or discontinuation of my application processing.	☐	☐	_____

		Yes	No	Initials
23.	I will follow all instructions provided to me during the testing sessions and hiring process.	☐	☐	_____
24.	I understand that I will receive only a "pass" or "fail" as a result of the Phase I test battery and the Phase II interview and written exercise. I understand that due to the high volume of applicants, FBI policy, and fair employment practices at the FBI, numerical test scores, cut scores, areas of deficiency or strength, percentiles, etc., will **not** be provided to me.	☐	☐	_____
25.	I understand that during the final stages of the hiring process, placement on a New Agent's Class list is **tentative.** A hiring decision is conditional upon the successful resolution of any outstanding inquires or issues.	☐	☐	_____
26.	I understand that I must successfully complete a 1.5 mile run within the established time frame.	☐	☐	_____
27.	I understand that prior to being placed in New Agents Training, I must meet the established height, weight, and body fat standards.	☐	☐	_____
28.	I understand that my appointment as a Special Agent is conditional and subject to budgetary limitations and authorized positions.	☐	☐	_____

Section 4– Job Requirements

The following are some **required and potentially difficult** aspects of the Special Agent position. You must be both **willing** and **able**, with or without reasonable accommodation (in accordance with the Rehabilitation Act of 1973 and Americans with Disabilities Act of 1990), to perform these aspects of the job in order to be considered for this position. Please read the following job requirements and indicate your response by answering **Yes** or **No** to each item and place your initials next to each response.

I am aware that as a Special Agent, I will be required to :

29.	Be available for FBI employment within 90 days of Phase II testing. Applicants may be required to accept no more than a two week notice to report to New Agent Training upon successful completion of the applicant process. Failure to do may result in disqualification for future consideration.	☐	☐	_____
30.	**(Active Duty Military Only in lieu of #29 above)** Provide a copy of my request to process out of the military upon successful completion of the polygraph examination. Further, I will accept a two-week notice to report to New Agent Training within two weeks of the date of any military discharge papers. I acknowledge that it is my choice to process out of the military, whether or not I am hired by the FBI.	☐	☐	_____
31.	If in military reserve, resign or be eligible to transfer to standby reserve status. Special Agents occupy "Key Federal Employee" positions and therefore may not be members of, or rejoin during FBI employment, military Ready Reserve units.	☐	☐	_____

		Yes	No	Initials
32.	Successfully complete New Agent Training at the FBI Academy in Quantico, Virginia for 16 weeks which includes physical fitness, firearms, defensive tactics, academics, practical exercises, self-study, and teamwork.	☐	☐	_____
33.	Successfully complete a two-year probationary period as a New Special Agent.	☐	☐	_____
34.	Commit to serving the FBI as a Special Agent for three years.	☐	☐	_____
35.	Drive a car.	☐	☐	_____
36.	Guard and defend myself and others in dangerous and unpredictable situations such as being physically assaulted or fired upon with gun fire (Personal safety may sometimes be in jeopardy).	☐	☐	_____
37.	Pursue and apprehend violators of the law (offenders may be unwilling to be detained and could be violent).	☐	☐	_____
38.	Use physical and/or deadly force if necessary.	☐	☐	_____
39.	Routinely carry firearms and **use** them, as appropriate, in a variety of life-threatening situations.	☐	☐	_____
40.	Maintain proficiency with FBI firearms.	☐	☐	_____
41.	Be assigned to any area within the FBI's jurisdiction (United States and Puerto Rico) in order to meet FBI needs on a temporary or permanent basis.	☐	☐	_____
42.	Maintain physical conditioning/fitness training required to perform duties (e.g., raids, arrests, firearms), to include exercises during training at the FBI Academy such as pull-ups, push-ups, sit-ups, two-mile run, shuttle run/sprint, and defensive tactics.	☐	☐	_____
43.	Be available at all times to meet the needs of the FBI, including, weekends holidays, and cancellation of scheduled vacations.	☐	☐	_____
44.	Work an average of 10 hours per day. Work overtime or work an irregular schedule as required.	☐	☐	_____
45.	Witness heinous crimes or crime scenes.	☐	☐	_____
46.	Talk to victims of crime, their family or friends.	☐	☐	_____
47.	Accept a starting salary of mid-$30,000s per year during the 16 weeks of training at the FBI Academy, and mid-$40,000s (not including locality pay, prior federal service credit, availability pay, etc.) upon successful completion of the FBI Academy.	☐	☐	_____

	Yes	No	Initials

I understand that:

48.   If I am hired, there will be at least a two week delay in the effective date of my medical coverage if I enroll as a new Federal employee in the Federal Employee Health Benefits program.   ☐ ☐ _____

49.   Federal law requires Special Agents to retire at the age of 57.   ☐ ☐ _____

Please read the following statement and sign in the area below.

Warning: Any intentional false statement in this document or willful misrepresentation will result in disqualification from the Special Agent position. If the misrepresentation is discovered after hiring, you may be subject to inquiry and suitable administrative or disciplinary action up to and including dismissal.

I hereby acknowledge that I have read this document entitled "Application Checklist for the Special Agent position," and to the best of my knowledge and belief, the declarations made by me on this form are true. I understand that it is my responsibility to request any reasonable accommodations under the Americans with Disabilities Act and Rehabilitation Act of 1973 which I require to complete the application, testing, or hiring process.

Applicant's Signature _____ Date _____

Applicant's Social Security Number_____

Applicant Coordinator's or SA Recruiter's Signature _____

Field Office_____ Date_____

APPENDIX B

Preliminary Application for Special Agent Position (FD-646)

In addition to requesting name, address, and telephone number information, the Preliminary Application for Special Agent Position asks for biographical information relating to your citizenship, military service, arrest record, employment history over the previous three years, educational background, foreign-language skills, and prior drug use. The preliminary application also asks whether you are a certified public accountant (CPA) and if you are a licensed driver. As with the Application Checklist for the Special Agent Position (FD-869), this form requires you to certify that you are willing to accept an initial assignment anywhere in the United States.

As the title of this form suggests, the preliminary application is submitted at the beginning of the hiring process along with the Application Checklist for the Special Agent Position, Special Agent Qualifications Questionnaire, and Applicant Background Survey. Like the application checklist, this form is used to determine whether minimum qualification standards for the special agent position have been met, although it provides the FBI with greater detail than the checklist. The preliminary application is a tool the FBI uses to eliminate applicants who do not meet minimum requirements, and also to identify the most competitive applicants.

As with other application forms, the preliminary application must be filled out as accurately as possible and your statements must be truthful. In fact, this form points out not only that withholding information or making false statements can lead to dismissal from the FBI, but also that you could be prosecuted criminally for doing so.

FEDERAL BUREAU OF INVESTIGATION

**Preliminary Application for
Special Agent Position
(Please Type or Print in Black Ink)**

Date: _____

FIELD OFFICE USE ONLY
Right Thumb Print
Div: Program:

I. PERSONAL HISTORY

Name in Full (Last, First, Middle)	List College Degree(s) Already Received or Pursuing, Major, School, and Month/Year:

Marital Status: ☐ Single ☐ Engaged ☐ Married ☐ Separated ☐ Legally Separated ☐ Widowed ☐ Divorced

Birth Date (Month, Day, Year)
Birth Place:

Social Security Number: (Optional)

Do you understand FBI employment requires availability for assignment anywhere in the U.S.?

Current Address

Street   Apt. No.

City   State   Zip Code

Home Phone _____

Area Code   Number

Work Phone _____

Area Code   Number

Are you: CPA ☐ Yes ☐ No   Licensed Driver ☐ Yes ☐ No   U. S. Citizen ☐ Yes ☐ No

Have you served on active duty in the U. S. Military? ☐ Yes ☐ No If yes, indicate branch of service and dates (month/year) of active duty. Include military school attendance (month/year):

How did you learn or become interested in FBI employment as a Special Agent?

Have you previously applied for FBI employment? ☐ Yes ☐ No
If yes, location and date:

Do you have a foreign language background? ☐ Yes ☐ No List proficiency for each language on reverse side.

Have you ever been arrested for any crime (include major traffic violations such as Driving Under the Influence or While Intoxicated, etc.)?
☐ Yes ☐ No If so, list all such matters on a continuation sheet, even if not formally charged, or no court appearance or found not guilty, or matter settled by payment of fine or forfeiture of collateral. Include date, place, charge, disposition, details, and police agency on reverse side.

II. EMPLOYMENT HISTORY

Identify your most recent three years FULL-TIME work experience, after high school (excluding summer, part-time and temporary employment).

From Month/Year	To Month/Year	Title of Position and Description of Work	# of hrs. Per week	Name/Location of Employer

III. PERSONAL DECLARATIONS

Persons with a disability who require an accommodation to complete the application process are required to notify the FBI of their need for the accommodation.

Have you used marijuana during the last three years or more than 15 times? ☐ Yes ☐ No

Have you used any illegal drug(s) or combination of illegal drugs, other than marijuana, more than 5 times or during the last 10 years? ☐ Yes ☐ No

All Information provided by applicants concerning their drug history will be subject to verification by a preemployment polygraph examination.

Do you understand all prospective FBI employees will be required to submit to an urinalysis for drug abuse prior to employment? ☐ Yes ☐ No

Please do not write below this line.

I am aware that willfully withholding information or making false statements on this application constitutes a violation of Section 1001. Title 18, U.S. Code and if appointed, will be the basis for dismissal from the Federal Bureau of Investigation. I agree to these conditions and I hereby certify that all statements made by me on this application are true and complete, to the best of my knowledge.

_____
Signature of applicant as usually written (**Do Not Use Nickname**)

The Federal Bureau of Investigation is an equal opportunity employer.

CONTINUATION SPACE TO PROVIDE ADDITIONAL INFORMATION

If necessary, attach continuation sheet(s) of the same size as this application, with your name and Social Security Number at the top of each sheet and each answer numbered the same as the question to which it refers.

GENERAL

This information is provided pursuant to Public Law 93-579 (Privacy Act of 1974), December 31, 1974, for individuals completing FBI employment application forms.

AUTHORITY

Title 28, Code of Federal Regulations, Section 0.137, authorizes the Director of the FBI to exercise power and authority vested in the Attorney General by law to take final action in matters pertaining to the employment, direction and general administration of personnel in the FBI. Your Social Security Account Number is requested under the authority of Executive Order 9397.

PURPOSE AND USE

The principal purpose of employment application forms is to collect information needed to determine qualifications, suitability, and availability of applicants for FBI employment and of current FBI employees for reassignment, reinstatement, transfer, or promotion. Your completed application may be used to examine, rate and/or assess your qualifications; to determine if you are entitled under certain laws and regulations such as Veterans' Preference, and restrictions based on citizenship, members of family already employed, and residence requirements; and to contact you concerning availability and/or interview. All or part of your completed FBI employment application form may be disclosed outside the FBI to:

1. Federal agencies upon request for an eligibility list of persons or individuals to consider for appointment, reassignment, reinstatement, transfer, or promotion.
2. State and local government agencies under the Intergovernment Personnel Act terms if you have expressed an interest in and availability for such employment consideration.
3. State and local government agencies under the President's Executive Program terms if you have expressed an interest in and availability for such employment consideration.
4. Federal agency investigators to determine your suitability for federal employment.
5. Federal, state, or local agencies to create other personnel records after you have been appointed.
6. To any appropriate entity responsible for investigating, prosecuting, or enforcing law, regulation, or contract, or for licensing (as to any indication of a violation of law, regulation, or contract, or of other matters bearing on licensing determinations, either on its face, or in conjunction with other information).
7. Appropriate federal, state, local, foreign or other public authority to elicit information, assistance, or cooperation in the background criminal, intelligence, or security investigation.
8. A requesting federal, state, local, foreign or other public authority to the extent the information is for employment, security, contracting, or licensing determinations by the requesting agency.
9. Federal agency selecting officials involved with internal personnel management functions.

EFFECTS OF NONDISCLOSURE

Because this employment application form requests mandatory data (qualifications and biographical information, etc.), it is in your best interest to answer all questions. Omission of an item means you might not receive full consideration for a position in which this information is needed. A false answer to a question in the employment application may be grounds for not employing you, or for dismissing you after you begin work, and may be punishable by fine or imprisonment (U.S. Code. Title 18, Section 1001). All statements are subject to investigation, including a check of your fingerprints, police records, and former employers. All information you give will be considered in reviewing your statement.

Special Agent Qualifications Questionnaire (FD-843)

The Special Agent Qualifications Questionnaire is a two-page form that requests personal data and details about college degrees you received and your major, any certifications or special skills you possess, your employment history and military service, and community service or volunteer work in which you have participated. You are also asked to indicate the earliest date you could report for FBI employment. Like the application checklist, preliminary application, and background survey, the qualifications questionnaire is submitted at the beginning of the application process.

The sole purpose of this form is to determine the competitiveness of each applicant. The FBI reviews information you provide and determines how well you measure up to other applicants based on the Bureau's needs at the time. As the form suggests, the FBI is particularly interested in special skills and certifications you may have. These include a pilot's license, foreign-language proficiency, CPA certification, a law degree, or an engineering certificate. This form also asks whether you have law enforcement, military, or direct supervisory experience and whether you have completed the FBI Honors Internship Program. All of these special skills, certifications, and experiences can be a plus. Be sure to list any awards, professional recognition, medals, community service or volunteer work, and your eligibility for Veteran's Preference, because these are also important in determining your competitiveness.

Information you provide on the qualifications questionnaire is verified during the phase II interview and the background investigation.

FD-843 (2-16-95)

FEDERAL BUREAU OF INVESTIGATION

SPECIAL AGENT QUALIFICATIONS QUESTIONNAIRE
(Please Type or Print in Ink)

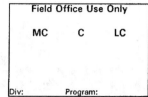

Field Office Use Only		
MC	C	LC
Div:	Program:	

Today's Date:_____

Applicants for the FBI Special Agent position are required to complete this short questionnaire. The competitiveness of every applicant will be determined based on the needs of the FBI. All information will be verified through future testing and background investigation procedures.

I. PERSONAL DATA

Name in Full: _____
             Last   First   Middle   Maiden

Soc. Sec. Number (Optional): _____ - ____ - _____ Birth Date (Mo/Day/Yr): _____ Current Age:_____

Current Address: _____
                 Street   Apt. No.

                 _____
                 City   State   Zip Code   Country

Home Phone: _____   Work Phone: _____
            Area Code   Number   Area Code   Number

Your FBI Recruiter's Name:_____

What would be the earliest date you could report for FBI employment (Month/Day/Year)?_____

II. ACADEMIC QUALIFICATIONS

Degree: _____ Date (Mo/Yr): _____ Major Field Of Study: _____

Degree: _____ Date (Mo/Yr): _____ Major Field Of Study: _____

Degree: _____ Date (Mo/Yr): _____ Major Field Of Study: _____

III. CERTIFICATIONS/SPECIAL SKILLS (check all that apply)

☐ Pilot's License: ____ Fixed Wing/Single Engine ____ Multi-Engine ___ Other: _____
  (please attach a copy of your pilot's license with proof of ratings)
☐ Foreign Language(s) in which you speak, read, and understand with native **fluency** (e.g., language is spoken in your family, you have lived in the foreign country, or you have taught the foreign language).

  Language(s):_____
☐ Have taken DPLT exam or FBI's Language Test for the foreign language(s). Date(s): _____
☐ Certified Public Accountant (CPA)   Date obtained:_____
☐ Bar Certification   State:_____ Date obtained:_____
☐ Professional Engineering Certificate   Date obtained:_____

Please list any other professional certifications, licenses, or special skills (e.g., technical, computer) that you have:

IV. WORK EXPERIENCE

Please list below information regarding your **full-time** work experience. Please provide each position in only one of the appropriate areas: supervisory, law enforcement/federal government/military, or other work experience.

A. Direct Supervisory Experience
(only include supervisory experience in which you had direct hiring/firing authority, responsibility for conducting performance evaluations, program authority, or financial accountability/budget responsibility):

Supervisory Position	Number of Subordinates Supervised	Employer/Organization	From Month/Yr	To Month/Yr

B. Law Enforcement/Federal Government/Military Experience

Law Enforcement/Federal Government/Military Position (Title and Grade)	Organization	From Month/Yr	To Month/Yr

C. Are you eligible to receive **Veteran's Preference** due to Military Service in a war, campaign, or expedition for which a medal or badge has been awarded?   Yes   No   (please attach a copy of your DD214 for verification)

D. Have you successfully completed the **FBI Honors Internship Program?** Yes   No   Dates? _____

E. Other Work Experience

Other Full-Time Position	Organization	From Month/Yr	To Month/Yr

F. Please list any **awards, medals, or other professional recognition** that you have received and the date (month/year) on which you received each:

G. Please list important **community service or volunteer work** you have participated in for at least one year during the last three years:

APPENDIX D

Applicant Background Survey (FD-804)

The Applicant Background Survey requests your name, date of birth, Social Security number, and information about your race and ethnicity, gender, and any disabilities you might have. You are required only to provide your name and date of birth and indicate the position for which you are applying. According to federal laws, listing your Social Security number and demographic data is voluntary.

The United States Code requires federal agencies to provide equal opportunities for job applicants and to carry out employment practices that are free from discrimination. The information you provide on this form is used in planning and monitoring Equal Employment Opportunity programs. The FBI uses this form to obtain demographic information in compliance with the Equal Employment Opportunity Commission's annual reporting requirements.

All applicants for special agent and professional support positions must submit this form. Information provided on the Applicant Background Survey is not used in determining basic qualifications, selecting applicants for further processing, or making appointment decisions.

FD-804 (4-29-91)

FEDERAL BUREAU OF INVESTIGATION

APPLICANT BACKGROUND SURVEY

(Please read the instructions below and read the Privacy Act
Statement on the reverse side before completing form)

Date: _____

1. Name (Last, First, MI):   Date of Birth:

2. Position Applied for: 3. Social Security Number

Your furnishing this information is voluntary. Please provide information on your race/ethnicity, sex, and disability status. In block 4, provide the race/ethnic code which indicates the group with which you identify yourself. Check the appropriate box in block 5, to show your sex. In block 6, enter your disability code. The codes are listed below.

4. Race/Ethnic Code: 5. Sex: ☐ Female ☐ Male   6. Disability Code:

RACE/ETHNIC CODES

A. **American Indian or Alaskan Native** - A person having origins in any of the original peoples of North America, and who maintains cultural identification through community recognition or tribal affiliation.
B. **Asian or Pacific Islander** - A person having origins in any of the original peoples of the Far East, Southeast Asia, the Indian subcontinent, or the Pacific Islands. This area includes, for example, China, India, Japan, Korea, the Philippine Islands and Samoa.
C. **Black, Not of Hispanic Origin** - A person having origins in any of the black racial groups of Africa. Does not include persons of Mexican, Puerto Rican, Cuban, Central or South American, or other Spanish cultures or origins (See Hispanic).
D. **Hispanic** - A person having Mexican, Puerto Rican, Cuban, Central or South American, or other Spanish cultures or origins **(Regardless of Race)**. Does not include persons of Portugese culture or origin.
E. **White, Not of Hispanic Origin** - A person having origins in any of the original peoples of Europe, North Africa, or the Middle East. Does not include persons of Mexican, Puerto Rican, Cuban, Central or South American, or other Spanish cultures or origins (See Hispanic). Also includes persons not included in other categories.

DISABILITY CODES

5 - I do not have a disability
6 - I have a disability but it is not listed below
16 - Hearing Impairment
23 - Vision Impairment
28 - Missing Extremities
64 - Partial Paralysis

71 - Complete Paralysis
82 - Convulsive Disorder
90 - Mental Retardation
91 - Mental or Emotional Illness
92 - Severe Distortion of Limbs and/or Spine

FBI/DOJ

PRIVACY ACT STATEMENT

You are requested to furnish this information under the authority of 42 U.S.C. &2000e-16, which requires that Federal employment practices be free from discrimination and provide equal employment opportunities for all. Solicitation of this information is in accordance with Department of Commerce Directive 15, "Race and Ethnic Standards for Federal Statistics and Administrative Reporting."

This information will be used in planning and monitoring equal employment opportunity programs. Your furnishing this information is voluntary. Your failure to do so will have no effect on you or on your Federal employment. If you fail to provide the information, however, then the employing agency will attempt to identify your race and national origin by visual perception.

You are requested to furnish your Social Security Number (SSN) under the authority of Executive Order 9397 (November 22, 1943). That Order requires agencies to use the SSN for the sake of economy and orderly administration in the maintenance of personnel records. Because your personnel records are identified by your SSN, your SSN is being requested on this form so that the other information you furnish on this form can be accurately included with your records. Your SSN will be used solely for that purpose. Your furnishing of your SSN is voluntary and failure to furnish it will have no effect on you; failure to provide it, however, may result in it being obtained from other agency sources.

APPENDIX E

Application for Employment (FD-140)

The Application for Employment is a 15-page form that requests a great deal of detailed information about your background. On this form, you must provide information relating to birth and citizenship, places of residence, educational achievements, employment history, military service, references and social acquaintances, foreign travel, association membership, civil and criminal court record, financial status, relatives, roommates, drug use, and availability for employment. A recent full-face photograph must also be attached.

Similar to the Special Agent Qualifications Questionnaire, this form is also used to determine your competitiveness with other applicants. The Special Agent Qualifications Questionnaire is reviewed to determine who will be invited to participate in phase I testing, whereas the Application for Employment is used to select a limited number of candidates who passed phase I testing to complete the phase II testing process. Only the most competitive applicants are chosen to continue in the hiring process. The FBI also uses this form in conducting your background investigation.

It is critical that you fill out the Application for Employment accurately and completely. Submitting an incomplete form could result not only in a delay in the processing of your application, but also your elimination from employment consideration.

FD-140 (Rev. 7-17-00)
Cover Page

Form Approval
(Exp. 5-31-02)
OMB No. 1110-0016

Application for Employment
Federal Bureau of Investigation

INSTRUCTIONAL INFORMATION SHEET

The Instructional Information Sheet has been prepared to assist you in completing the application for FBI employment. If a question does not apply to you, please indicate "N/A" in the appropriate space. If you need additional space for any question on the application or want to give additional information, you must use the FD-140a for Sections II and IV and/or you may use plain sheets that are the same size as this application for any other question. You should number each answer to correspond to each question and include your name and Social Security Account Number at the top of each continuation sheet.

Type or legibly print your answers in **black ink**. If your form is illegible, it will not be accepted.

Note: Persons with disabilities who require accommodations to complete the application process should notify the FBI of their needs.

COMMON OMISSIONS

Incomplete information will delay the processing your application. Therefore, answer each question as thoroughly as possible. In Part XIV, we have found that some applicants omit the middle names of relatives. If a relative does not have a middle name, indicate "NMN," meaning no middle name. If you are unable to furnish complete information concerning your parents or relatives, give a justifiable explanation as to why you cannot do so.

If you served in the Armed Forces, indicate in Part II, by each address, whether you lived on or off base. Be sure to include overseas tours. If you have relatives who are currently in the military, indicate their complete addresses and whether they reside on or off base.

TRANSCRIPTS

Official transcripts of all college courses will be necessary if you are applying for a specialty position. Examples of speciality positions are Computer Scientist, Electronics Technician, Laboratory Aide/Technician, Budget Analyst, Operating Accountant, and Financial Analyst. Attach your transcripts to your application so that we can determine your qualifications for the position. If you are unsure as to whether the position you are applying for requires transcripts, contact your local FBI office.

CERTIFICATIONS

If you are applying for Special Agent under the Accounting Program, you may need certification of your academic qualifications. Contact your local FBI office for further information.

HATCH ACT REFORM PROVISIONS

The Hatch Act Reform Amendments of 1993, 5 U.S.C. § 3303, prohibit the FBI from accepting oral or written statements from congressional or political sources that are **unsolicited** recommendations for your appointment to an employment position.

**YOU MAY DETACH THIS INFORMATION SHEET, BUT INCLUDE
ALL OTHER SHEETS WITH YOUR COMPLETED APPLICATION.**

FD-140 (Rev. 7-17-00)

Form Approval
(Exp. 5-31-02)
OMB No. 1110-0016

Application for Employment
Federal Bureau of Investigation

EFFECTS OF NONDISCLOSURE AND PENALTIES FOR INACCURATE OR FALSE STATEMENTS

The employment application forms request both mandatory and optional information. If you omit answering an item, however, you may not receive full consideration for a position; and without your social security number, we cannot process your application. Consequently, it is in your best interest to answer all of the questions. The U.S. Criminal Code, Title 18 § 1001, provides that knowingly falsifying or concealing a material fact is a felony that may result in fines of up to $10,000 or 5 years in prison, or both. Under 5 U.S.C. § 8315, a false answer to questions relating to membership in the Communist Party, U.S.A., or other communist or fascist organizations could deprive you of your right to an annuity when you reach retirement age. Deliberately and materially making false or fraudulent statements on this form will be grounds for not granting you a security clearance and not hiring you or for firing you after you begin work. In addition, these violations will become part of your permanent record for future employment.

You are applying for a sensitive position, and your trustworthiness and suitability for FBI employment is vital to your eligibility for a security clearance. Consequently, your prospects for placement and a security clearance are better if you answer all questions honestly and completely. An investigation of your statements will include checking fingerprints, police records, and former employers. Should questions on any of your statements arise, you will be given an adequate opportunity to respond, and your comments will be included in the official record. As a further condition of employment, you will be administered a polygraph examination. This examination will focus on your truthfulness on the FBI application form, which includes questions on prior drug use. Please note that you can be disqualified for FBI employment if you have done any of the following:

- used marijuana during the last 3 years,
- used marijuana more than 15 times,
- used an illegal drug or combination of illegal drugs, other than marijuana, more than 5 times,
- used an illegal drug or combination of illegal drugs, other than marijuana, during the last 10 years,
- sold an illegal drug for profit,
- used an illegal drug while employed in a law enforcement or prosecutorial position or while in a position of high-level responsibility or public trust,
- failed an FBI polygraph examination regarding prior drug use, even if the extent of use would not have been disqualifying,
- failed an FBI polygraph examination regarding truthfulness/candor on an FBI employment application, or
- failed an FBI polygraph examination regarding contact with non-U.S. Intelligence Services.

Printed Name
_____

Signature (as usually written, without nicknames)
_____

Social Security Account Number
_____

Date
_____

(Public Burden and Privacy Act Statements on next page)

1

PUBLIC BURDEN INFORMATION The public burden reporting for this collection of information is estimated to be 8 hours per response. This estimate includes reviewing instructions, searching information sources, and gathering and reporting the information. You may send your comments on the time estimate and other aspects of data collection, including suggestions for reducing the time it takes to complete this form to the Fraud Section, Criminal Division, U. S. Department of Justice, Washington, D.C. 20535-0001, and to the Office of Management and Budget, OMB Number 1110-0016, Washington, D.C. 20535-0001.

AUTHORITY

The FBI investigates and assesses suitability and security issues of federal employment primarily under 5 U.S.C. §§ 3301 and 9101 and Executive Orders 10450 and 12968. The Director of the FBI exercises power and authority vested in the Attorney General to take final action on the employment, direction, and general administration of FBI personnel under 28 C.F.R. § 0.137. The Bureau requests your Social Security Account Number (SSAN) under Executive Order 9397.

PRIVACY ACT NOTICE

Pursuant to the Privacy Act of 1974, 5 U.S.C. § 552a, we are providing the following information on principal purposes and routine uses for individuals completing the FBI employment application forms.

PRINCIPAL PURPOSES AND ROUTINE USES

The principal purpose of this form is to collect information to determine the qualifications and suitability of FBI employment applicants and to determine the reassignment, reinstatement, transfer, or promotion of current FBI employees. By law and regulation, we may evaluate your application to determine, for example, if you are entitled to Veterans' Preference and if you are restricted by citizenship, family members already employed, or residence requirements. We may also use your application to contact you for an interview and to verify your availability for employment. The further purpose of this form is to collect information for an FBI background investigation to establish your eligibility for a required security clearance and for other authorized purposes within the Department of Justice. Your SSAN identifies you throughout your federal career from job application to retirement. We may use your SSAN to accurately identify your records and to process your application for employment. We may use your SSAN to seek information about you from employers, schools, banks, and other individuals who know you. Your SSAN may also be used in studies and computer matches with other government files that, for instance, may pertain to unpaid student loans or parent locators. Furthermore, all or part of your completed FBI application form may be disclosed outside the Department of Justice to the following:

1. Federal agencies requesting lists of individuals who are eligible for appointment, reassignment, reinstatement, transfer, or promotion.

2. State or local government agencies under either the Intergovernmental Personnel Act or the President's Executive Program when you have expressed an interest in such employment.

3. Federal agency investigators to determine suitability for federal employment.

4. Selecting officials who are involved with the internal personnel management of federal agencies.

5. Appropriate federal, state, local, foreign, or other public authorities conducting criminal, intelligence, or security background investigations.

6. Federal, state, or local agencies creating other personnel records after you have been appointed to an agency position.

7. Appropriate entities responsible for licensing or for investigating, prosecuting, or enforcing law, regulation, or contract.

8. Federal, state, local, foreign, or other public authorities if there is a request for information on employment, security, contracting, or licensing determinations.

9. The news media or general public when the disclosure of factual information would be in the public interest and would not constitute an unwarranted invasion of privacy.

10. Officials or employees of other federal agencies to assist in the performance of their duties, including the White House for employment, security, or access purposes and for matters of constitutional, statutory, or other official duties of the President.

11. Non-FBI employees acting in furtherance of a Department of Justice function.

12. Courts or adjudicative bodies when the FBI has an official interest in the proceedings.

13. Identified persons or entities to publish notice in the **Federal Register** of the routine use of information.

Application for Employment
Federal Bureau of Investigation

Position for which you are applying:

☐ Special Agent   ☐ Clerical   ☐ Honors Intern   Date: ....

☐ Professional/Technical (Specify): ....

I. PERSONAL HISTORY

1. Name in Full (Last, First, Middle)	2. List all other names you have used including nicknames. If female, furnish your maiden name. If you have used a surname, other than your true name, give the time period and the circumstances under which you used this name. If you legally changed your name, give the date, place, and court in which this occurred.

3. Birth Date (Month, Date, Year)	4. Birthplace (City, State, Country, Zip Code). If foreign born to American parent(s), attach a copy of State Department Form 240 - Report of Birth Abroad of a Citizen of the United States.

5. Age	6. Sex ☐ Female ☐ Male	7. Social Security Account Number (See Privacy Act Notice on Cover Page)

8. Marital Status:

☐ Never Married   ☐ Engaged   ☐ Married   ☐ Separated   ☐ Legally Separated   ☐ Divorced   ☐ Widowed

a. Give marriage date and place (City, State, Zip Code).

b. Give the dates, places (City, State, Zip Code), and reason for all separations, divorces, or annulments.

9. Citizenship

a. Country of current citizenship: .... b. Citizenship acquired by: ☐ Birth ☐ Naturalization

c. Date and place (City, State, Zip Code) of naturalization: ....

d. Naturalization Certificate Number: .... e. Alien Registration Number: ....

f. Name used when entering the United States ....

g. If you are or were a dual citizen of the United States and another country, provide the name of that country: ....

II. RESIDENCES

List all places where you have lived and account for all time periods. Begin with your most recent place of residence and work back to age 16. Be sure to indicate the actual physical location of your residence. Do not use a post office box as an address, and do not list a permanent address when you are actually living at school. During military service, be sure to list each place of residence, including your base or ship/home port.

★ Note: If you need additional space, attach FD-140a (Continuation Sheet to FD-140).

Month/Year - Month/Year	Street Address	Apt.#	City (County)	State	Zip Code	Telephone Number
1. to Present						( )
Apartment Complex/Landlord	Street Address	Apt.#	City (County)	State	Zip Code	

Month/Year - Month/Year	Street Address	Apt.#	City (County)	State	Zip Code	Telephone Number
2. to						( )
Apartment Complex/Landlord	Street Address	Apt.#	City (County)	State	Zip Code	

Month/Year - Month/Year	Street Address	Apt.#	City (County)	State	Zip Code	Telephone Number
3. to						( )
Apartment Complex/Landlord	Street Address	Apt.#	City (County)	State	Zip Code	

The Federal Bureau of Investigation is an equal opportunity employer.

Field Office	
SEARCHED	INDEXED
SEARCHED	FILED
FBI-	

Headquarters	
67-	
SEARCHED	NUMBERED
THREE	

3

II. RESIDENCES (con't)

Month/Year - Month/Year	Street Address		Apt.#	City (County)		State	Zip Code	Telephone Number
4. to								( )
Apartment Complex/Landlord	Street Address		Apt.#	City (County)			State	Zip Code

Month/Year - Month/Year	Street Address		Apt.#	City (County)		State	Zip Code	Telephone Number
5. to								( )
Apartment Complex/Landlord	Street Address		Apt.#	City (County)			State	Zip Code

III. EDUCATION

1. High School

Name of High School from which you graduated or issuer of GED	Address (City, State, Zip Code)	From Month/Year	To Month/Year

2. College or University

Names and Addresses of all Colleges or Universities Attended (City, State, Zip Code)	Subject		From Month/Year	To Month/Year	Degree Received	GPA
	Major	Minor				
#1						
#2						
#3						

3. Specialized Schools

Name and Address of School (City, State, Zip Code)	Study or Specialization	Certificate/ Degree received	From Month/Year	To Month/Year
#1				
#2				

4. Was any disciplinary action taken against you while you were in school or were you dismissed or suspended from school for academic reasons?
☐ Yes ☐ No   If yes, provide the name of the school, the action, and the date of action below.

School	Action	Date

4

IV. EMPLOYMENT

List your employment activities, beginning with the present (#1) and working back to age 16. You should list all full-time work, part-time work, military service, temporary military duty locations over 90 days, self-employment, other paid work, and all periods of unemployment. The entire period must be accounted for without breaks, but you need not list employments before your 16th birthday. If you need additional space, attach FD-140a (Continuation Sheet to FD-140).

• **Code.** Use one of the codes listed below to identify the type of employment:

1 - Active military duty stations
2 - National Guard/Reserve
3 - U.S.P.H.S. Commissioned Corps

4 - Other Federal employment
5 - State Government (Non-Federal employment)
6 - Self-employment (Include business name and /or name of person who can verify)

7 - Unemployment (Include name of person who can verify)
8 - Federal Contractor (List contractor, not Federal agency)
9 - Other

1. Month/Year-Month/Year to Present | Code | Employer/Name/Military Duty Location | Your Position Title/Military Rank

Address of Employment | City (County) | State | Zip Code | Telephone Number ( )

Immediate Supervisor | Telephone Number of Supervisor ( ) | Reason for Leaving

Salary/Earnings _____ per ____ Ending $_____ per ____ | Average No. of Hrs. per week .... ☐ Full Time ☐ Part Time | Level of Security Clearance (if applicable)

Work Description (Describe your specific duties and, if applicable, include all supervisory, managerial, scientific, and professional experience.)

2. Month/Year-Month/Year | Code | Employer/Name/Military Duty Location | Your Position Title/Military Rank

Address of Employment | City (County) | State | Zip Code | Telephone Number ( )

Immediate Supervisor | Telephone Number of Supervisor ( ) | Reason of Leaving

Salary/Earnings Starting $_____ per ____ Ending $_____ per ____ | Average No. of Hrs. per week ☐ Full Time ☐ Part Time | Level of Security Clearance

Work Description (Describe your specific duties and, if applicable, include all supervisory, managerial, scientific, and professional experience.)

3. Has any of the following happened to you? If Yes, begin with the most recent occurrence and go backward, providing date fired, quit, or left, and other information requested. ☐ Yes ☐ No Attach additional sheets as necessary.
• **Code.** Use the following codes and explain the reason your employment ended:

1 - Fired from a job
2 - Quit a job after being told you'd be fired
3 - Left a job by mutual agreement following allegations of misconduct

4 - Left a job by mutual agreement following allegations of unsatisfactory
5 - Left a job for other reasons under unfavorable circumstances

Month/Year	Code	Specify Reason	Employer's Name and Address (Include City/Country if outside U.S.)	State	Zip Code

4. To your knowledge, have you ever had a clearance or access authorization denied, suspended, or revoked, or have you ever been debarred from government employment? ☐ Yes ☐ No If Yes, give date of action and agency. **Note:** An administrative downgrade or termination of a security clearance is not a revocation.

Month/Year	Department or Agency Taking Action	Month/Year	Department or Agency Taking Action

5

V. MILITARY RECORD

1. Did you register with the Selective Service System as required. ☐Yes ☐No   If yes, provide the following:

Registration Number .... Location (City, State, Zip Code) ....

If no, provide reason:..

2. Have you served on active duty in the United States Armed Forces? ☐Yes ☐No   If yes, attach a copy of each DD-214 received and proceed to question 3. If no, proceed to Part VI.

3. Branch of military service:

4. Dates of active duty (Month, Date, Year)	5. Military Serial Number or SSAN:
From: ....To:	6. Are you a member of the Reserve? ☐Yes ☐No
From: ....To:	☐Ready ☐Standby
	Branch of Service: ....

7. Was any disciplinary action taken against you while you were in the service? ☐Yes ☐No If applicable, be sure to include nonjudicial punishment and Article 15s. If yes, provide details. ....

8. Have you served in the National Guard? ☐Yes ☐No If yes, provide dates, unit location, and name of Commanding Officer.

9. a. Do you claim Veterans Preference? ☐Yes ☐No
   b. If yes, indicate dates of service and attach DD-214. ....
   c. If claiming 10-point Veterans Preference, in addition to your DD-214, you must provide a Standard Form 15 (Application for 10-point Veteran Preference) with appropriate documentation.

VI. REFERENCES/SOCIAL ACQUAINTANCES

List three people who know you well and live in the United States. They should be good friends, peers, colleagues, college roommates, etc., whose combined association with you covers as well as possible the last 10 years. Do not list your spouse, former spouse, or other relatives, and try not to list anyone who is listed elsewhere on this form.

1. Complete Name

Home Address ....

_____
(Last, First, Middle)

(City, State, Zip Code) ....

Yrs. Acq.	Occupation

Home Phone (Including Area Code) ....

DOB or Approximate Age

Business Address ....

Business Phone (Including Area Code) ....

2. Complete Name

Home Address ....

_____
(Last, First, Middle)

(City, State, Zip Code) ....

Yrs. Acq.	Occupation

Home Phone (Including Area Code) ....

DOB or Approximate Age

Business Address ....

Business Phone (Including Area Code) ....

3. Complete Name

Home Address ....

_____
(Last, First, Middle)

(City, State, Zip Code) ....

Yrs. Acq.	Occupation

Home Phone (Including Area Code) ....

DOB or Approximate Age

Business Address ....

Business Phone (Including Area Code) ....

6

VII. FOREIGN TRAVEL

1. List all foreign countries you have visited. (Include travel while serving in the United States Armed Forces.) Under "Reasons for Travel" indicate whether the travel was for business, pleasure, education, or other. Attach additional sheets as necessary.

Passport Number: _____ Date issued _____

Countries Visited	From Month/Year	To Month/Year	Reasons for Travel

2. Have you served in the Armed Forces of a foreign country? ☐ Yes ☐ No If yes, specify country, type of service, and dates of service.

3. Do you or members of your immediate family, including in-laws, have relatives now residing outside the United States? (Do not include relatives living abroad who are in the Armed Forces or employed by the United States Government.) ☐ Yes ☐ No If yes, provide information requested below.

Name	Age	Relationship	Frequency of Contact	City	Country	Country of Citizenship

4. Have you or members of your immediate family, including in-laws, had contact with foreign diplomatic establishments or their representatives in the U.S. or abroad, which include commercial, consular, news media, and trade or travel organizations? ☐ Yes ☐ No If yes, explain the circumstances on a separate page.

5. Have you or members of your immediate family, including in-laws, been employed by or acted as a consultant for a foreign government, firm, or agency? ☐ Yes ☐ No If yes, attach a separate page explaining the circumstances.

6. Have you or members of your immediate family, including in-laws, had contact with a foreign government, its establishments (embassies or consulates), or its representatives (either inside or outside the United States) for other than official government business? (Do not include routine visa applications and border-crossing contacts.) ☐ Yes ☐ No If yes, attach a separate page explaining the circumstances.

VIII. ASSOCIATION RECORD

1. Have you been an officer or a member of or contributed to an organization that is dedicated to the violent overthrow of the United States Government and that engages in illegal activities with the specific intent to further that end? ☐ Yes ☐ No If yes, provide details.

2. Have you engaged in acts or activities designed to overthrow the United States Government by force? ☐ Yes ☐ No If yes, provide details.

IX. COURT RECORD

1. Have you been a party to a civil court action? ☐ Yes ☐ No If yes, provide the requested information below.

Month/Year	Nature of Action	Result of Action	Names of parties, (identify plaintiff and defendant) the court and address (city, county, state, zip code; or country if a court outside the U.S.)

2. Have you ever been arrested or charged with any violation including traffic, but excluding parking tickets? ☐ Yes ☐ No If yes, list all such matters even if not formally charged or no court appearance, or found not guilty, or matter settled by payment of fine or forfeiture of collateral. Attach additional sheets as necessary.

Date	Place and Department	Charge	Court and Place	Disposition	Details

7

IX. COURT RECORD (continued)

3. To your knowledge, have any members of your immediate family been arrested? ☐ Yes ☐ No If yes, list all such matters even if not formally charged or no court appearance, or found not guilty, or matter settled by payment of fine or forfeiture of collateral. Attach additional sheets as necessary.

Date	Place and Department	Charge	Court and Place	Disposition	Details

X. FINANCIAL STATUS

1. Have you ever been over 120 days delinquent on any debt(s) or had any debt placed for collection? ☐ Yes ☐ No

2. Are you currently delinquent on any debt(s)? ☐ Yes ☐ No

3. Have you ever filed a petition under any chapter of the bankruptcy code (to include Chapter 13)? ☐ Yes ☐ No

4. Have you ever had your wages garnished or had any property repossessed for any reason? ☐ Yes ☐ No

5. Have you ever had a lien placed against your property for failing to pay taxes or other debts? ☐ Yes ☐ No

6. Have you ever had any judgments filed against you? ☐ Yes ☐ No

7. Are you currently delinquent or have you ever been in default on any student loan? ☐ Yes ☐ No

If you answered "Yes" to items 1-7, provide the information requested below:

Month/Year	Action Taken	Amount	Name Action Occurred Under	Name/ Address of Court or Agency Handling Case	City	Zip Code

8. Are you current on all federal, state and local tax debts? (Include individual and employer tax debts that apply to you).
   ☐ Yes ☐ No If no, provide details.

9. Do you have income from sources other than your salary or your spouse's salary? ☐ Yes ☐ No If yes, specify the source and amount

XI. SPECIAL QUALIFICATIONS AND SKILLS

1. Do you have foreign language abilities? ☐ Yes ☐ No If yes, indicate your foreign language proficiency by rating each category of ability as "slight," "good" or "fluent."

Name of Language	Speak	Understand	Read	Write

2. Are you a member of the bar? ☐ Yes ☐ No If yes, give the date of membership and the state below. Also indicate if any complaints or grievances were ever filed against you. (If applicable)

Date	State	Grievance/Complaint Information

3. Are you a Certified Public Accountant? ☐ Yes ☐ No If yes, give the date of membership and the state below. Also indicate if any complaints or grievances were ever filed against you. (If applicable)

Date	State	Grievance/Complaint Information

4. a. Are you a licensed automobile driver? ☐ Yes ☐ No b. Are you a licensed motorcycle driver? ☐ Yes ☐ No
   Do you possess a Commercial Driver's License? ☐ Yes ☐ No If yes to a., b., or c. indicate the following:

   State: .... Expiration Date: .... License # (s): ....

   State: .... Expiration Date: .... License # (s): ....

5. Do you have any special skills for which certification or licensing is required? (Nurse, Emergency Medical Technician, Pilot, Real Estate, Cosmetology, etc.)

....

8

XII. RELATIVES

All applicants must give complete information concerning their close relatives and in-laws. Relatives include spouse, parents, stepparents, siblings, step and half siblings, children, and stepchildren. This information will be verified through a background investigation. If you have been married more than once, give the requested information for each former spouse. For deceased relatives, give the requested information and indicate the decedent's last residence and year of death. If you or your spouse were raised by legal guardians or others, give the requested information on them as well as the biological parents. If you are engaged to be married, indicate this in Part 1, Block 8, and give information on your future spouse and future in-laws in Part XII, Blocks 21 through 26, clearly indicating that they are future relationships. For any relatives (excluding in-laws) who were born outside the United States to American parents, attach a copy of State Department Form - 240.

1. FATHER (Last, First, Middle)	2. MOTHER (Last, First, Middle) (Maiden)
Address (City, State, Zip Code)	Address (City, State, Zip Code)
Name of Firm or Employer	Name of Firm or Employer
Address of Employer (City, State, Zip Code)	Address of Employer (City, State, Zip Code)
Date of Birth Place of Birth	Date of Birth Place of Birth

3. SPOUSE (Last, First, Middle) (Maiden)	4. FORMER SPOUSE (Last, First, Middle) (Maiden)
Address (City, State, Zip Code)	Address (City, State, Zip Code)
Name of Firm or Employer	Name of Firm or Employer
Address of Employer (City, State, Zip Code)	Address of Employer (City, State, Zip Code)
Date of Birth Place of Birth	Date of Birth Place of Birth

5. CHILD (Last, First, Middle) (Maiden)	6. CHILD'S SPOUSE (Last, First, Middle) (Maiden)
Address (City, State, Zip Code)	Address (City, State, Zip Code)
Name of Firm or Employer	Name of Firm or Employer
Address of Employer (City, State, Zip Code)	Address of Employer (City, State, Zip Code)
Date of Birth Place of Birth	Date of Birth Place of Birth

9

XII. RELATIVES (continued)	
7. CHILD (Last, First, Middle) (Maiden)	**8. CHILD'S SPOUSE** (Last, First, Middle) (Maiden)
Address (City, State, Zip Code)	Address (City, State, Zip Code)
Name of Firm or Employer	Name of Firm or Employer
Address of Employer (City, State, Zip Code)	Address of Employer (City, State, Zip Code)
Date of Birth　　　　　Place of Birth	Date of Birth　　　　　Place of Birth
9. BROTHER (Last, First, Middle)	**10. BROTHER'S SPOUSE** (Last, First, Middle) (Maiden)
Address (City, State, Zip Code)	Address (City, State, Zip Code)
Name of Firm or Employer	Name of Firm or Employer
Address of Employer (City, State, Zip Code)	Address of Employer (City, State, Zip Code)
Date of Birth　　　　　Place of Birth	Date of Birth　　　　　Place of Birth
11. BROTHER (Last, First, Middle)	**12. BROTHER'S SPOUSE** (Last, First, Middle) (Maiden)
Address (City, State, Zip Code)	Address (City, State, Zip Code)
Name of Firm or Employer	Name of Firm or Employer
Address of Employer (City, State, Zip Code)	Address of Employer (City, State, Zip Code)
Date of Birth　　　　　Place of Birth	Date of Birth　　　　　Place of Birth
13. BROTHER (Last, First, Middle)	**14. BROTHER'S SPOUSE** (Last, First, Middle) (Maiden)
Address (City, State, Zip Code)	Address (City, State, Zip Code)
Name of Firm or Employer	Name of Firm or Employer
Address of Employer (City, State, Zip Code)	Address of Employer (City, State, Zip Code)
Date of Birth　　　　　Place of Birth	Date of Birth　　　　　Place of Birth

10

XII. RELATIVES (continued)	
15. SISTER (Last, First, Middle) (Maiden)	**16. SISTER'S SPOUSE** (Last, First, Middle)
Address (City, State, Zip Code)	Address (City, State, Zip Code)
Name of Firm or Employer	Name of Firm or Employer
Address of Employer (City, State, Zip Code)	Address of Employer (City, State, Zip Code)
Date of Birth Place of Birth	Date of Birth Place of Birth
17. SISTER (Last, First, Middle) (Maiden)	**18. SISTER'S SPOUSE** (Last, First, Middle)
Address (City, State, Zip Code)	Address (City, State, Zip Code)
Name of Firm or Employer	Name of Firm or Employer
Address of Employer (City, State, Zip Code)	Address of Employer (City, State, Zip Code)
Date of Birth Place of Birth	Date of Birth Place of Birth
19. SISTER (Last, First, Middle) (Maiden)	**20. SISTER'S SPOUSE** (Last, First, Middle)
Address (City, State, Zip Code)	Address (City, State, Zip Code)
Name of Firm or Employer	Name of Firm or Employer
Address of Employer (City, State, Zip Code)	Address of Employer (City, State, Zip Code)
Date of Birth Place of Birth	Date of Birth Place of Birth
21. FATHER-IN-LAW (Last, First, Middle)	**22. MOTHER-IN-LAW** (Last, First, Middle) (Maiden)
Address (City, State, Zip Code)	Address (City, State, Zip Code)
Name of Firm or Employer	Name of Firm or Employer
Address of Employer (City, State, Zip Code)	Address of Employer (City, State, Zip Code)
Date of Birth Place of Birth	Date of Birth Place of Birth

11

219

XII. RELATIVES (continued)	
23. SPOUSE'S BROTHER (Last, First, Middle)	24. SPOUSE'S BROTHER (Last, First, Middle)
Address (City, State, Zip Code)	Address (City, State, Zip Code)
Name of Firm or Employer	Name of Firm or Employer
Address of Employer (City, State, Zip Code)	Address of Employer (City, State, Zip Code)
Date of Birth Place of Birth	Date of Birth Place of Birth
25. SPOUSE'S SISTER (Last, First, Middle) (Maiden)	26. SPOUSE'S SISTER (Last, First, Middle) (Maiden)
Address (City, State, Zip Code)	Address (City, State, Zip Code)
Name of Firm or Employer	Name of Firm or Employer
Address of Employer (City, State, Zip Code)	Address of Employer (City, State, Zip Code)
Date of Birth Place of Birth	Date of Birth Place of Birth

12

XIII. COTENANTS

List all individuals with whom you have resided in the last 5 years, for a period of 30 days or more. Do not include relatives listed in section XII above (Attach additional sheets if necessary.)

1. Name (Last, First, Middle) (Maiden)	2. Name (Last, First, Middle) (Maiden)
Current Address (City, State, Zip Code)	Current Address (City, State, Zip Code)
Home Telephone Number	Home Telephone Number
Name of Firm or Employer	Name of Firm or Employer
Address of Employer (City, State, Zip Code)	Address of Employer (City, State, Zip Code)
Work Telephone Number	Work Telephone Number
Date of Birth Place of Birth	Date of Birth Place of Birth
Dates of Residence From: (Month, Day, Year) To: (Month, Day, Year)	Dates of Residence From: (Month, Day, Year) To: (Month, Day, Year)

XIV. CITIZENSHIP OF RELATIVES/COTENANTS

Are any close relatives or cotenants naturalized or non-United States citizens? ☐ Yes ☐ No If yes, provide the information below. (You do not need to list this information for in-laws unless they currently reside with you). Attach additional pages, if necessary.

Full Name	Name Used When Entering U.S.	Relationship to Applicant	Alien Registration Number	Naturalization Number, Date, and Place of Naturalization (City, State, Zip Code)

XV. FRIENDS OR ACQUAINTANCES EMPLOYED BY THE FBI

Full Name	Location	Length of Acquaintance

XVI. PHYSICAL DATA

1. Height Without Shoes	3. Persons with a disability who require an accommodation to complete the application process are required to notify the FBI of their need for the accommodation.
2. Weight Without Clothes	

13

221

XVII. PERSONAL DECLARATIONS

1. Have you used marijuana during the last 3 years? ☐ Yes ☐ No

2. Have you used marijuana more than 15 times? ☐ Yes ☐ No

3. Have you used an illegal drug or combination of illegal drugs, other than marijuana, more than 5 times? ☐ Yes ☐ No

4. Have you used an illegal drug or combination of illegal drugs, other than marijuana, during the last 10 years? ☐ Yes ☐ No

5. Have you used an illegal drug while employed in a law enforcement or prosecutorial position? ☐ Yes ☐ No

6. Have you used an illegal drug while employed in a position of high-level responsibility or public trust? ☐ Yes ☐ No

7. Have you ever sold illegal drugs? ☐ Yes ☐ No   If yes, provide details.

8. Do you understand that all prospective FBI employees will be required to submit to a urinalysis for drug abuse prior to employment? ☐ Yes ☐ No

9. List all federal agencies and any state or local law enforcement agencies to which you have applied for employment.

10. Has any organization listed in number 9 above investigated, interviewed, tested, or polygraphed you? If so, indicate the name of the agency and the date and type of pre-screening method.

11. Are you now or have you been a member of a foreign or domestic organization, association, movement, group, or combination of persons that is totalitarian, fascist, communist, or subversive or that has adopted or shows a policy of advocating or approving acts of force or violence to deprive other persons of their rights under the Constitution of the United States or that seeks to alter the form of Government of the United States by unconstitutional means? ☐ Yes ☐ No   If yes, provide details.

12. Have you been a member of a foreign intelligence organization, or have you supported or had any connection with its activities? ☐ Yes ☐ No   If yes, provide details.

13. All information on this application will be investigated. Are you therefore aware of any information about yourself or anyone with whom you are or have been closely associated (including relatives and roommates) that tends to reflect unfavorably on your reputation, morals, character, abilities, or loyalty to the United States? ☐ Yes ☐ No   If yes, provide complete details.

XVIII. AVAILABILITY OF APPLICANT

1. Have you previously submitted an application for employment to the FBI? ☐ Yes ☐ No

Date: ....   Position: ....

2. Are you willing to relocate to Washington, D.C., or to another duty station at your own expense? ☐ Yes ☐ No

3. If appointed as a Special Agent, do you agree to serve a minimum of 3 years, and do you clearly understand that you must be available for an assignment wherever your services are needed? ☐ Yes ☐ No

4. If applying for a position which duties typically require travel, are you prepared to accept temporary duty assignments anywhere worldwide? ☐ Yes ☐ No

5. What is the earliest date that you would be available for employment?

6. How much notice do you need to report for work?

7. Do you understand that if you are appointed to a support position, you are not assured of an appointment to Special Agent even if you qualify for the position in the future? ☐ Yes ☐ No

14

XIX. PHOTOGRAPH

All Applicants - For identification, attach an unmounted full-face photograph of yourself, no larger than 3/4 x 2 1/2 inches. Print your name plainly on the back of the photograph. The photograph must be taken no more than 3 months prior to the date of this application. Please note that this photograph, as well as other materials that you submit, will become the property of the FBI and will not be returned.

ATTENTION - THIS STATEMENT MUST BE SIGNED BY THE APPLICANT

I understand that I will be required to submit to a pre-employment polygraph examination to assist the Federal Bureau of Investigation in determining my qualifications for a Top Secret Security Clearance and suitability for employment.

I understand that all appointments are probationary for a period of one year, except for Special Agents and Forensic Examiners which have a probationary period of two years, during which time I must demonstrate my fitness for continued employment with the Federal Bureau of Investigation. I understand that, in many parts of the FBI, it has been necessary to establish regular night and midnight shifts, as well as weekend duty, and that I may be required to work such schedules as needs arise. I further understand that any appointment offered to me will be contingent on the results of a complete character and fitness investigation, and I am aware notwithstanding a State Expungement Order concerning criminal history that willfully withholding information or making false statements on this application will be grounds for dismissal from the Federal Bureau of Investigation and constitutes a violation of Section 1001, Title 18 of the U.S. Criminal Code. I agree to these conditions and hereby certify that all of my statements on this application are, to the best of my knowledge, true and complete.

Finally, I understand that as an applicant for employment with the Federal Bureau of Investigation, I have been notified that if I believe I have been discriminated against because of race, color, religion, sex, sexual orientation, national origin, age (must be at least 40 years old) or disability (mental or physical or both), or as a reprisal for previous involvement in the EEO process, I must contact an EEO Counselor at any FBI field office or at FBI Headquarters **within 45 calendar days** of an alleged discriminatory action. I also understand that if I fail to contact a counselor within 45 days, it is likely that I may forfeit my right to pursue a claim of discrimination.

Printed Name

Signature (as usually written, without nicknames)

Date

15

FD-140a (7-17-00)

CONTINUATION SHEET FOR FD-140

INSTRUCTIONS: Use this form to continue your answers to Sections II. Residences and IV. Employment. Follow the instructions on the FD-140 and give information in the same sequence. Use as many continuation sheets as needed.

Your Name: Social Security Number:

II. RESIDENCES (continued)

Month/Year - Month/Year	Street Address	Apt.#	City (County)	State	Zip Code	Telephone Number ( )
Apartment Complex/Landlord	Street Address	Apt.#	City (County)	State		Zip Code

(Entries 1 through 7, same structure repeated)

IV. EMPLOYMENT (continued)

1. Month/Year-Month/Year	Code	Employer/Name/Military Duty Location		Your Position Title/Military Rank

Address of Employment	City (County)	State	Zip Code	Telephone Number ( )

Immediate Supervisor	Telephone Number of Supervisor	Reason for Leaving

Salary/Earnings   Average No. of Hrs. per week   Level of Security Clearance

Starting $_____ per ____ Ending $_____ per ____ ☐ Full Time ☐ Part Time

Work Description (Describe your specific duties and, if applicable, include all supervisory, managerial, scientific, and professional experience.)

IV. EMPLOYMENT (Continued)

| 2. Month/Year-Month/Year | Code | Employer/Name/Military Duty Location | | Your Position Title/Military Rank |

Address of Employment   City (County)   State   Zip Code   Telephone Number ( )

Immediate Supervisor   Telephone Number of Supervisor   Reason for Leaving

Salary/Earnings   Average No. of Hrs. per week   Level of Security Clearance (if applicable)

Starting $_____ per ____ Ending $_____ per ____   ☐ Full Time ☐ Part Time

Work Description (Describe your specific duties and, if applicable, include all supervisory, managerial, scientific, and professional experience.)

| 3. Month/Year-Month/Year | Code | Employer/Name/Military Duty Location | | Your Position Title/Military Rank |

Address of Employment   City (County)   State   Zip Code   Telephone Number ( )

Immediate Supervisor   Telephone Number of Supervisor   Reason for Leaving

Salary/Earnings   Average No. of Hrs. per week   Level of Security Clearance (if applicable)

Starting $_____ per ____ Ending $_____ per ____   ☐ Full Time ☐ Part Time

Work Description (Describe your specific duties and, if applicable, include all supervisory, managerial, scientific, and professional experience.)

| 4. Month/Year-Month/Year | Code | Employer/Name/Military Duty Location | | Your Position Title/Military Rank |

Address of Employment   City (County)   State   Zip Code   Telephone Number ( )

Immediate Supervisor   Telephone Number of Supervisor   Reason for Leaving

Salary/Earnings   Average No. of Hrs. per week   Level of Security Clearance (if applicable)

Starting $_____ per ____ Ending $_____ per ____   ☐ Full Time ☐ Part Time

Work Description (Describe your specific duties and, if applicable, include all supervisory, managerial, scientific, and professional experience.)

APPENDIX F

Worldwide Mobility Agreement (FD-918)

FBI special agents and certain professional support employees must be willing to accept permanent transfers or temporary duty (TDY) assignments anywhere in the world, and all FBI employees must be available for TDY assignments away from their permanent offices. To ensure that applicants understand this policy, they are required to complete a one-page Worldwide Mobility Agreement.

In addition to special agents, those serving in several professional support positions are subject to permanent transfers. These personnel include automotive workers and mechanics, computer specialists, data systems programmers, electronics technicians, financial analysts and accounting technicians, investigative specialists, forensic examiners, and language specialists. The FD-918 form asks applicants for these positions to certify that they are willing to accept a permanent or temporary duty (TDY) assignment worldwide.

According to the Bureau's TDY policy, which is described on the form, the FBI first seeks qualified volunteers for temporary duty before making nonvoluntary TDY assignments. In the certification block of this form, you must indicate whether you "...accept these terms without reservation." Any applicant who is unwilling to accept the terms of the FBI Worldwide Mobility Agreement will not be considered for FBI employment.

FD-918 (4-10-00)

WORLDWIDE MOBILITY AGREEMENT

My application is for the position of _____ in the FBI.
I am therefore responding to this agreement under section A or B accordingly.

A. I have applied for either a Special Agent position or one of the following
support positions: Automotive Worker/Mechanic, Computer Specialist, Data
Systems Programmer, Electronics Technician, Financial Analyst/Accounting
Technician, Investigative Specialist in the Special Surveillance Group Program,
Forensic Examiner, or Language Specialist; therefore:

1. As a condition of employment with the FBI, I fully understand that I will be
subject to and will remain completely available for **temporary duty (TDY)**
anywhere worldwide according to the needs of the Bureau. ☐ Yes ☐ No

2. As a condition of employment with the FBI, I fully understand that I will be subject
to and will remain completely available for **permanent transfer** anywhere
worldwide according to the needs of the Bureau. ☐ Yes ☐ No

3. I accept these terms without reservation. ☐ Yes ☐ No

B. I have applied for a support position that is not among the positions listed in
section A above; nevertheless:

1. As a condition of employment with the FBI, I fully understand that I will be subject to
and will remain available for **temporary duty (TDY)** anywhere worldwide according
to the needs of the Bureau. I am aware that the Bureau will first seek qualified
volunteers and that managers are instructed to make maximum possible use of such
volunteers for **TDY** assignments. If, however, volunteers are unavailable or
inadequate in numbers, I am willing to perform **TDY** anywhere worldwide as a
condition of employment, unless I am precluded by a disability that warrants
reasonable accommodation. ☐ Yes ☐ No

2. I accept these terms without reservation. ☐ Yes ☐ No

_____
Name (print)

_____   _____
Signature   Date

FBI\DOJ

APPENDIX G

Desirable Weight Ranges

The FBI is committed to having a workforce that is physically fit. Strength and endurance are especially important for special agents because they are often faced with strenuous and dangerous situations. In an effort to select candidates for the special agent position who will be able to perform law enforcement responsibilities safely and effectively—and succeed during demanding physical training in the New Agent Training program—the FBI provides the Desirable Weight Ranges chart, as shown on the following page.

These height and weight figures, as well as the body fat percentages shown at the bottom of the chart, serve as a guide for special agent candidates to follow. It is important to note that these are only *desirable* weight ranges for various heights, and not *required* weight ranges. In other words, if your height and weight are reasonably proportionate and close to the figures on the chart, you could still be considered for employment even though your numbers are outside the desirable range. The Bureau makes these determinations on a case-by-case basis. Of course, if you are significantly overweight or underweight, the FBI is not likely to hire you and hope you will make adjustments later.

The Desirable Weight Ranges chart is only one tool used to evaluate physical fitness. Prior to appointment, special agent candidates are given a physical examination and their medical history is also reviewed. They must also complete a 1.5-mile timed run. The final determination concerning suitability to use firearms, participate in raids, execute defensive tactics, and perform other essential functions of the job rests with the FBI's chief medical officer.

Males	
Height	**Weight in Pounds**
5' 4"	117–163
5' 5"	120–167
5' 6"	124–173
5' 7"	128–178
5' 8"	132–183
5' 9"	136–187
5' 10"	140–193
5' 11"	144–198
6' 0"	148–204
6' 1"	152–209
6' 2"	156–215
6' 3"	160–220
6' 4"	169–231
6' 5"	174–238

Females	
Height	**Weight in Pounds**
5' 0"	96–138
5' 1"	99–141
5' 2"	102–144
5' 3"	105–149
5' 4"	108–152
5' 5"	111–156
5' 6"	114–161
5' 7"	118–165
5' 8"	122–169
5' 9"	126–174
5' 10"	130–179
5' 11"	134–185
6' 0"	138–190

Body Fat Requirements
Males: 19%
Females: 22%

APPENDIX H

Foreign Language Assessment Questionnaire

The Foreign Language Assessment Questionnaire is a three-page form that must be submitted by special agent applicants who would like to qualify for entry under the Bureau's language program. To qualify for this entry program, you must pass a language-proficiency test that focuses on listening comprehension, reading comprehension, and translation, and possess a bachelor's degree in any discipline. In addition, you must be proficient in a language that meets the needs of the FBI at the time.

In this six-part form, you are asked to assess your language proficiency by answering "yes" or "no" to 33 questions. Part One includes questions that focus primarily on your conversational abilities in public and social gatherings. Parts Two through Five are mostly concerned with your ability to discuss personal and employment experiences, problem-solving situations, and other matters while using appropriate vocabulary and grammar. Part Six relates to your overall experience in speaking the language.

Only special agent applicants use this form. Candidates for employment as a language specialist or contract linguist, which are professional support positions, must provide an assessment of their language proficiency in accordance with the FBI's Language Proficiency Self-Assessment Chart, as shown in appendix I.

FEDERAL BUREAU OF INVESTIGATION
LANGUAGE TRAINING AND ASSESSMENT UNIT

SELF-APPRAISAL FORM (SAF) FOR SPEAKING PROFICIENCY

Name:_____ Date:_____

Language:_____ Division:_____

      In order to help us provide appropriate language training for our applicants, please answer the following questions regarding your ability to speak the foreign language you have indicated above. Place a Y for "Yes" or an N for "No" on the line to the left of each question to express what you think you can or cannot do in the language. Place a U for "Unsure" if you cannot make up your mind whether or not you can do what is described. Part Six is self-explanatory.

Part One

_____ Can you tell other people basic information about your background and family?

_____ Can you order a meal in a restaurant?

_____ Can you get a room in a hotel or tell a taxi driver where you want to go?

_____ Can you buy a needed item of clothing or a bus or train ticket?

_____ Can you respond correctly to standard questions about your nationality, marital status, occupation, date and place of birth, background and family, etc?

_____ Can you introduce people at informal social gatherings and use appropriate expressions when saying goodbye to someone?

_____ Can you ask someone how to get from where you are to your hotel, a restaurant, a bank, the post office, or a similar public place?

Part Two

_____ Can you describe your present or most recent job or professional activity in some detail?

_____ Can you give detailed information about your family, your home, or the weather today?

_____ Can you describe in detail a person or place that is very familiar to you?

____ Can you tell the facts of what has been reported recently on television news or in the newspaper?

____ Can you tell in detail about a trip you took or some other everyday event that happened in the recent past?

____ Can you give detailed information about your family's or your future plans or an event that you expect will happen in the future, e.g., a planned vacation or a project you want to work on?

Part Three

____ Can you express your opinion on a subject which you feel strongly about and support that opinion effectively in the face of strong counter-arguments?

____ Can you use the language to speculate at length about how some change in history or the course of human events would have affected your life or civilization, e.g., how would our world be different without the invention of the computer?

____ Are you able to speak about abstract topics such as the theory or concepts that underlie the job or profession you are presently involved in?

____ Can you use the language to solve problems arising in diverse and unexpected situations such as those having to do with neighbors, public officials, the police, or repair persons in the service industry?

Part Four

____ Can you use the language sufficiently effectively to convince a good friend with health problems to give up smoking, or a substance-dependent coworker to seek professional help?

____ Do you have the linguistic skill necessary to advise your boss, a colleague, or another professional on the best course of action to take in a delicate work-related matter?

____ Are you able to alter your speech deliberately depending on whether you are talking to a close friend, an employee, a university professor, etc.?

____ Can you use the language sufficiently well to act as a formal interpreter for a high-ranking U.S. government official making a state visit to the country where the language is spoken?

Part Five

_____ In discussions on all subjects, is your vocabulary always extensive and precise enough to enable you to convey your exact meaning?

_____ Do you have a broad grasp of the idioms, colloquialisms, and cultural references used in the language?

_____ When you are conversing with well-educated native speakers of the language, do they react to you in the same way they do to each other?

Part Six

_____ English is my first language.

_____ This (the language you indicated on the first page) is my first language.

_____ I learned this language in school.

_____ I learned this language in the country where it is spoken.

_____ My family speaks this language at home.

_____ This language was my major/minor in college.

_____ I speak this language on a frequent basis.

_____ I feel I need more training in this language.

_____ I am a native speaker of this language as I was raised and educated through secondary education or higher in this language.

(date of revision: 06/14/01)

APPENDIX I

Language Proficiency Self-Assessment Chart

The following chart reflects proficiency standards that are generally accepted throughout the United States government community. These standards are applied by the FBI during the Applicant Self-Assessment process. Candidates for language specialist and contract linguist positions are required to assess both their English and foreign language fluency levels in speaking, listening, reading, and writing on a scale of 0 to 5.

Level	Speaking	Listening	Reading	Writing
0	**No Proficiency:** Unable to function in the spoken language.	**No Proficiency:** No practical understanding of the spoken language.	**No Proficiency:** No practical ability to read the language.	**No Proficiency:** No functional writing ability.
0+	**Memorized Proficiency:** Able to satisfy immediate needs using rehearsed utterances.	**Memorized Proficiency:** Sufficient comprehension to understand a number of memorized utterances in areas of immediate needs.	**Memorized Proficiency:** Can recognize all the letters in the printed version of an alphabetic system and high-frequency elements of a syllabary or a character system.	**Memorized Proficiency:** Writes using memorized material and set expressions.
1	**Elementary Proficiency:** Able to satisfy minimum courtesy requirements and maintain very simple face-to-face conversations on familiar topics.	**Elementary Proficiency:** Sufficient comprehension to understand utterances about basic survival needs and minimum courtesy and travel requirements.	**Elementary Proficiency:** Sufficient comprehension to read very simple connected written material in a form equivalent to usual printing or typescript.	**Elementary Proficiency:** Sufficient control of the writing system to meet limited practical needs.

(continues)

(continued)

Level	Speaking	Listening	Reading	Writing
1+	**Elementary Proficiency, Plus:** Can initiate and maintain predictable face-to-face conversations and satisfy limited social demands.	**Elementary Proficiency, Plus:** Sufficient comprehension to understand short conversations about all survival needs and limited social demands.	**Elementary Proficiency, Plus:** Sufficient comprehension to understand simple discourse in printed form for informative social purposes.	**Elementary Proficiency, Plus:** Sufficient control of the writing system to meet most survival needs and limited social demands.
2	**Limited Working Proficiency:** Able to satisfy routine social demands and limited work requirements.	**Limited Working Proficiency:** Sufficient comprehension to understand conversations on routine social demands and limited job requirements.	**Limited Working Proficiency:** Sufficient comprehension to read simple, authentic written material in a form equivalent to usual printing or typescript on subjects within a familiar context.	**Limited Working Proficiency:** Able to write routine social correspondence and prepare documentary materials required for most limited work requirements.
2+	**Limited Working Proficiency, Plus:** Able to satisfy most work requirements with language usage that is often, but not always, acceptable and effective.	**Limited Working Proficiency, Plus:** Sufficient comprehension to understand most routine social demands and most conversations on work requirements as well as some discussions on concrete topics related to particular interests and special fields of competence.	**Limited Working Proficiency, Plus:** Sufficient comprehension to understand most factual material in nontechnical prose, as well as some discussions on concrete topics related to special professional interests.	**Limited Working Proficiency, Plus:** Shows ability to write with some precision and in some detail about most common topics.

Level	Speaking	Listening	Reading	Writing
3	**General Professional Proficiency:** Able to speak the language with sufficient structural accuracy and vocabulary to participate effectively in most formal and informal conversations on practical, social, and professional topics.	**General Professional Proficiency:** Able to understand the essentials of all speech in a standard dialect, including technical discussions within a special field.	**General Professional Proficiency:** Able to read within a normal range of speed and with almost complete comprehension a variety of authentic prose material on unfamiliar subjects.	**General Professional Proficiency:** Able to use the language effectively in most formal and informal written exchanges on practical, social, and professional topics.
3+	**General Professional Proficiency, Plus:** Is often able to use the language to satisfy professional needs in a wide range of sophisticated and demanding tasks.	**General Professional Proficiency, Plus:** Comprehends most of the content and intent of a variety of forms and styles of speech pertinent to professional needs, as well as general topics and social conversations.	**General Professional Proficiency, Plus:** Can comprehend a variety of styles and forms pertinent to professional needs.	**General Professional Proficiency, Plus:** Able to write the language in a few prose styles pertinent to professional and educational needs.
4	**Advanced Professional Proficiency:** Able to use the language fluently and accurately on all levels normally pertinent to professional needs.	**Advanced Professional Proficiency:** Able to understand all forms and styles of speech pertinent to professional needs.	**Advanced Professional Proficiency:** Able to read fluently and accurately all styles and forms of the language pertinent to professional needs.	**Advanced Professional Proficiency:** Able to write the language precisely and accurately in a variety of prose styles pertinent to professional and educational needs.

(continues)

(continued)

Level	Speaking	Listening	Reading	Writing
4+	**Advanced Professional Proficiency, Plus:** Speaking proficiency is regularly superior in all respects, usually equivalent to that of a well-educated, highly articulate native speaker.	**Advanced Professional Proficiency, Plus:** Increased ability to understand extremely difficult and abstract speech as well as ability to understand all forms of speech pertinent to professional needs, including social conversations.	**Advanced Professional Proficiency, Plus:** Nearly native ability to read and understand extremely difficult or abstract prose, a very wide variety of vocabulary, idioms, colloquialisms, and slang.	**Advanced Professional Proficiency, Plus:** Able to write the language precisely and accurately in a wide variety of prose styles pertinent to professional and educational needs.
5	**Functionally Native Proficiency:** Speaking proficiency is functionally equivalent to that of a highly articulate, well-educated native speaker and reflects the cultural standards of the country where the language is natively spoken.	**Functionally Native Proficiency:** Comprehension equivalent to that of an educated native listener.	**Functionally Native Proficiency:** Reading proficiency is functionally equivalent to that of a well-educated native reader.	**Functionally Native Proficiency:** Has writing proficiency equal to that of a well-educated native.

FBI Field Offices and Resident Agencies

Alabama
Mobile Field Office

FBI Mobile Division
One St. Louis Centre
1 St. Louis Street—3rd Floor
Mobile, AL 36602
(334) 438-3674
http://mobile.fbi.gov/

Resident Agencies of the Mobile Field Office

- Dothan, AL
- Mobile, AL
- Montgomery, AL
- Selma, AL
- Monroeville, AL
- Opelika, AL

Birmingham Field Office

FBI Birmingham Division
Room 1400
2121 8th Avenue North
Birmingham, AL 35203
(205) 326-6166
http://birmingham.fbi.gov/

Resident Agencies of the Birmingham Field Office

- Florence, AL
- Huntsville, AL
- Gadsden, AL
- Tuscaloosa, AL

Alaska
Anchorage Field Office

FBI Anchorage Division
101 East Sixth Avenue
Anchorage, AK 99501
(907) 276-4441
http://anchorage.fbi.gov/

Resident Agencies of the Anchorage Field Office

- Juneau, AK
- Fairbanks, AK

Arizona
Phoenix Field Office

FBI Phoenix Division
Suite 400
201 East Indianola Avenue
Phoenix, AZ 85012
(602) 279-5511
http://phoenix.fbi.gov/

Resident Agencies of the Phoenix Field Office

- Flagstaff, AZ
- Gallup, NM
- Kingman, AZ
- Lakeside, AZ
- Sierra Vista, AZ
- Tucson, AZ
- Yuma, AZ

Both the Phoenix and the Albuquerque field offices have agents working from the Gallup resident agency.

Arkansas
Little Rock Field Office

FBI Little Rock Division
24 Shackleford West Boulevard
Little Rock, AR 72211
(501) 221-9100
http://littlerock.fbi.gov/

Resident Agencies of the Little Rock Field Office

- El Dorado, AR
- Fayetteville, AR
- Fort Smith, AR
- Hot Springs, AR
- Jonesboro, AR
- Texarkana, AR
- West Memphis, AR

California
Los Angeles Field Office

FBI Los Angeles Division
Federal Building—Suite 1700
11000 Wilshire Boulevard
Los Angeles, CA 90024
(310) 477-6565
http://losangeles.fbi.gov/

Resident Agencies of the Los Angeles Field Office

- LAX Airport
- Long Beach, CA
- Riverside, CA
- Santa Maria, CA
- Victorville, CA
- Lancaster, CA
- Palm Springs, CA
- Santa Ana, CA
- Ventura, CA
- West Covina, CA

Sacramento Field Office

FBI Sacramento Division
4500 Orange Grove Avenue
Sacramento, CA 95841
(916) 481-9110
http://sacramento.fbi.gov/

Resident Agencies of the Sacramento Field Office

- Bakersfield, CA
- Fairfield, CA
- Modesto, CA
- South Lake Tahoe, CA
- Chico, CA
- Fresno, CA
- Redding, CA
- Stockton, CA

San Diego Field Office

FBI San Diego Division
Federal Office Building
9797 Aero Drive
San Diego, CA 92123
(858) 565-1255
http://sandiego.fbi.gov/

Resident Agencies of the San Diego Field Office

- Carlsbad, CA
- El Centro, CA

San Francisco Field Office

FBI San Francisco Division
13th Floor
450 Golden Gate Avenue
San Francisco, CA 94102
(415) 553-7400
http://sanfrancisco.fbi.gov/

Resident Agencies of the San Francisco Field Office

- Concord, CA
- Hayward, CA
- Oakland, CA
- Palo Alto, CA
- San Jose, CA
- San Rafael, CA
- Santa Rosa, CA
- Watsonville, CA

Colorado
Denver Field Office

FBI Denver Division
Federal Building—Room 1823
1961 Stout Street—18th Floor
Denver, CO 80294
(303) 629-7171
http://denver.fbi.gov/

Colorado Resident Agencies of the Denver Field Office

- Boulder, CO
- Colorado Springs, CO
- Durango, CO
- Fort Collins, CO
- Glenwood Springs, CO
- Grand Junction, CO
- Pueblo, CO

Connecticut
New Haven Field Office

FBI New Haven Division
600 State Street
New Haven, CT 06511
(203) 777-6311
http://newhaven.fbi.gov/

Resident Agencies of the New Haven Field Office

- Bridgeport, CT
- Meriden, CT

Delaware

Delaware is under the jurisdiction of the Baltimore Field Office.

Baltimore Field Office

FBI Baltimore Division
7142 Ambassador Road
Baltimore, MD 21244
(410) 265-8080
http://baltimore.fbi.gov/

Delaware Resident Agencies of the Baltimore Field Office

- Dover, DE
- Wilmington, DE

District of Columbia
Washington Metro Field Office

Federal Bureau of Investigation
Washington Metro Field Office
601 Fourth Street Northwest
Washington, DC 20535
(202) 278-2000
http://washingtondc.fbi.gov/

Resident Agencies of the Washington Metro Field Office

- Falls Church, VA

Florida
Jacksonville Field Office

FBI Jacksonville Division
Suite 200
7820 Arlington Expressway
Jacksonville, FL 32211
(904) 721-1211
http://jacksonville.fbi.gov/

Resident Agencies of the Jacksonville Field Office

- Daytona Beach, FL
- Fort Walton Beach, FL
- Gainesville, FL
- Ocala, FL
- Panama City, FL
- Pensacola, FL
- Tallahassee, FL

Miami Field Office

FBI Miami Division
16320 Northwest Second Avenue
North Miami Beach, FL 33169
(305) 944-9101
http://miami.fbi.gov/

Resident Agencies of the Miami Field Office

- Fort Pierce, FL
- Key West, FL
- Homestead, FL
- West Palm Beach, FL

Tampa Field Office

FBI Tampa Division
Federal Building—Room 610
500 Zack Street
Tampa, FL 33602
(813) 273-4566
http://tampa.fbi.gov/

Resident Agencies of the Tampa Field Office

- Clearwater, FL
- Lakeland, FL
- Naples, FL
- Sarasota, FL
- Fort Myers, FL
- Melbourne, FL
- Orlando, FL

Georgia
Atlanta Field Office

FBI Atlanta Division
Suite 400
2635 Century Parkway Northeast
Atlanta, GA 30345
(404) 679-9000
http://atlanta.fbi.gov/

Resident Agencies of the Atlanta Field Office

- Albany, GA
- Augusta, GA
- Columbus, GA
- Gainesville, GA
- Rome, GA
- Savannah, GA
- Thomasville, GA
- Athens, GA
- Brunswick, GA
- Dublin, GA
- Macon, GA
- Rossville, GA
- Statesboro, GA
- Valdosta, GA

Hawaii
Honolulu Field Office

FBI Honolulu Division
Room 4-230
300 Ala Moana Boulevard
Honolulu, HI 96850
(808) 566-4300
http://honolulu.fbi.gov/

Resident Agencies of the Honolulu Field Office

- Kailua-Kona, HI
- Wailuku, HI
- Mongmong, Guam
- Puerto Rico, Saipan, Northern Mariana Islands

Idaho

Idaho is under the jurisdiction of the Salt Lake City Field Office.

Salt Lake City Field Office

FBI Salt Lake City Division
257 Towers Building #1200
257 East—200 South
Salt Lake City, UT 84111
(801) 579-1400
http://saltlakecity.fbi.gov/

ID Resident Agencies of the Salt Lake City Field Office

- Boise, ID
- Idaho Falls, ID
- Pocatello, ID
- Coeur d'Alene, ID
- Lewiston, ID
- Twin Falls, ID

Illinois
Chicago Field Office

FBI Chicago Division
Room 905
219 South Dearborn Street
Chicago, IL 60604
(312) 431-1333
http://chicago.fbi.gov/

Resident Agencies of the Chicago Field Office

- Lisle, IL
- Rolling Meadows, IL
- Rockford, IL
- Tinley Park, IL

Springfield Field Office

FBI Springfield Division
Suite 400
400 West Monroe Street
Springfield, IL 62704
(217) 522-9675
http://springfield.fbi.gov/

Resident Agencies of the Springfield Field Office

- Carbondale, IL
- Champaign, IL
- Decatur, IL
- Effingham, IL
- Fairview Heights, IL
- Normal, IL
- Peoria, IL

Indiana

Indianapolis Field Office

FBI Indianapolis Division
Federal Building—Room 679
575 North Pennsylvania Street
Indianapolis, IN 46204
(317) 639-3301
http://indianapolis.fbi.gov/

Resident Agencies of the Indianapolis Field Office

- Bloomington, IN
- Evansville, IN
- Fort Wayne, IN
- Lafayette, IN
- Merrillville, IN
- Muncie, IN
- New Albany, IN
- South Bend, IN
- Terre Haute, IN

Iowa

Iowa is under the jurisdiction of the Omaha Field Office.

Omaha Field Office

FBI Omaha Division
10755 Burt Street
Omaha, NE 68114
(402) 493-8688
http://omaha.fbi.gov/

Iowa Resident Agencies of the Omaha Field Office

- Cedar Rapids, IA
- Davenport, IA
- Des Moines, IA
- Sioux City, IA
- Waterloo, IA

Kansas

Kansas is under the jurisdiction of the Kansas City (MO) Field Office.

Kansas City Field Office

FBI Kansas City Division
1300 Summit
Kansas City, MO 64105
(816) 512-8200
http://kansascity.fbi.gov/

Kansas Resident Agencies of the Kansas City Field Office

- Garden City, KS
- Salina, KS
- Topeka, KS
- Wichita, KS

Kentucky
Louisville Field Office

FBI Louisville Division
Room 500
600 Martin Luther King, Jr. Place
Louisville, KY 40202
(502) 583-3941
http://louisville.fbi.gov/

Resident Agencies of the Louisville Field Office

- Ashland, KY
- Bowling Green, KY
- Covington, KY
- Elizabethtown, KY
- Frankfort, KY
- Hopkinsville, KY
- Lexington, KY
- London, KY
- Owensboro, KY
- Paducah, KY
- Pikeville, KY

Louisiana
New Orleans Field Office

FBI New Orleans Division
2901 Leon C. Simon Drive
New Orleans, LA 70126
(504) 816-3000
http://neworleans.fbi.gov/

Resident Agencies of the New Orleans Field Office

- Alexandria, LA
- Baton Rouge, LA
- Lafayette, LA
- Lake Charles, LA
- Monroe, LA
- Shreveport, LA

Maine

Maine is under the jurisdiction of the Boston Field Office.

Boston Field Office

FBI Boston Division
One Center Plaza—Suite 600
Boston, MA 02108
(617) 742-5533
http://boston.fbi.gov/

Maine Resident Agencies of the Boston Field Office

- Augusta, ME
- Bangor, ME

Maryland
Baltimore Field Office

FBI Baltimore Division
7142 Ambassador Road
Baltimore, MD 21244
(410) 265-8080
http://baltimore.fbi.gov/

Maryland Resident Agencies of the Baltimore Field Office

- Annapolis, MD
- Bel Air, MD
- Calverton, MD
- Frederick, MD
- Salisbury, MD

Massachusetts
Boston Field Office

FBI Boston Division
One Center Plaza—Suite 600
Boston, MA 02108
(617) 742-5533
http://boston.fbi.gov/

Massachusetts Resident Agencies of the Boston Field Office

- Hudson, MA
- Lowell, MA
- Lakeville, MA
- Springfield, MA

Michigan
Detroit Field Office

FBI Detroit Division
26th Floor
McNamara Federal Building
477 Michigan Avenue
Detroit, MI 48226
(313) 965-2323
http://detroit.fbi.gov/

Resident Agencies of the Detroit Field Office

- Ann Arbor, MI
- Clinton Township, MI
- Grand Rapids, MI
- Lansing, MI
- St. Joseph, MI
- Troy, MI
- Bay City, MI
- Flint, MI
- Kalamazoo, MI
- Marquette, MI
- Traverse City, MI

Minnesota
Minneapolis Field Office

FBI Minneapolis Division
Suite 1100
111 Washington Avenue South
Minneapolis, MN 55401
(612) 376-3200
http://minneapolis.fbi.gov/

Minnesota Resident Agencies of the Minneapolis Field Office

- Bemidji, MN
- Duluth, MN
- Mankato, MN
- Rochester, MN
- St. Cloud, MN
- St. Paul, MN

Mississippi
Jackson Field Office

FBI Jackson Division
Federal Building—Room 1553
100 West Capitol Street
Jackson, MS 39269
(601) 948-5000
http://jackson.fbi.gov/

Resident Agencies of the Jackson Field Office

- Columbus, MS
- Greenville, MS
- Gulfport, MS
- Hattiesburg, MS
- McComb, MS
- Meridian, MS
- Oxford, MS
- Pascagoula, MS
- Southaven, MS
- Tupelo, MS

Missouri
Kansas City Field Office

FBI Kansas City Division
1300 Summit
Kansas City, MO 64105
(816) 512-8200
http://kansascity.fbi.gov/

Missouri Resident Agencies of the Kansas City Field Office

- Jefferson City, MO
- Joplin, MO
- St. Joseph, MO
- Springfield, MO

St. Louis Field Office

FBI St. Louis Division
2222 Market Street
St. Louis, MO 63103
(314) 231-4324
http://stlouis.fbi.gov/

Resident Agencies of the St. Louis Field Office

- Cape Girardeau, MO
- Hannibal, MO
- Kirksville, MO
- Rolla, MO
- St. Peters, MO

Montana

Montana is under the jurisdiction of the Salt Lake City Field Office.

Salt Lake City Field Office

FBI Salt Lake City Division
257 Towers Building #1200
257 East—200 South
Salt Lake City, UT 84111
(801) 579-1400
http://saltlakecity.fbi.gov/

Montana Resident Agencies of the Salt Lake City Field Office

- Billings, MT
- Browning, MT
- Glasgow, MT
- Havre, MT
- Helena, MT
- Kalispell, MT
- Missoula, MT

Nebraska
Omaha Field Office

FBI Omaha Division
10755 Burt Street
Omaha, NE 68114
(402) 493-8688
http://omaha.fbi.gov/

Nebraska Resident Agencies of the Omaha Field Office

- Grand Island, NE
- Lincoln, NE
- North Platte, NE

Nevada
Las Vegas Field Office

FBI Las Vegas Division
John Lawrence Bailey Building
700 East Charleston Boulevard
Las Vegas, NV 89104
(702) 385-1281
http://lasvegas.fbi.gov/

Resident Agencies of the Las Vegas Field Office

- Carson City, NV
- Elko, NV
- Reno, NV

New Hampshire

New Hampshire is under the jurisdiction of the Boston Field Office.

Boston Field Office

FBI Boston Division
One Center Plaza—Suite 600
Boston, MA 02108
(617) 742-5533
http://boston.fbi.gov/

New Hampshire Resident Agencies of the Boston Field Office

- Bedford, NH
- Portsmouth, NH

New Jersey
Newark Field Office

FBI Newark Division
Market Street—22nd Floor
1 Gateway Center
Newark, NJ 07101
(973) 792-3000
http://newark.fbi.gov/

Resident Agencies of the Newark Field Office

- Atlantic City, NJ
- Franklin Township, NJ
- Garret Mountain, NJ
- Red Bank, NJ
- Trenton, NJ

The Newark Field Office has jurisdiction over all counties in New Jersey except Camden, Gloucester, and Salem, which fall under the Philadelphia (PA) Field Office.

New Mexico
Albuquerque Field Office

FBI Albuquerque Division
415 Silver Avenue Southwest #300
Albuquerque, NM 87102
(505) 224-2000
http://albuquerque.fbi.gov/

Resident Agencies of the Albuquerque Field Office

- Farmington, NM
- Gallup, NM
- Las Cruces, NM
- Roswell, NM
- Santa Fe, NM

Both the Phoenix and the Albuquerque field offices have agents working from the Gallup resident agency.

New York
Albany Field Office

FBI Albany Division
200 McCarty Avenue
Albany, NY 12209
(518) 465-7551
http://albany.fbi.gov/

New York Resident Agencies of the Albany Field Office

- Binghamton, NY
- Burlington, VT
- Ithaca, NY
- Kingston, NY
- Plattsburgh, NY
- Rutland, VT
- Syracuse, NY
- Utica, NY

The Albany Field Office also has jurisdiction over 14 counties in Vermont. These counties are covered by the Burlington and Rutland Resident Agencies of the Albany Field Office.

Buffalo Field Office

FBI Buffalo Division
One FBI Plaza
Buffalo, NY 14202
(716) 856-7800
http://buffalo.fbi.gov/

Resident Agencies of the Buffalo Field Office

- Elmira, NY
- Jamestown, NY
- Niagara Falls, NY
- Rochester, NY

New York Field Office

FBI New York Division
26 Federal Plaza—23rd Floor
New York, NY 10278
(212) 384-1000
http://newyork.fbi.gov/

Resident Agencies of the New York Field Office

- Goshen, NY
- Kew Gardens, NY
- New Rochelle, NY
- JFK International Airport, NY
- Melville, NY

North Carolina
Charlotte Field Office

FBI Charlotte Division
Wachovia Building—Suite 900
400 South Tyron Street
Charlotte, NC 28285
(704) 377-9200
http://charlotte.fbi.gov/

Resident Agencies of the Charlotte Field Office

- Asheville, NC
- Fayetteville, NC
- Greenville, NC
- Raleigh, NC
- Elizabeth City, NC
- Greensboro, NC
- Hickory, NC
- Wilmington, NC

North Dakota

North Dakota is under the jurisdiction of the Minneapolis Field Office.

Minneapolis Field Office

FBI Minneapolis Division
Suite 1100
111 Washington Avenue South
Minneapolis, MN 55401
(612) 376-3200
http://minneapolis.fbi.gov/

North Dakota Resident Agencies of the Minneapolis Field Office

- Bismarck, ND
- Grand Forks, ND
- Fargo, ND
- Minot, ND

Ohio
Cincinnati Field Office

FBI Cincinnati Division
550 Main Street—Room 9000
Cincinnati, OH 45202
(513) 421-4310
http://cincinnati.fbi.gov/

Resident Agencies of the Cincinnati Field Office

- Athens, OH
- Cambridge, OH
- Columbus, OH
- Dayton, OH
- Middletown, OH
- Portsmouth, OH

Cleveland Field Office

FBI Cleveland Division
Federal Building—Room 3005
1240 East 9th Street
Cleveland, OH 44199
(216) 522-1400
http://cleveland.fbi.gov/

Resident Agencies of the Cleveland Field Office

- Akron, OH
- Canton, OH
- Elyria, OH
- Lima, OH
- Mansfield, OH
- Painesville, OH
- Sandusky, OH
- Toledo, OH
- Youngstown, OH

Oklahoma
Oklahoma City Field Office

FBI Oklahoma City Division
3301 West Memorial Drive
Oklahoma City, OK 73134
(405) 290-7770
http://oklahomacity.fbi.gov/

Resident Agencies of the Oklahoma City Field Office

- Ardmore, OK
- Durant, OK
- Elk City, OK
- Enid, OK
- Lawton, OK
- McAlester, OH
- Muskogee, OK
- Norman, OK
- Stillwater, OK
- Tulsa, OK
- Vinita, OK
- Woodward, OK

Oregon
Portland Field Office

FBI Portland Division
Crown Plaza Building—Suite 400
1500 Southwest 1st Avenue
Portland, OR 97201
(503) 224-4181
http://portland.fbi.gov/

Resident Agencies of the Portland Field Office

- Bend, OR
- Eugene, OR
- Pendleton, OR
- Salem, OR

Pennsylvania
Philadelphia Field Office

FBI Philadelphia Division
William Green Jr. Federal Building
600 Arch Street—8th Floor
Philadelphia, PA 19106
(215) 418-4000
http://philadelphia.fbi.gov/

Resident Agencies of the Philadelphia Field Office

- Allentown, PA
- Ft. Washington, PA
- Harrisburg, PA
- Newtown Square, PA
- Scranton, PA
- Cherry Hill, NJ
- State College, PA
- Williamsport, PA

The Philadelphia Field Office also has jurisdiction over three counties in New Jersey. These counties are covered by the Cherry Hill Resident Agency of the Philadelphia Field Office.

Pittsburgh Field Office

FBI Pittsburgh Division
U.S. Post Office Building
700 Grant Street—Suite 300
Pittsburgh, PA 15219
(412) 471-2000
http://pittsburgh.fbi.gov/

Resident Agencies of the Pittsburgh Field Office

- Beckley, WV
- Charleston, WV
- Clarksburg, WV
- Erie, PA
- Huntington, WV
- Johnstown, PA
- Martinsburg, WV
- Charleroi, PA
- New Castle, PA
- Wheeling, WV

The Pittsburgh Field Office has jurisdiction over western Pennsylvania and the state of West Virginia.

Rhode Island

Rhode Island is under the jurisdiction of the Boston Field Office.

Boston Field Office

FBI Boston Division
One Center Plaza—Suite 600
Boston, MA 02108
(617) 742-5533
http://boston.fbi.gov/

Rhode Island Resident Agencies of the Boston Field Office

- Providence, RI

South Carolina
Columbia Field Office

FBI Columbia Division
151 Westpark Boulevard
Columbia, SC 29210
(803) 551-4200
http://columbia.fbi.gov/

Resident Agencies of the Columbia Field Office

- Aiken, SC
- Charleston, SC
- Greenville, SC
- Rock Hill, SC

- Beaufort, SC
- Florence, SC
- Myrtle Beach, SC
- Spartanburg, SC

South Dakota

South Dakota is under the jurisdiction of the Minneapolis Field Office.

Minneapolis Field Office

FBI Minneapolis Division
Suite 1100
111 Washington Avenue South
Minneapolis, MN 55401
(612) 376-3200
http://minneapolis.fbi.gov/

South Dakota Resident Agencies of the Minneapolis Field Office

- Aberdeen, SD
- Rapid City, SD

- Pierre, SD
- Sioux Falls, SD

Tennessee
Knoxville Field Office

FBI Knoxville Division
Duncan Federal Building #600
710 Locust Street
Knoxville, TN 37902
(865) 544-0751
http://knoxville.fbi.gov/

Resident Agencies of the Knoxville Field Office

- Chattanooga, TN
- Greeneville, TN
- Oak Ridge, TN

- Cleveland, TN
- Johnson City, TN
- Winchester, TN

Memphis Field Office

FBI Memphis Division
Eagle Crest Building #3000
225 North Humphreys Boulevard
Memphis, TN 38120
(901) 747-4300
http://memphis.fbi.gov/

Resident Agencies of the Memphis Field Office

- Columbia, TN
- Clarksville, TN
- Cookeville, TN
- Jackson, TN
- Nashville, TN

Texas
Dallas Field Office

FBI Dallas Division
Suite 300
1801 North Lamar Street
Dallas, TX 75202
(214) 720-2200
http://dallas.fbi.gov/

Resident Agencies of the Dallas Field Office

- Abilene, TX
- Amarillo, TX
- DFW Airport, TX
- Fort Worth, TX
- Lubbock, TX
- Lufkin, TX
- Plano, TX
- San Angelo, TX
- Sherman, TX
- Texarkana, TX
- Tyler, TX
- Wichita Falls, TX

Houston Field Office

FBI Houston Division
2500 East T.C. Jester
Houston, TX 77008
(713) 693-5000
http://houston.fbi.gov/

Resident Agencies of the Houston Field Office

- Beaumont, TX
- Bryan, TX
- Conroe, TX
- Corpus Christi, TX
- Texas City, TX
- Victoria, TX

El Paso Field Office

FBI El Paso Division
Suite 3000
660 South Mesa Hills Drive
El Paso, TX 79912
(915) 832-5000
http://elpaso.fbi.gov/

Resident Agencies of the El Paso Field Office

- Midland, TX

San Antonio Field Office

FBI San Antonio Division
U.S. Post Office Courthouse Building
615 East Houston Street #200
San Antonio, TX 78205
(210) 225-6741
http://sanantonio.fbi.gov/

Resident Agencies of the San Antonio Field Office

- Austin, TX
- Del Rio, TX
- McAllen, TX
- Brownsville, TX
- Laredo, TX
- Waco, TX

Utah
Salt Lake City Field Office

FBI Salt Lake City Division
257 Towers Building #1200
257 East—200 South
Salt Lake City, UT 84111
(801) 579-1400
http://saltlakecity.fbi.gov/

Utah Resident Agencies of the Salt Lake City Field Office

- Monticello, UT
- Provo, UT
- Vernal, UT
- Ogden, UT
- St. George, UT

Vermont

Vermont is under the jurisdiction of the Albany Field Office.

Albany Field Office

FBI Albany Division
200 McCarty Avenue
Albany, NY 12209
(518) 465-7551
http://albany.fbi.gov/

Vermont Resident Agencies of the Albany Field Office

- Burlington, VT
- Rutland, VT

Virginia
Richmond Field Office

FBI Richmond Division
1970 East Parham Road
Richmond, VA 23228
(804) 261-1044
http://richmond.fbi.gov/

Resident Agencies of the Richmond Field Office

- Bristol, VA
- Charlottesville, VA
- Fredericksburg, VA
- Lynchburg, VA
- Richmond, VA
- Roanoke, VA
- Winchester, VA

Norfolk Field Office

FBI Norfolk Division
150 Corporate Boulevard
Norfolk, VA 23502
(757) 455-0100
http://norfolk.fbi.gov/

Resident Agencies of the Norfolk Field Office

- Hampton, VA

Washington
Seattle Field Office

FBI Seattle Division
1110 Third Avenue
Seattle, WA 98101
(206) 622-0460
http://seattle.fbi.gov/

Resident Agencies of the Seattle Field Office

- Bellingham, WA
- Everett, WA
- Olympia, WA
- Richland, WA
- Silverdale, WA
- Spokane, WA
- Tacoma, WA
- Vancouver, WA
- Wenatchee, WA
- Yakima, WA

West Virginia

West Virginia is under the jurisdiction of the Pittsburgh Field Office.

Pittsburgh Field Office

FBI Pittsburgh Division
U.S. Post Office Building
700 Grant Street—Suite 300
Pittsburgh, PA 15219
(412) 471-2000
http://pittsburgh.fbi.gov/

West Virginia Resident Agencies of the Pittsburgh Field Office

- Beckley, WV
- Charleston, WV
- Clarksburg, WV
- Huntington, WV
- Martinsburg, WV
- Wheeling, WV

Wisconsin

Milwaukee Field Office

FBI Milwaukee Division
330 East Kilbourn Avenue #600
Milwaukee, WI 53202
(414) 276-4684
http://milwaukee.fbi.gov/

Resident Agencies of the Milwaukee Field Office

- Eau Claire, WI
- Green Bay, WI
- Pleasant Prairie, WI
- La Crosse, WI
- Madison, WI
- Wausau, WI

Wyoming

Wyoming is under the jurisdiction of the Denver Field Office (except for Yellowstone National Park, which is covered by the Salt Lake City Field Office).

Denver Field Office

FBI Denver Division
Federal Building—Room 1823
1961 Stout Street—18th Floor
Denver, CO 80294
(303) 629-7171
http://denver.fbi.gov/

Wyoming Resident Agencies of the Denver Field Office

- Casper, WY
- Cheyenne, WY
- Jackson Hole, WY
- Lander, WY

INDEX

G